The Fear of Insignificance

The Fear of Insignificance

Searching for Meaning in the Twenty-First Century

Carlo Strenger

THE FEAR OF INSIGNIFICANCE: SEARCHING FOR MEANING IN THE TWENTY-FIRST CENTURY
Copyright © Carlo Strenger, 2011.

First published in 2011 by PALGRAVE MACMILLAN® in the United States—a division of St. Martin's Press LLC, 175 Fifth Avenue, New York, NY 10010.

Where this book is distributed in the UK, Europe and the rest of the world, this is by Palgrave Macmillan, a division of Macmillan Publishers Limited, registered in England, company number 785998, of Houndmills, Basingstoke, Hampshire RG21 6XS.

Palgrave Macmillan is the global academic imprint of the above companies and has companies and representatives throughout the world.

Palgrave® and Macmillan® are registered trademarks in the United States, the United Kingdom, Europe and other countries.

ISBN: 978-0-230-10895-0 (hardcover)
ISBN: 978-0-230-11375-6 (paperback)

Library of Congress Cataloging-in-Publication Data

Strenger, Carlo.
    The fear of insignificance : searching for meaning in the twenty-first century / Carlo Strenger.
        p. cm.
    Includes bibliographical references.
    ISBN 978–0–230-10895–0 (alk. paper)
    1. Existential psychology. 2. Existentialism. 3. Individuation (Psychology).
I. Title.
    BF204.5.S745 2010
    150.19'2–dc22   2010030276

A catalogue record of the book is available from the British Library.

Design by Scribe Inc.

First edition: February 2011

D 10 9 8 7 6 5 4 3 2

Printed in the United States of America.

For Julia

Contents

Introduction: Our Historical Moment   1

Part I The Defeat of Mind

1   The Years of the Golden Calf   9
2   "Just Do It": The Celebrity Culture and the Designed Self   23
3   The Defeat of Mind: Relativism and Pop Spirituality   47

Part II From the "I" Commodity to the Drama of Individuality

4   The Drama of Individuality   71
5   From "Just Do It" to Active Self-Acceptance   89
6   Paring Down Life to the Essentials: An Epicurean Proposal   103

Part III Reclaiming Our Minds

7   Escaping the Platonic Cave   121
8   Religion and Science: Civilized Disdain and Epicurean Laughter   149
9   Toward World Citizenship and a Coalition of Open Worldviews   171

Notes   193

Index   211

Introduction

Our Historical Moment

We are awakening from a period that Immanuel Kant would have called one of <u>dogmatic slumber</u>.[1] But as opposed to the dogmatic slumbers of previous centuries governed by metaphysical and religious beliefs that Kant dismantled in his *Critique of Pure Reason* (1781), the last decades will probably go into history as the age of mindless fantasies of omnipotence and of thoughtless free market dogmatism.

After the fall of the Berlin Wall in 1989 the proponents of unfettered free markets, who had taken the reins of the economy during the years of Ronald Reagan and Margaret Thatcher, went into a triumphalist mood: the demise of Communism and the dissolution of the Soviet Union and its sphere of influence were taken to be proof that the gospel of the free market was now the only world religion of universal validity.[2]

The value of everything ranging from companies to religions and from music records to ideas was determined through ranking and rating systems: stock markets, rating agencies, bestseller lists, or number of hits on the web. It was a matter of logic to extend this commoditization to human beings,[3] and this commoditization was accelerated by the new global infotainment system. One of this system's main activities was to rank people for its own purposes: it needed global celebrities for global marketing and advertising. As a result it promoted two models of the good life around the globe: celebrity—a quantification of how well you are known—and financial success.

The new ranking systems determined the value of the individual by a number of factors ranging from the number of friends on Facebook, through the number of entries on Google, and to the position of the ever-growing number of listings of the most influential, most popular, sexiest, most powerful, or wealthiest people in cities, countries, and, ultimately, around the globe.

A new species was born: Homo globalis, the large class of people whose identity is strongly defined by their being plugged into global infotainment.

Now that Homo globalis was commoditized, it was no longer just the holder of a portfolio but became the portfolio itself, traded around the globe through the infotainment system.

The commoditization of the self induced permanent instability of self-esteem and doubt about the sense of leading a significant life. The result was constant existential unease ineffectively addressed by a combination of psychotropic medication and quick-fix spiritual advice by self-help gurus who spread the gospel that celebrity and wealth were just a matter of will-power and courage.

The current meltdown of the financial markets has awoken us from the neoliberal belief that capitalism captures the essence of what it means to live a rich human life. The demise of this dogma was sealed with the bankruptcy of Lehman Brothers, which showed even to the most recalcitrant that a historical period had come to its end.[4]

The victim of the age of the golden calf, the decades governed by the commoditization of everything, has not just been the economy, even though the havoc inflicted on the lives and livelihood of scores of millions is terrible. The real casualty is the idea of the free world and the free society, which has been perverted into the mindless dogma that what really matters must be measurable in economic terms. Great harm was done to the core idea of the open society that thrives on critical, trenchant thought, the enduring legacy of the European Enlightenment.[5]

How can Homo globalis's malaise be addressed? The claim of this book is that the ideas needed to reconstruct the core values of what John Stuart Mill defended in *On Liberty*[6] are to be found in the cultural and intellectual history of the West.[7]

The first idea is that the drama of human development rather than the resulting commodity is the core of human life. The infotainment system has made us forget that the true drama of human life is the process through which we become individuals with character, voice, and a worldview. The point is to live lives that are our own creation rather than adapting to the demands of the global marketplace.

Existentialism developed this idea by showing that we live with the tension between our cultural heritage and the ability to criticize it; between our desires and our possibilities; and the need to turn the base materials of our lives, which we did not choose, into a life that is truly ours. In these respects we are like bricoleurs, artists who make do with what they find in their backyards and do not buy their materials in stores that could cater to their whims. Our individuality is the result of our struggle to integrate these tensions and to live them fruitfully rather than trying to resolve them into an illusory harmony.

The second idea was originally formulated in classical Greece. The idea that we can liberate our minds and reach for ever more truth has been the cornerstone of the Western philosophical tradition. Plato's great parable of the cave, his image of humans as creatures led by circumstances of birth, who mistake illusion for reality, is a great allegory of the process that philosophies of all cultures have called upon us to undergo: to examine the most fundamental tenets of our worldviews mercilessly.[8]

This idea received its latest formulation in the European Enlightenment, defined by Kant as "the liberation of man from self-imposed tutelage." To be truly free, humans need to address the most basic issues of existence through an arduous process of intellectual effort. These questions range from the nature of the good life and the good society to the question of how we can move from erroneous belief to true knowledge. Without coherent worldviews our lives lack the structure that provides us with meaning; and without criteria of cogency, we have no way of anchoring those worldviews beyond how well ideas sell in the marketplace, a notoriously fickle yardstick of quality. While I have no illusion that consensus can be achieved on the deepest questions of existence, I hope to show that we can at least argue these issues articulately.

This book proposes a reassessment of what it means to live a valuable life. A rapprochement is to be expected between European cultural sensibilities, characterized by a love of cultural and intellectual depth, and the tremendous intellectual energies of the Americans who have been relegated to the sidelines of mainstream culture during the last decades.

Hopefully this may contribute to the development of world citizenship[9] in the deepest sense. As opposed to glib forms of cosmopolitanism,[10] it is not just facile worldliness, but the realization that globalization has come to the point where there is no way around cooperation across divides of religion and ideology—a task only possible if we are able and willing to see our worldviews as human creations. *yes & no*

Reconnecting to the central ideas of our culture requires arduous work, and this book outlines aspects of the mental discipline[11] required for living in a Free World as a world citizen. And it also opens the vista of leading lives infinitely richer than those that were prescribed during the age of the golden calf.

***

This book attempts to provide a diagnosis for the malaise of Homo globalis and then argues for two distinct yet connected ways to address it. Here is a brief outline of the book's structure and argument.

Part I focuses on diagnosing the plight of Homo globalis.

Chapter 1 gives an outline of the cultural and existential changes that have been induced by the global infotainment system and sketches the book's theoretical perspective. It will show the depth of our need to feel that we are significant and how this need is rooted in our biological nature, particularly as it has been understood by existential philosophy, psychology, and its new offspring: experimental existential psychology.

Chapter 2 focuses on two features of the global culture driven by the infotainment system: it uses Nike's phenomenally successful "just do it" campaign, which celebrated its twentieth anniversary in 2008, to show how it captures an essential aspect of the spirit of the age: anything is possible and two things are desirable—fame and riches—both of which are measurable and constantly rated and ranked throughout the world. The chapter argues that the seeming objectivity of these rankings leads members of Homo globalis to feel that their place on these scales determines their value—to the detriment of the 99.999 percent of us who do not figure in these rankings. Those who do figure in them live in constant fear of losing their visibility in the list of the richest, sexiest, and most adored celebrities—and thus the persistent fear of insignificance arises.

Chapter 3 analyzes some of the resources through which members of Homo globalis try to assuage their persistent fears of insignificance: the booming self-help culture and pop spirituality. The chapter's central argument is that many of the products of these two phenomena are based on shaky intellectual foundations (to put it mildly) and argues that incoherent worldviews are unlikely to provide us with meaning of enduring value. It describes the relativist atmosphere that has made our culture overly tolerant of intellectual constructs devoid of coherence.

From here the book branches out in two directions: Part II provides an existentialist alternative to the conception of the self that has been promoted in the "just do it" culture described in Chapter 2. Part III calls for reestablishing a culture of reasoned argument as an antidote to the mindless relativism and anti-intellectualism described in Chapter 3. It can be read independently of Part II for those primarily interested in the idea of how a culture based on reason might look.

Part II develops an existentialist picture of individuality quite different from that of the "just do it" culture: it argues that the central task of individuals is to shape the base materials of our lives into a coherent creation that is our life. In doing so it attacks the idea that the individual's essence is prescribed by ethnicity, religion, race, or gender, as has been argued by the fashionable politics of identity. Instead, it calls for a reflective individualism; each of us must decide what the central themes of our lives will be and not accept that being Jewish, Muslim, gay, a woman, or black is what must determine all of our lives.

Chapter 4 shows that all of us are born into a family, culture, and language that we did not choose. For many of us this generates the task of choosing what of our background and upbringing we accept, what we reject, and how we turn our lives into our creation. This task is often arduous and conflictual. The chapter's central thesis is that a life well lived is not one in which these tensions are resolved, but one in which they are lived fully and productively, as shown through the lives of Barack Obama, Somali-born activist and writer Ayaan Ali Hirsi, and Jewish novelist Philip Roth.

Chapter 5 argues that the "just do it" culture has made it impossible to shape our lives according to their inner logic because it has claimed that anything is possible and that we can take on anything we like. This is patently false, and one of the tasks all of us need to tackle is to understand our strengths and weaknesses. As opposed to the Adidas slogan *Impossible Is Nothing*, all of us have limitations. The chapter's argument is that realizing the existence of limitations is not a process of resignation. Instead it proposes the notion of *active self-acceptance* through which we reach a positive conception of our individuality with its potentials and limits.

Chapter 6 tackles the question, "If not everything is possible, how do I determine what my life is about? How do I know what really matters to me?" This process has been made almost impossible by a culture that values youth more than anything else. We are supposed to be successful very early, and hence the process of acquiring self-knowledge is made almost impossible. To counteract this myth that youth is when we make all the central decisions of our lives, the chapter shows through some examples how humans often reach true self-knowledge rather late, and how many lives become more fulfilled only when through reflection we come to a reasoned conclusion regarding what we want to focus on.

Part III launches a full-blown attack on the relativism and anti-intellectualism about worldviews that has been fashionable in the last decades. It argues for a return to exacting standards of argumentation and calls on members of Homo globalis to invest time and energy in the intellectual foundations of their worldviews. Its goal is to develop a psychology of world citizenship, of the mental and emotional abilities needed to live responsibly in an interconnected world. If we, as members of Homo globalis, do not try to influence our fate, humanity is about to self-destruct. Involving ourselves in the world's affairs and investing time and energy in understanding them is a much better basis for living a significant life than buying into pop spirituality.

Chapter 7 shows the great downside of political correctness, the idea that beliefs need to be respected just because somebody holds them, no matter how irrational, odious, or incoherent they are. This tolerance has

led to the point where all three Abrahamic religions have developed fundamentalist strands that have influenced world affairs in catastrophic ways.
The chapter's argument is that Plato's ideas that we are not condemned to
the beliefs that have been instilled in us in childhood and that we can rise
above these beliefs and use reason to build our worldview still have validity.
This chapter is a plea for the ideal of liberal education, the part of our studies not geared toward making money, to make us more competent citizens
of the world.

Chapter 8 tackles one of the deepest reasons why Homo globalis tends
to shy away from debating issues of worldview: arguments about religion
tend to get us nowhere, so why bother? The result has been the idea of
political correctness: we need to respect each other's beliefs. But this, I
argue, is a psychological impossibility: how can we respect beliefs that we
take to be shallow, irrational, or immoral? We may, at best, be able to tolerate them. Hence I suggest an alternative to the ideology of political correctness, which I call *civilized disdain*. By this I mean the position that respects
the humanity of all but allows for the disdain that we feel toward beliefs
that we take to be unacceptable.

Chapter 9 finally asks the question, where are we headed? Existential
psychology has shown that humans are very unlikely to give up their beliefs
no matter how destructive or irrational they are. Are we therefore doomed
to destroy the planet through warfare, nuclear terror, and ecological ruin?
The chapter presents the nonzero principle active in biological and cultural
evolution: non-zero-sum situations are more likely to be adaptive than
zero-sum situations. This is what has created ever more complex organisms and cultures. But what will win—our irrationality or nonzeroness?
We cannot know, and yet the chapter calls on Homo globalis to bet on the
nonzero principle, to form a coalition of all those who want to be citizens
of the world, and to take responsibility for the planet and humanity as
a whole.

Part I

The Defeat of Mind

1

The Years of the Golden Calf

September 11, 2001, or 9/11, will probably come to be seen as the onset of the twenty-first century. This will create problems for future historians because a strong case has been made that the twentieth century ended with the fall of the Berlin Wall in 1989. How, then, will the years between 1989 and 2001 be classified? My suggestion is that these years might be viewed as a brief period during which the West believed that its values and culture had triumphed. Francis Fukuyama's thesis that history had come to an end can well be understood as the idea that the West's takeover of the world was on the way to completion.[1]

More than anything, 9/11 is an indication for the depth of the human need for meaning and identity. Looking at al Qaeda and the perpetrators of 9/11 from a purely psychological point of view shows how wrong the idea has been that capitalism and democracy are enough to sustain human beings existentially. Mohammed Atta and his fellow al Qaeda members were neither poor nor uneducated. In fact they had gotten to know each other while studying for degrees at Western universities. Their motivation for killing themselves along with thousands of innocent victims was their seething rage at what they experienced as the humiliation of Islam at the hands of high-handed American policies.

The West had welcomed them to acquire knowledge and technological expertise through its institutions of higher learning. But their encounter with the West created the opposite of what many would have expected. They felt nothing but disdain and hatred at the liberty and, as they saw it, mindless, soulless materialism and hedonism of the Western world. When they encountered Osama bin Laden's call to purify Islam of the putrefying influence of the West, they finally found meaning and a calling: they would show the world that Western dominance and superiority was but a sham, and that Islam would ultimately triumph.

It is easy to disqualify suicide terrorism as a fringe phenomenon and an indication of extreme psychopathology. Research shows otherwise:[2]

in-depth interviews with intercepted suicide bombers by psychologically trained researchers did not find any psychopathology that would allow predicting who will turn into a suicide bomber. If anything, suicide bombing, though extreme, is a manifestation of the depth of the human need for meaning. More than anything, we humans need to feel that we live lives that matter.

The roots of this desire are to be found far back in our evolutionary history. The human species at some point in its evolution made a momentous transition, possibly the most dramatic step in the evolution from being merely a more intelligent animal to being distinctly human: our species acquired the notion of death and the realization that each of us will die.[3]

There are powerful arguments for the thesis that this is the step that made our species fully human. Philosophers of all cultures and ages have claimed that the ability to live well with the knowledge of death is crucial to living a good life. And, as opposed to many other philosophical theses that survive only as parts of intellectual and cultural history, the idea that death awareness—referred to in psychological studies as mortality salience—is one of the defining characteristics of our life has received powerful empirical validation.

Existential philosophy had claimed that coming to terms with finitude is at the center of human existence throughout the twentieth century, particularly in Martin Heidegger's *Being and Time* (1927) and Jean-Paul Sartre's *Being and Nothingness* (1943).[4] Heidegger and Sartre analyzed the most basic structures of human existence. Heidegger put the point in his unique style when he said that *Dasein* (literally "being-there," Heidegger's term for human existence) *stands out into nothingness.* By this Heidegger denoted two related aspects of *Dasein*: First, humans, whether consciously or not, constantly make choices, and each choice we make prevents other courses of action or life options from being actualized. Second, human existence is characterized by the awareness that it is *finite.* We know that our time is limited, and that we will die. This immensely heightens the impact of the terminal nature of our choices. Not only did we not actualize some possibilities by choosing to act as we did, but also the finite amount of time we have to live means that we did not have the option of rewinding our lives, so to speak, and trying other options as well.

It was one of Heidegger's seminal insights that awareness of finitude and freedom inevitably generates existential anxiety, which is so difficult to bear that we most of the time fend off this awareness. In Heidegger's terms, most of the time, we live in a state of inauthenticity. Instead of being aware of freedom and finitude, we live as if there are no choices, as if customs, social norms, expectations, and worldview determine completely how we live. This inauthenticity is a defense that allows us to live our lives without being flooded by anxiety.[5]

Existentialism ceased to be en vogue during the last decades. Its emphasis on the tragic dimension of human life did not square well with the mindless optimism of a culture that thrived on the idea that anxiety was for the weak-minded and should be taken care of pharmacologically. Hence, along with other great paradigms of psychodynamic thought, existentialism had been relegated to the archives of intellectual history, which in turn was studied by fewer and fewer students who were mostly busy getting degrees that would help them to launch lucrative careers as quickly as possible.

While general culture was busy with economic escapism, existential philosophy gradually regained a life of its own—which first occurred on the sidelines of academia. Irvin Yalom[6] showed that existentialism provided a valuable framework for clinical practice. The ideas of anthropologist Ernest Becker, particularly his last two books—*The Denial of Death* (1974) and the posthumously published *Escape from Evil* (1975)—reformulated some of the core ideas of existentialism in a way closer to evolutionary biology. He argues that evolution has created an impossible situation for the human species. Like all other animals, we are terrified of anything that could lead to our death. But unlike other animal species, we as humans *know of our death*.

Yet we simply cannot bear this knowledge. Becker's momentous hypothesis is that *the denial of death is one of the strongest motivators of the human species.* But how can we deny something that we know? The primary answer is that in order not to feel exposed to the naked terror of death, humans buy into worldviews that have two functions: First, they provide us with meaning. They tell us what we are here for, how to structure our lives. Second, these worldviews protect us by giving us the experience of being part of a larger whole. Belonging to a uniquely valuable group (religion, nation, or race) as defined by the worldview, makes us *eo ipso* valuable and thus bolsters our self-esteem.

In the late 1980s a new research paradigm of social psychology and the theory of motivation and personality based on Becker's ideas emerged: experimental existential psychology (EEP).[7] EEP is quite extraordinary in that it has turned a philosophical theory into a testable empirical theory with quite spectacular success, and we will encounter some of its specific results in the course of this book.

The central tenet of existential psychology is that only an animal that knows time is limited can ask, "Do I live a life worth living?" Only such an animal is preoccupied with the question whether life as a whole is good, valiant, and successful.[8] And this question camouflages the unbearable terror, which is awareness of the passage of time and the reality of death. Terror management theory,[9] one of the most successful paradigms of experimental existential psychology, has established beyond any doubt that we humans invest enormous energies to deny death, and that the denial of death is one of the most powerful motivators of the human psyche: we cannot really accept that we will die.

The Psychological Function of Self-Esteem and Worldviews

Worldviews provide us with what Ernest Becker has called symbolic immortality. Each worldview states that the group and its mission on earth are there to stay beyond our individual death. By contributing to the larger group, its task on earth and its continuity, we feel that something of us will survive our physical death. It also lowers the looming threat of the feeling of being an insignificant speck in a universe that is indifferent to us.

The denial of death is responsible for humankind's greatest achievements and for some of its most abominable traits. Behavior as diverse as building cathedrals, writing literature, and creating art, but also the initiation of wars and suicide bombings, are all linked to our need to defend ourselves against mortality.[10] If 9/11 proves anything, it is that human beings are willing to lose their lives and kill thousands of innocent people for only one reason: to preserve the worldview that provides them with meaning.

Existential psychology shows that there are basically three ways in which we defend against the terror induced by death awareness: one is attachment to significant figures, spouses, family, and close friends;[11] the second is to bolster self-esteem; and the third is to cling to cultural worldviews that imbue our lives with meaning.[12]

These three elements are interlinked developmentally. As infants and toddlers, we are completely dependent on adults to take care of us. Their expression of love and support provides us with the sense that we are safe against the dangers of the world. As we grow up and our social awareness widens, our primary caretakers (normally parents) cease to be our only frame of reference. The positive feedback we receive from an ever-widening circle becomes crucial for our self-esteem, which bolsters our sense of security.[13]

The diameter of the relevant circle increases as we grow up. Our kindergarten teacher and our little peer group broadens to a school class, a whole school, possibly a youth organization, to our peers and teachers at college, and so on.

Once we belong more or less safely, a second issue arises: self-esteem has an essential comparative element. Every group of animals is organized in hierarchies. We are genetically programmed to move up this hierarchy as high as possible. For both sexes this means access to resources; for males it means more access to females that will carry their offspring; for females it means protection by a stronger male and genes that are likely to increase the fitness of offspring.[14]

All mammals are also known to have a safety valve that prevents the fight for supremacy (which is mostly physical for nonhumans) from being lethal. When a male loses in the fight for the position of alpha male, there is a sharp drop in testosterone (the male sexual hormone associated, among others, with self-esteem and aggression) and serotonin (the neurotransmitter known to be instrumental in determining our mood).

This is manifested in body language that expresses dejection and the knowledge that we need to give up. This mechanism, which is equivalent to a mild and transient depression, is of great importance. It makes the animal relinquish the fight, acquiesce in its position, and thus prevents the physical harm or even death that is likely to result from continued challenge.

Of course we know all this from our lives. If you tune into a tennis match on television, you very quickly know which of the players is now playing better even if you don't see the result. If one of them is on a good streak, his gait between points is bouncy, his gaze aggressive, and his posture upright. The other player often looks frustrated, nervous, insecure, dejected, and beaten at worst.

We humans have inherited from our animal ancestors their natural disposition to strive for dominance and to defeat their opponents.[15] Players who have won a game show a sharp increase in testosterone and a moderate increase in serotonin, while those who have lost show a corresponding decrease. The same holds true for the physiology of two people who have competed for a promotion.

In advanced civilizations self-esteem is mostly no longer a function of beating somebody in direct competition. It is rather that we measure our achievement vis-à-vis a whole culture. The question now arises: What is your field of comparison? What are the criteria according to which you assess your value? What is the group within which you strive for status? To whom do you compare yourself?

The Emergence of Homo Globalis

The frame of reference for comparison changed radically in the last decades. The process of *globalization* that went into high gear in the 1980s with the deregulation of the financial markets became a tangible reality for anybody with an investment portfolio on October 19, 1987, the day that has gone into history as Black Monday. A severe fall of the Hong Kong Stock Exchange rapidly moved through the time zones, raced through Europe, and hit Wall Street where the Dow Jones lost 22.6 percent within a single day.

Many felt the impact of globalization in ways they did not necessarily understand. In its first stages, global connectedness was clear for those who made strategic decisions, like moving manufacturing jobs to countries with cheaper labor, whereas workers who lost these jobs did not quite understand how this came about. This also happened to lawyers or accountants who had conducted their practices for decades without worrying about the new global trend and were suddenly faced with the emergence of global law firms and accounting giants like Ernst & Young, Andersen, and KPMG with whom they couldn't compete.

But soon global consciousness became a reality for anyone with cable television. Operation Desert Storm, the first invasion of Iraq in 1991, with its embedded reporters, allowed viewers around the globe to share the experience of the troops that moved into Kuwait and Iraq in real time. It also made clear to everybody that what happens at a point on the globe that many couldn't even find on the map had powerful implications everywhere. September 11, 2001, brought this to new heights. Within minutes after CNN broke the news of the first jet crashing into the South Tower, the world was glued to television screens, thus creating the first terrorist act to be transmitted globally and to instantly change the way people from New York to Canberra and from Karachi to Buenos Aires experienced the world.

Culturally the power of global interconnectedness hit upon the young generation through the emergence of MTV, which started broadcasting in 1981 and soon turned into a global phenomenon. New art forms like the music video spread around the world within a few years and created a lingua franca for youngsters around the world.

The emergence of the Internet[16] truly changed ordinary people's daily experience dramatically. In the past it would take many years of hard work to introduce concepts, ideas, and brands that had global recognition value. Now images, ideas, and information travelled the globe at the speed of light. The Internet enabled brands and concepts such as Google and YouTube within months to span the globe and change people's lives in ways ranging from the way people did research to how they conducted their social lives. MySpace allowed people to peek into the most private aspects of lives that were on the other side of the earth. YouTube made it possible for Muslim preachers in Egypt to reach believers in Oregon; Amazon.com made it possible to order Stephen King's latest novel on the day it was published, no matter where you resided.

Homo globalis is a reality. In his seminal 1992 work, *The End of History and the Last Man*, Francis Fukuyama[17] argued that liberal democracy and free market capitalism were the political and economic arrangement that would take hold of the whole world. With some regret he had also predicted that Homo globalis would sign up for bourgeois values; no large philosophical questions would be asked anymore, and the Last Man (a term Fukuyama borrowed from Nietzsche) would settle into questions no deeper than what car to buy and how to get good insurance for it.

But reality turned out to be very different. Tom Friedman[18] tellingly entitled his analysis of globalization *The Lexus and the Olive Tree*. "Lexus" was an example of the brands that commanded instant recognition anywhere on earth. The olive tree was used by Friedman as a symbol for national, religious, and ethnic identities. These had not disappeared or merged into global identities, but, as Friedman was keen to point out, often hardened and reached for ways to become more deeply rooted under the threat of the leveling influence of global capitalism and Western (or, more precisely, American) culture that was pumped around the world through the global infotainment system. Globalization in fact led to an ever growing clash between what political scientist Benjamin Barber[19] called "Jihad vs. McWorld." Along with thinkers like historian of religion Karen Armstrong,[20] Barber argued that many forms of fundamentalism were distinctly modern phenomena driven by globalization. They made a strong case that modern fundamentalism was a completely new movement that could only be understood within the context of the impact of global capitalism. Political philosopher John Gray[21] made a strong case that al Qaeda could only be understood within the context of hypermodernity.

Symbolic Immortality and the Global Playing Field

For Homo globalis, maintaining meaning and identity became ever more complex. No culture was now immune from the influx and influence of foreign cultures, ways of life, religions, and technological achievements. It became ever more difficult to feel that your belief system had exclusive validity, and that the group that defined your identity was uniquely valuable.

An Egyptian Pharaoh presumably knew about adjacent cultures, and the Classical Greek's awareness of other cultures is historically documented. Ancient Greeks called non-Greeks *hoi barbaroi*, those barbarians (literally: those without a real language); to them it was clear that the only frame of reference relevant for their self-esteem was Greece. You knew pretty well what you had to do to be respected and who you wanted to be remembered by after your death.

A Dutch merchant of the seventeenth century knew quite a bit about the world, because his wealth depended on importing goods from around the globe to Europe. But there wasn't the slightest doubt that culturally Christendom was the only frame of reference that really mattered. The Netherlands of the seventeenth century was unique at the time because it was characterized by a belief in tolerance and a remarkable ability to accept religious diversity. Nevertheless a Dutch merchant's daily dealings were limited to those that he could communicate with directly, and this is what primarily defined his self-esteem.

As opposed to the Dutch merchant a few centuries ago, we have immediate access to audiovisual information about every corner of the globe. This is essentially the new element in the existential situation of the inhabitant of the global village. The question is, how do you define your place in a global playing field? How can you feel that your worldview is intrinsically meaningful if there are so many alternatives?

The global playing field now proposed a simple answer to the question of how cultures and worldviews could be valued. They needed to be ranked according to a quantitative measure. Mathematics is, after all, the most objective of sciences. Advanced economics became governed by an ever growing, blind belief in the power of quantification. The value of *everything* had to be expressible in some number. This seemed obvious in the domain of economics, which was ostensibly about quantity to begin with. The nation or culture you belonged to could be ranked by its per capita gross domestic product—that is, by how fast its economy grew. The city you lived in could be ranked by how many global companies had their headquarters there.

Companies were ranked all the time, and the measures multiplied to make the ranking game more interesting. It was no longer just whether you were the largest company; you could also be the fastest-growing, the most profitable company; the company rated most inventive by some rating agency; the company rated most fun to work at.

Never mind that Nobel Laureate Daniel Kahaneman and his deceased coresearcher Amos Twersky had argued for years that all of these models were based on wrong assumptions on how the human mind worked; or that George Soros, who had proven that he could play the markets like a grand piano said that the market's functioning was inherently flawed and irrational; or that future Nobel Laureate Paul Krugman kept saying that the American economy was not generating any real value and that the numbers were lying.[22] But the quantification mind-set said that the numbers *couldn't* be lying. Quantification was the gospel of the golden calf, and doubting it was nothing but a quaint remainder of those who had not yet grasped the new religion.

The Great Delusion

We are awaking from more than two decades of what history will probably come to judge as a strange, worldwide delusion of omnipotence. Historians will find many reasons for what Alan Greenspan, one of the architects of the global economic meltdown at a certain moment called "irrational exuberance." For more than two decades we were all swept into two illusions.

The first was that there were no real problems left for humanity to solve. We had it all figured out: free markets, representative democracy, and human rights were the three ideas that had conquered the world.[23] With the fall of the Berlin Wall, the last great obstacle to world peace and prosperity had been removed. We lived at the end of history, after the end of ideology. Whatever was left to solve was basically a matter of good management. The world just needed to be turned over to economists to fix. The International Monetary Fund (IMF) and the World Bank, in unison with the U.S. Federal Reserve, headed through most of this period by the guru of endless economic growth through deregulation, Alan Greenspan, would fix states that had not yet quite aligned with the holy rules of the Free Market.

There was really no more use asking deep questions about the nature of the good life and the good society. Philosophical questions were for the sickly minded, left behind in the race for riches and celebrity. The point was to get ahead in life; existential questions could, after all, be answered by picking one of the world religions off the shelf. If none quite fitted, there was an endless supply of new fusion spiritualities that could be adapted to your specific needs and desires.

The second illusion was that in a world of endless economic growth, the world was up for grabs, open 24/7 for those who had the guts and the imagination to reach for the stars. You could be anything you wanted. You could shape yourself and your life as you wished, and along the way become immensely rich. The good life depended on whether you went ahead to "just do it."

The examples of those who had just done it were plentiful. Michael Jordan had taught the world to fly; Michael Jackson had shown that you could build your fantasyland through sheer talent; Bill Gates had shown that you could become the world's richest man in no time. The Wachowski brothers showed that you could turn your childhood infatuation with Japanese comics and kung fu movies into a spectacular trilogy that would gross billions.

The deification of endless economic growth and the myth of "just do it" together were the foundation of the age of the golden calf. Margaret Thatcher and Ronald Reagan had preached its gospel: greed was good. We were all responsible for ourselves, and we shouldn't expect anything from the state or society. Nevertheless unfettered capitalism would, ultimately, benefit all. Reagan's theory of trickledown economics stated that the riches amassed at the top of the pyramid would end up making money for everybody.

For an ever growing number of people in the developed world, this actually seemed to work. Richard Florida[24] christened this group the *creative class*: the professionals ranging from journalists, designers, and academics to doctors, lawyers, engineers, and senior executives who were in high demand, could pick from what seemed an endless supply of exciting jobs, and could speed up their careers through diagonal moves across companies, universities, hospitals, and an ever growing number of new media.

True: there were some worrying indicators; the income gap between the wealthy and the poor grew at a staggering pace. Some party poopers claimed that something was wrong with a financial system that allowed a single speculator to topple a currency. Some found the idea unpalatable that global companies could force ever new tax breaks onto governments by the simple threat of moving their management and operations elsewhere, particularly if these companies paid their CEOs five hundred times the average salary of its employees. Others again claimed that the new financial instruments that were flooding the market were too opaque to be assessed realistically. But nobody wanted to listen. The golden calf was too attractive to be questioned. Hence critics were dutifully discarded as Cassandras, and, if necessary, fired from their jobs to stop disturbing the party.[25]

The gospel of quantification pushed its way into domains that had previously been untouched by it. High culture had, for a long time, resisted the pressure of quantification. The value of paintings, compositions, books, and ideas had not been measured by how many people had watched, listened to, read, or believed them. There was supposed to be something like an intrinsic value to the creations of high culture. Universities, the supposed sanctuary of high culture, were, as yet, supposed to be beyond quantification, too.

These bulwarks of high culture were crumbling quickly from the 1980s onwards. The iconic event was probably the series of concerts in the 1990s that came to be known as "The Three Tenors" that united opera stars Placido Domingo, Luciano Pavarotti, and Jose Carreras in a single show that became a great financial success. While some argued that this project acquainted many who would never have listened to it otherwise with opera, others saw this as an indication that classical music was gradually being killed by being chopped into user-friendly sound-bites in which the three tenors screamed high Cs in unison. In parallel, an ever growing number of symphony orchestras needed to close down because of financial difficulties, as attendance at classical music concerts dropped dramatically.

The value of a record was quite simple: it depended on how many were sold; the same went for books. Paintings were different: there could be only one of them—so the value was a matter of the price it fetched at Sotheby's or Christie's. Some of the buyers of Van Goghs, Cezannes, or Picassos may have known little about the painting's place in the development of the painter or an artistic school. But they had an irrefutable proof for the value of what they now owned: the money it had fetched at an auction that had been conducted globally.

Even religions, which sprouted at the pace of three new religions a day (yes, religion was a growth business), could now be measured quantitatively. The Catholic Church was worried by declining market share in the Western world, whereas Islam could proudly announce that it was on the way to overtake Christianity as the world's largest religion. Then again, some of the new churches, which were run as sophisticated marketing operations, could claim that they were fastest growing (some of them acquired constituencies measuring millions and funds measuring billions a few years after inception).

So why care about whether a belief system made any sense, whether it was a patchwork put together from incompatible historical sources like Indian Astrology and Kabbalah? Why should you subject it to critical examination? Why should you care whether it stood up to critical examination? Why should you check whether the latest spiritual guru your company had brought in for a little feel-good effect made any sense or whether he just put together some platitudes dressed up with Eastern sounding terms? If the guru had been hired by other *Fortune* 500 companies and commanded high fees, he must be good; if a book like *The Secret* sold millions of copies, here was a good reason to buy it.

The same held true for political belief systems. The two Bush administrations pushed to its ultimate conclusion the concept that ideas are measured only by how well they can be marketed. Truth and coherence ceased to be of any importance. If there was no case for either the connection between Saddam Hussein's regime and al Qaeda or its having piles of weapons of mass destruction, the case was simply made up.[26] With the efficient help of Karl Rove, Bush managed to get himself reelected, because his constituency no longer cared about the truth value of his ideas. The age of the golden calf had come to its pinnacle: Ideas and belief systems had become commodities whose value was determined by supply and demand, like any other.

The Global I-Commodity Market

It was only a matter of logic to extend this model of quantitative ranking to human beings. By the inner logic of the game of quantifying value, money was the simplest measure, because it could be counted easily. Of course riches had played an important role in human affairs before. But now wealth was no longer just a measure of what you could afford, how safe you were and how much power you had. It became an indication of your value as a human being. The locution "he's worth X dollars" became more than a shortcut; it became a literal truth.

The next step was to find other ways of ranking humans. The spread of global capitalism and the craze for quantification and rankings created what I will call the *global I-Commodity Market*, and the result is the I-Commodity. Like every commodity its value depends on myriads of factors ranging from the rise or fall of supply and demand, the marketing success of competitors and so on. The measures and ranking multiply: while writing these pages I looked up the various *Forbes* lists, the *Times 100* list, and *People Magazine*. I double-checked some facts about Google founders Larry Page and Sergei Brin, Steve Jobs, Oprah Winfrey, Tiger Woods, and Philip Roth. I didn't have to move from my chair to do so, and the info was not only textual; I could watch any number of videos, photos, and interviews that I wanted.

The problem is the sheer *size* of the field of comparison, which for the first time in history has become truly global. Of course most of us are not constantly busy measuring our place in the global playing field (if we did, it would probably lead to a sharp increase in suicides), but this global field is there as an implicit background to what we do.

Here we come to the dark secret of Homo globalis: the same computer monitor that makes creative work so much easier also provides an endless stream of information about the feats of the global world-class, information that invariably impacts Homo globalis's self-esteem. The mechanism that helped our ancestors not to fight to the death in the struggle for status, giving up and experiencing a mild depression, now becomes the basis of an epidemic. In the global I-Commodity Market each of us is beaten by some spectacular achievement somewhere in the globe thousands of times, daily.

Two of our age's icons, Larry Page and Sergei Brin, now in their midthirties, have literally changed the world. Never mind the fact that they each have an estimated net worth close to $20 billion. Their achievement goes way beyond the incredible financial and marketing success they have experienced. They changed the way we use the World Wide Web and made it a matter of course for us that the first results of our searches almost invariably are what we were really looking for (anyone still remember the frustration of the early search engines that brought you endless, useless sites?). In doing so they have also created another global rating scale, the number of Google entries each of us has, and their ranking status.

Even the supposed sanctuary of western culture, academia, is at this point largely ruled by a rating system. It is, of course, supposed to be a completely objective system (even though there have been often acrimonious debates about its value) that combines the impact factors of the scientific journals in which you have been published and the number of citations that your work receives. In theory there should be one single number that measures your current market evaluation in your discipline.

So what matters more: the number of citations you have, or the number of Google entries? Or shouldn't all this be eclipsed by the fact that *Vanity Fair* has carried a profile on you? Or should you really care more about eternity and do research that may not get much media exposure, but might become a long-term contribution to your field?

The value of the I-Commodity is a complex amalgam of the various ranking systems. And we haven't even started to speak about the more local ranking systems. Are you popular with your friends? Do society columns write about you—and if they do, will this lower your ranking in academia? Do you easily get good tables at top restaurants on crowded evenings? How many New Years wishes do you get?

There are ranking systems that quite explicitly rank the self proper, without direct reference to any achievement: they are the purest expression of the global I-Commodity Market. The various social network sites do exactly that. Take Facebook: the most immediate datum of your commodity value is the number of friends you have. But there are further measures: how many of your friends are well connected? How many of them are celebs? In other words: when someone looks at your friends in Facebook, how many of them will make people think that you are valuable or important?

It has actually come to the point where the ultimate snobbery is that of *not* having a profile in Facebook, LinkedIn, Zoom-Info, or one of the many, many other social networking websites. Instead, you long to be a member of Smallworld, an exclusive website for the rich and famous to be joined by invitation only, the jet set that wants to be informed about the (presumably) most prestigious social events in the world.

Your ranking on the global I-Commodity Market not only impacts your self-esteem; it also determines your possibilities—and these possibilities in turn impact on your self-esteem and well-being. It could be argued that you can only count as a Homo globalis if you are recognized by some of the global ranking systems. If you weren't, you wouldn't get a position in one of the organizations that choose their employees or members according to their standing in the relevant ranking system.

In other words, Homo globalis is no longer just a manager or the owner of a self-portfolio. Homo globalis *is now the portfolio itself*; a commodity whose daily value depends on a myriad of factors, most of which are not under our control. The global "I" commodity market's credo has therefore become "I am ranked, therefore I am."

It is very difficult to ascertain what the impact of this global I-Commodity Market is on Homo globalis's well-being. There is research that shows that there is a dramatic increase in anxiety disorders, depression, and a huge rise in the use of antidepressant and antianxiety medication, mostly SSRIs (selective serotonin reuptake inhibitors like Prozac, Paxil, Zoloft, etc.).[27] Even though these results are problematic, because most of this research is funded by the companies that produce the drugs, they indicate an existing trend, and are as such frightening.

In any case they only point to the tip of the iceberg. Below the radar of explicitly psychopathological research there is a much more pervasive phenomenon: many members of Homo globalis suffer from a pervasive existential panic and from a persistent sense of failing to live lives that truly matter. I will show that most of this suffering is not psychopathological in nature, but reflects the impact of the global I-Commodity Market on us all.

2

"Just Do It"

The Celebrity Culture and the Designed Self

Conventional wisdom has it that we live in a hyperindividualist age. But in many ways individuality has been diminished by the impact of the global I-Commodity Market. The global I-Commodity Market is a node in a network of markets and rating systems. There seems to be no historical and cultural depth, no inner anchoring to the self; and it is almost impossible to maintain a true sense of individuality beyond the rating of the global I-Commodity Market. Lives are reduced to careers and the narration of one's lifetime looks more like a series of achievement graphs in the domain of career, excitement, and fleeting attachments than the biography of a human being with depth.

The good life seems to be reduced to the question how well we are doing on the global I-Commodity Market: Is our career sufficiently spectacular? Have we achieved the recognition we seek? Is our lifestyle multifaceted and stylish enough? Have we succeeded in maintaining a cool image even though we are working around the clock to keep up with the global Joneses?

Too often we confuse living a life with having a career. We are pressured into telling about our lives as marketable curriculum vitae: with titles we have acquired, positions we have held, and successes that were measurable. As David Brooks has pointed out, *The New York Times*'s wedding announcements sometimes sound more like mergers between two career paths than like unions between human beings.[1]

The infotainment system keeps feeding us images of what the enviable life looks like. The state of mind generated by the global I-Commodity Market makes enviableness into a central measure of whether we have made it or not. Would our lives look good on the pages of *House and Garden*? Charlotte, one of the characters in the HBO television series *Sex and*

.. *City*, indeed sees a central success in the possibility that her Park Avenue apartment will be photographed for this magazine—at the very moment when her marriage is falling apart. Carrie Bradshaw, the series' narrator, and Samantha, the lusty public relations consultant, are constantly worried about being invited to the right parties, wearing the right clothes, and the right brands.

While the characters of *Sex and the City* are, on purpose, slightly over-drawn, they reflect many contemporary members of the global creative class's concerns quite well. Even our sex lives are anxiously monitored to make sure that we are doing well on the indices of the global I-Commodity Market that are constantly updated with the latest information by pieces in *Cosmopolitan*, *Esquire*, and other sources of information about the lifestyle of those who are doing well.

I harbor no illusions about the centrality of the human propensity to worry about our status and to compare ourselves to others. Furthermore my intention is neither to vilify nor to condemn what is after all a very human trait, which along with many deleterious effects, also leads many to high achievement. And we should not forget that our need to compare endlessly between each other feeds our insatiable appetite for gossip with ever new information about achievements, failures, scandals, and successes— certainly one of the pleasures of life. But during the age of the golden calf, the obsession to compare the self and its achievements rose to proportions that all but took over the identities of members of Homo globalis.

Just Do It!

One of the most successful advertising campaigns in history was Nike's "just do it" campaign. During the 2008 Olympics, Nike celebrated the campaign's twentieth birthday with a video titled "Courage," which starts with "everything you need is already inside" followed by the phrase "I got soul but I'm not a soldier" from The Killers' song, "All These Things I've Done." Within sixty seconds we see split seconds of athletes who have endorsed Nike through the decades: from Carl Lewis to Michael Johnson (both world-record holders and multiple Olympic gold medalists); from John McEnroe to Roger Federer and Maria Sharapova (all ATP number one players and the latter a WTA top-seeded player); and of course the man who more than anybody else symbolizes the Nike *spirit*—Michael Jordan, generally recognized as the greatest basketball player in history. The last shot is of the South African athlete who attempted to qualify for the normal Olympics, even though he is missing both legs.[2]

There is nothing that can't be done. "Impossible is nothing," as the slogan of Nike's prime competitor, German company Adidas says. These slogans define a period in history pretty much spanning Nike's "just do it" (abbreviated as JDI) campaign. It was a period in time that seemed to prove that indeed everything is possible.

A number of interrelated technological, social, and political developments evolved into an atmosphere that created the feeling that human history had taken a new turn. Limitations and divisions that had defined the human condition and global history for centuries seemed to disappear.

In 1989, one year after the onset of the JDI campaign, the Berlin Wall fell. Within a few years, the Soviet Union was dismantled and all Middle and Eastern Europe replaced Communist regimes with liberal democracy. Also in 1989, a formerly obscure researcher at the U.S. State Department, Francis Fukuyama, was catapulted into stardom by a paper titled "The End of History." Its argument, greatly expanded in the 1992 book of the same name,[3] was that there were powerful reasons to believe that liberal democracy was the final political arrangement in history because it suits human nature: it provides efficient economic arrangement and also meets the human need for recognition and self-determination. It looked as if the ideological divisions that had plagued the twentieth century were finally relegated to the past. Humans were about to fulfill the Enlightenment dream of managing their affairs rationally and thus attain peace and stability.

A new generation of politicians burst onto the global scene, which by virtue of their personalities no less than by their political message, embodied this hope for a new world. In 1992 Bill Clinton, the youngest president since John F. Kennedy, was elected in the United States. He was the first baby boomer to become the most powerful person on earth, and he had it all figured out: he would combine capitalist efficiency with the social conscience of American liberalism. He was soon joined on the other side of the Atlantic by Tony Blair, a charismatic youngster who at age 44 took the British Labour Party to the first of his three consecutive victories riding on the slogan "Cool Britannia." Together they defined the new ethos that was about to take over the world: the *third way*, a worldview beyond Left and Right and beyond the ideological tensions of the past that would lead the world into a new age of harmony.[4]

Along with these political developments came technological innovations that promised to link the newly unified humanity into a seamless web of instant communication. In 1989, CERN, the European Organization for Nuclear Research, opened its first external Internet using TCP/IP, the protocol that would become the lingua franca spanning the world. Within a few years, the Internet turned from an obscure tool used by the Pentagon, NASA, and organizations like CERN into a phenomenon that would change the world. From 1992 to 2006, the number of Internet hosts would grow from zero to more than 350 million while billions of dollars were invested in optical-fiber networks that could carry all this information around the globe.[5]

This revolution did not just benefit government agencies, large companies, and armies. Computing power became available to almost everybody in the developed world. In 1998 a hard disk with 150 MB storage capacity cost $8,755. Today a desktop with a built-in hard disk of 750 GB can be bought for less than $1,000. The personal computer (PC) was relatively rare in 1988. As of June 2008, it was estimated that there were more than one billion computers in the world.

In 1990 there were slightly more than 5.5 million cellular phone users in the United States. In 2005 this number had grown to 219 million in the United States and to more than 2.1 billion worldwide. In the late 1990s cellular phones were able to connect to the web; and in 1999, BlackBerry introduced the first phone that enabled users to access their email at any place where there was cellular coverage. The global communication network was now literally in everyone's pocket and the launch of the iPhone in 2007 closed the circle: users can now surf the web with this smartphone, enjoy the graphics, and listen to weeks of music stored on the same device.

The breakthrough in communications technology also catapulted the scale of economic success stories into the stratosphere. In 1985 Microsoft founded by Paul Allen, Bill Gates, and Steven Ballmer offered its first user-friendly operating system, Microsoft Windows. In 1986 the company was launched in an initial public offering and its market capitalization instantaneously went to more than half a billion dollars. As of September 2008, its market capitalization was $230 billion and had come to dominate the market of PC operating systems worldwide. Bill Gates, its main shareholder and chairman, was the wealthiest man on the globe with a personal fortune that exceeded $80 billion before he founded the Bill and Melinda Gates Foundation with an initial donation of $25 billion.[6]

In 1994 the first search engines enabling people to find things on the web were launched. In 1998 two 27-year-old Stanford students, Larry Page and Sergey Brin, founded Google with $100,000 of seed capital. This company would soon change the way the Internet was used. By 2008, the company had a market capitalization approaching $200 billion. The story of Google became paradigmatic for the age. Not only had the two youngsters become multibillionaires within a very short time, but they also left an imprint on the world and now galloped toward their goal of revolutionizing access to the whole of human knowledge. The sky was no longer the limit.[7]

The two decades from 1988 to 2008 do not define a generation in the usual sociological sense; they are not a birth cohort like the baby boomers or Generation X. What defined these two decades was that globalization became a lived reality for an ever-growing number of humans. The deregulation of the financial markets in the 1980s made globalization a fact for corporations and their executives. But the enormous boom in communication technology during the last two decades made globalization a lived reality for anybody with an Internet connection.

Particularly since the onset of efficient search engines, the amount and range of information, entertainment, imagery, and video have become staggering. There are hardly any corners of the world, any social, historical, economic, technological, medical information, as well as gossip about anybody on the globe that are not accessible through the fingertips.

Members of Homo globalis are defined by the feeling that being plugged into the worldwide infotainment network is in a deep sense definitive of their experience of their place in the world. I use a subjective definition because Homo globalis's age ranges from youngsters to midlifers who feel that their frame of reference has changed. For many of them, daily lives and their work are literally involving global communication on a minute-by-minute basis. Financial markets are abuzz 24 hours a day and there is never a moment in which one of the markets around the globe is not working. The Internet has reached the point where most major newspapers have websites that are updated 24/7, 365 days a year.

There is no commodity that is not traded around the globe and around the clock. This is true not only for the more traditional commodities like raw materials but also for the commodity that now makes up a large percentage of all developed economies: information, texts, images, music, software, and scientific and technological research are being produced, marketed, published, and traded in an endless stream distributed through a network literally functioning at the speed of light.

The Impact of the Global Infotainment Network on Personal Identity

It has become commonplace to say that the explosion of information technology has produced a social, economic, and cultural revolution comparable in its extent and impact of the industrial revolution that went under way in the late eighteenth century. The latter dramatically changed the lives of the population in the newly industrial world. While in agrarian societies the vast majority of the population lived in rural areas, this revolution led to an ever growing concentration of the population in cities, destroying the social fabric of small communities and leading to the shift from community to society (*Gemeinschaft* and *Gesellschaft*) as the German sociologist Ferdinand Tönnies argued.[8]

Within the span of a century the frame of reference for most humans in developed economies completely changed. From being embedded in communities in which most people knew each other, they moved into a framework ruled by abstract rules and regulation rather than by custom and ritual. They could no longer count on their neighbors knowing them, never mind caring about them. Autonomy and self-management became virtues more important than loyalty.

The upside of the loss of being embedded in a community was higher mobility. At least in theory, it was now possible to be socially mobile in ways that could not be dreamed of in agrarian societies. The distinction between aristocracy and ordinary mortals was abolished. At least in principle, circumstances of birth no longer set the limit of where you could go and how far you could evolve. While de facto mobility was still curtailed by many, primarily economic factors, Western societies began to evolve to a state closer to the ideal of meritocracy. Gradually, abilities and motivation rather than circumstances of birth determined fate.

Large proportions of the population did not experience much of this mobility. Workers in a Manchester textile plant were very unlikely to make it out of their misery into the relative safety, stability, prosperity, and status of the middle classes. Neither the necessary capital for developing a business nor the financial means to receive the education necessary for joining the professions that guaranteed entry into the middle classes was within the working class's reach.

The twentieth century gradually increased social mobility, particularly after World War II, during the unprecedented boom of economic growth in the developed economies. In the United States the G.I. Bill made higher education affordable to more people than ever before, and in most European universities, education was available without tuition to all who fulfilled the academic requirements. The higher education system grew exponentially, eroding the limits that differentiated between the working class, lower-middle class, and upper-middle class.

In the late 1980s, something happened. You would have expected that the explosion in communication technologies should have led to a decentralization of economic activity. In some respects it did. It was no longer necessary to have management and production at one place. Multinational corporations began to move production to countries with lower labor costs; Nike did so efficiently—and notoriously—by moving most of its production to China into sweatshop-like environments. Already by the end of the 1980s cars were produced making use of parts manufactured in countries spanning the globe.

Yet in parallel a new development set in. Sociologist Saskia Sassen coined the term "global cities" for the hubs that became the effective centers of the world economy. When she originally did her research in the late 1980s, she thought there were three such cities: New York, London, and Tokyo. In the early 2000s in the second edition of *The Global City* she had added a vast number of cities to this list ranging from Zurich to Shanghai, Paris to Hong Kong, and so on.

Sassen defined global cities by their concentration of headquarters of multinational corporations. It turned out that the new communication technologies had not eliminated the need for face-to-face contact between the leading players of the global economy. The upper tiers of management and the companies and firms that provided financial, legal, and advertising services to the multinationals crowded into a limited number of places on the globe.

Within a very short time a new class evolved at the border of the upper and the upper-middle classes, which led Secretary of Labor and now University of California, Berkeley, public policy professor Robert Reich to speak of the "New Rich-Rich Gap." He writes,

> A new group is emerging at the very top. They're CEOs and CFOs of global corporations, and partners and executives in global investment banks, law firms, and consultancies. Unlike most national symbolic analysts, these global symbolic analysts conduct almost all their work in English, and share with one another an increasingly similar cosmopolitan culture.
>
> Most global symbolic analysts have been educated at the same elite institutions—America's Ivy League universities, Oxford, Cambridge, the London School of Economics or the University of California, Berkeley. They work in similar environments—in glass-and-steel office towers in the world's largest cities, in jet planes and international-meeting resorts. And they feel as comfortable in New York, London or Geneva as they do in Hong Kong, Shanghai or Sydney. When they're not working—and they tend to work very hard—they live comfortably, and enjoy golf and first-class hotels. Their income and wealth far surpass those of national symbolic analysts.[9]

In terms of income this group did fabulously well. The average salary of employees at Goldman Sachs in 2007 was $661,490 a year and Lehman Brothers (before it was wiped out, of course) was in the mid-$300,000 range. Senior partners of the law firms catering to corporate clients took home high six- or low seven-figure incomes, and so did the partners in the leading consulting, auditing, and advertising firms who implemented worldwide marketing and branding strategies.

The boards of global multinationals gave their CEOs stratospheric remunerations. In the United States the typical CEO of a large company made more than four hundred times the average salary of its employees, and upper tiers of management also received bonuses and option packages that turned them into millionaires many times over.

Add to this the growing number of high-tech entrepreneurs and the upper levels of their companies that made phenomenal fortunes when their startup companies were taken public, and the new class of those who managed the wealth of the new upper class.

Reich points out that a growing number of service workers are making their living by servicing the lives of this new upper class. I should add that this holds true for the economies of global cities in general that are focused increasingly on this upper class.

The impact of this new upper class was felt most strongly by the traditional upper-middle class Reich calls the "national symbolic analysts." The first impact is quite concrete. Global cities became unaffordable for a growing number of people with real estate prices and rents shooting through the roof into stratospheric heights. The economies of global cities became centered on catering to the needs of this new upper class.

The second impact was psychological. I have, for example, worked with physicians who felt like complete idiots. "I have studied and specialized for fifteen years, and I'm starting to make money only now. I feel like a complete idiot when I look at my classmates who dropped out of medicine and moved to some biotech company or a fund that invests in them. They have more money now than I'll make in a lifetime!"

These physicians represent the larger group of the traditional professions who feel largely disenfranchised. First, they feel financially stressed. They need to work very hard just to get their kids through college and they still feel that they have difficulties maintaining the lifestyles that they were led to expect when they chose their professions.

Second, they feel that the status that they expected when they entered their professions eludes them. If doctors or lawyers could once reasonably expect to be respected in their communities, most of them, except a few stars plugged into the system of Reich's "international symbolic analysts," don't make the type of money needed to afford a lifestyle with the prestige that was associated with the traditional professions in the past.

My father was a lawyer in Basel, Switzerland; a relatively small city, it was very well off because of the concentration of leading pharmaceutical companies like Roche, Ciba-Geigy, and Sandoz (which merged into Novartis) that had their headquarters and research and development (R&D) in Basel. In the 1960s and 1970s there were just about two hundred lawyers in Basel. As a young child, walking through the city center with my dad was a reassuring experience. Every few steps somebody would greet him, and he would, in old-fashioned European manner, lift his hat to greet back.

There was a class of very wealthy patrician families in Basel. Most of them had been in the city for centuries and they included the owners of Roche (to this date largely owned by a few families). Yet they did not set the tone of the city's general atmosphere. It was the educated middle class, lawyers like my father, physicians, researchers in the chemical industry, architects, and university professors that defined the cultural atmosphere and the horizon of expectations for those who, like me, were about to choose their professional course. It was clear that the established professions would provide you with both the financial means and a gratifying status. The upper classes were there, but they did not define the middle class's horizon of expectation.

This was to change dramatically with the rise of the new upper class. The next generation of lawyers would already compete for the large corporate accounts that would raise their income and status into a different sphere. Within a short span of time, Reich's national symbolic analysts would come to feel that they were largely left behind.

Sociologist Dalton Conley has aptly termed the resulting state of mind as the "economic red-shift effect."[10] Professionals who move into the $200,000 bracket, which not long ago was considered to be a high income, now feel that while they are making more money, the goal of feeling well off is actually receding into a distance. Instead of feeling better off, they feel that they are working around the clock without getting anywhere, a phenomenon that was described by *Forbes* magazine as the "seething resentment of the rich against the super-rich."

I believe that besides the tangible economic problems that the economic structure of the global cities inflicts on all strata of the middle class and Conley's economic red-shift effect, there is an additional phenomenon.

Existential psychology has shown the depth of the human need to matter, make a difference, and feel a significant purpose in this world. We all need to feel that we do something that matters within the frame of reference that defines our experiential world. The question is, what is this frame of reference?

Those who belong to the group of national symbolic analysts may be highly competent and do interesting work, but their impact and reach is limited to their immediate environment. During most of my father's career, starting in the mid-1950s, this mattered far less, because the frame of reference was not yet global. But those who are "only" national symbolic analysts feel left out, because the global infotainment system has become the Homo globalis's frame of reference. Even if they are not part of the relatively small elite that is involved in running business at a global level, they cannot help but be aware of the diminishing importance of what they do.

Add to this the many national symbolic analysts who have lost their independence through the new global developments. For lawyers it is becoming increasingly difficult to be competitive in a market that has come to be dominated by ever larger firms able to provide 24/7 services, providing their global clients with legal services at very high speed. The same holds true for consultants, accountants, and advertisers whose environment has changed dramatically with the advent of global firms like McKinsey, Ernst & Young, and McCann Erickson.

Within a local environment, individual practitioners of the professions were established brands even though they wouldn't call themselves that. You would just talk about the good standing and name of a professional. Within a global context, positioning became dependent on being associated with a brand that had global standing.

David Rothkopf has argued that the world is run by what he calls the "superclass,"[11] a group that he estimates to number about six thousand people. They are the new Davos men, the thin elite composed of heads of state, the upper echelons of the world's most powerful companies, and the few individuals whose personal wealth provides them with global influence. Without necessarily buying into Rothkopf's definition, he certainly captures a reality. The new global upper class has strongly impacted both the economic and the existential reality of the vast majority of those who are not within this echelon.

The impact of globalization on cultural production and the arts was similar. Until a few decades ago the publishing business was defined by publishing houses—like Alfred Knopf, Robert Strauss, Robert Giroux, Germany's Samuel Fischer, and Paris's Gaston Gallimard—whose owners deeply cared about literature and who knew and nurtured their authors personally. The economics of publishing made it possible to publish books that would sell a few thousand copies and put literary and intellectual quality over the demands of the mass market.

Within a few decades the economics of scale took over. Independent publishers were bought up by large companies and consolidated into the powerhouses of the global infotainment sector.[12] Today a few infotainment giants like Viacom, Sony, and Bertelsmann own many of the leading publishers; and the managers of international publishing mostly have little actual connection to books and literature. When previously independent publishers are bought up, their backlists are often slashed on the basis of nothing but sales numbers, depriving both authors and the reading public of often-valuable titles.

In parallel, the last decades have seen the decline and death of most independent booksellers who have given way to giants like Barnes & Noble, Waterstone, FNAC, and of course Internet giant Amazon.com. As a result publishers fight for the prime shelf space and entrance tables of those book chains whose bargaining power runs so high that they can influence titles and design of books.

Similar developments have taken place in the music and film business. Enormous power is concentrated with a few major studios, recording companies, and cable networks. The result is what John Seabrook has called "Nobrow Culture"[13] in which marketing considerations have almost completely overruled judgments of quality to the point where it has become unclear whether there is any quality left except for ranking and sales success. What is sometimes euphemistically called the democratization of taste really means that the market puts pressure to produce what appeals to the lowest common denominator.

Why Not Just Do It?

The impact of these developments on Homo globalis's material and psychological reality is enormous. On the one hand the possibilities of those who want to live more individualized forms of life are more limited. From lawyers to booksellers and from accountants to playwrights, the pressure to conform to the demands of the global markets is enormous.

On the other hand there is the endless lure of the highly publicized success stories of global entrepreneurs and the emergence of the new class of star CEOs and global celebrities. "Just do it" was more than an advertising slogan. It was a lived reality. If the 1980s had produced spectacular business success and great wealth for the stars of the financial sector, the 1990s and early 2000s dwarfed those stories. From Steven Jobs to Mark Zuckerberg, from Eminem to Beyoncé Knowles, there is plenty of proof that you can make it to the top of the global heap. It seemed that anybody with guts, inventiveness, and a computer linked to the Internet could become an incredible success story. From e-Bay to Google and from YouTube to Facebook, the stories that seemingly proved that the sky is the limit kept multiplying.

Let us now analyze the psychological effect of one of the most successful ad campaigns in history: Nike's JDI. Let me start with my favorite ad. Michael Jordan's 30-second "Failure" commercial.[14] We see Jordan exit a black SUV, striding slowly toward the player's entrance, presumably in a stadium. He is greeted by ordinary mortals—security personnel, cleaners, and so on—who look at him admiringly. He is dressed in a gray suit, black overcoat, and white shirt. His wardrobe provides a sense both of size and strength and of quiet elegance. In the background, Jordan's bass voice softly recounts the statistics of his failures: missed shots, missed game-defining shots entrusted to him, and lost games. His final words opening the door to the stadium are "I failed over and over and over again in my life. That's why I succeed."

The production is subdued, with quiet, pent-up energy. The lighting is focused, giving the color video almost a black and white quality. Jordan is filmed in slow motion, emphasizing the inner power and elegance.

The text works beautifully. By recounting his failures, Jordan helps the viewer to create a connection with him, a demigod. We all know what failure is like. Probably 99.9999 percent of us do not and will never know what success on Michael Jordan's scale is like. But the text suggests that we just might know what success is like if we don't quit.

The subtext of immortality and demigod status becomes more explicit in the "Look Me in the Eye" commercial. We do not see Michael Jordan; we only hear his voice throughout the video. We see close-ups of young people—most of them black and some white; some are in athletic stadiums and some on basketball courts. The two backgrounds suggest poor neighborhoods. Some of the faces look angry or doubtful; all of them are defiant.

The video text reads, "Look me in the eye. It's OK if you're scared. So am I. But we're scared for different reasons. I'm scared of what I won't become. You're scared of what I could become. Look at me. I won't let myself end where I started. I won't let myself finish where I began. I know what is in me, even if you can't see it yet. Look me in the eyes. I have something more important than courage. I have patience. I will become what I know I am." Then we see the video caption: "Become Legendary."

Here is another example: we see Maria Sharapova, who occupied the ATP number one spot through some months in 2008. She walks through the hotel (it seems to be the Waldorf), and the chorus of onlookers sings, "I feel pretty" from *West Side Story*. The subtext is the denigration of good-looking women who are not taken seriously by anybody. Sharapova avoids looking anybody in the eye, focused inside herself, through the journey to Flushing Meadows Centre Court, where commentator John McEnroe (a former ATP champion) is part of the taunting chorus.

The music stops as her opponent serves and Sharapova returns with a powerful backhand that thunders past her opponent into the back of the court. McEnroe comments "Ouch."

This time Nike makes skilled use of the pain of many women who are not taken seriously because they are women, and even less so if they are good-looking, because they encounter the nagging doubt of the environment about whether they achieved their place in society or work through their looks. Sharapova has indeed encountered a lot of prejudice, and commentators seemed to be ill at ease with her combination of great beauty and her tennis prowess.

"Just do it" makes a connection between the new demigods, the sports celebrities, and us ordinary mortals. The goal of the commercials is, obviously, to get us to buy the shoes and apparel used by the endorsers and thus magically connect our drab selves and mediocre talent to those who have reached the pinnacle of their sports and along the way have gained both fame and riches. But my point is not to criticize our advertising culture.

The Psychology of Heroism and Striving for Fame

Nike's campaign would never have been as successful as it has been, and would never have turned Nike into a company with a market capitalization of more than $50 billion and sales exceeding $33 billion if it didn't link to a deep and pervasive theme.

The theme is as old as the human capacity for storytelling, and it is one of the deepest themes in all of mythology. The heroes of all myths face doubts. They feel that they have a calling but they do not know whether they can live up to their destinies. The drama of the psychological birth of the hero is facing fear, doubt, and hesitation; knowing that reaching for the stars entails the risk of failure, ridicule, even injury or death; and knowing that by not trying, you forfeit the possibility of greatness.

Greek mythology has the great advantage of putting themes that have been relegated into the unconscious by modern culture into bright light. The heroes of Greek mythology are all motivated by gaining immortal fame. They are even willing to die physically for the possibility that all generations to come will tell the tale of their bravery.

The findings of experimental existential psychology (EEP) show that Greek mythology gets it right. Our fear of death, insignificance, and vanishing into nothingness is so tremendous that there are many who are willing to die for the symbolic immortality that heroism bestows on us.

Self-esteem is one of the most effective buffers for our fears of insignificance and death. This has been shown by a type of experiment typical of EEP. The experimental group was given a boost to their self-esteem by some positive feedback on their performance on a task, whereas the control group wasn't. Subjects were then shown stimuli involving some mortality salience—the awareness of one's own death. The two groups were then tested for worldview defense. The results were as predicted. The group whose self-esteem had been bolstered made *less* use of worldview defense than the control group.

This indicates that indeed self-esteem is quite a successful defense against our fear of death. Part of this is for purely physiological reasons: when an event increases our self-esteem, serotonin, and testosterone increase, and we feel empowered and strong. This much we have in common with animals. Just look at your dog when he has managed to catch the stick you threw in midair, shakes it with a killing gesture, and walks toward you, tail high, and gait sprightly. This is what we see on the tennis court, when one of the players has fired a winning shot past her opponent, screaming "yesssss!" and pumping her fist, or in the boxing ring when the winner has knocked out his opponent. Triumph creates a rush that is immensely pleasurable and increases our vitality, and yes, our self-esteem.

But in talking about day-to-day self-esteem management, we cannot rely on this rush all the time, and most of our self-esteem is not based on beating opponents or short-term successes. Our long-term self-evaluation is a function of being valued in our cultural framework; knowing that who we are and what we do are appreciated; that our work as lawyers, designers, journalists, or physicians is good; that our clients appreciate us; and that we are producing value is a state that becomes part of our self-conception. Here the physiological effect is less pronounced, and our self-esteem is not a matter of short rushes.

One aspect of such self-esteem is certainly a function of the intrinsic pleasure of doing something well. This is what Mihaly Csikszentmihalyi has called the state of "flow,"[15] immersion in an activity that we are good at and that we value intrinsically. Flow does not depend on the appreciation of others; it is intrinsically pleasurable and valuable. Csikszentmihalyi's research indicates that flow is one of the best predictors of well-being.

We are concerned here with the second aspect of self-esteem. It is the sense that on the scale of our cultural frame of reference we are ranked high and that we are valuable and esteemed. One of the experiments of existential psychology shows that when we feel we are being valued within our cultural framework, we are less afraid of dying. The reason is that we feel that, like the Greek heroes, our contribution to the larger whole to which we belong, our culture, is leaving a mark—a mark that could possibly outlast our physical lives. Yet this is mostly not an explicit thought. We do not think consciously every time we feel good about ourselves that we might be remembered beyond our deaths. We just feel good about ourselves and strengthened. We unconsciously equate what we do as a contribution to a whole larger than ourselves, and we want to feel that we are appreciated for that.

This is what pushes painters, writers, and composers to labor tirelessly toward creations that will make them immortal. It is what drives entrepreneurs to build the most spectacular buildings, the most powerful companies, or the most recognizable brands. It is what drives youngsters to go from audition to audition in the hope that one day they will be famous actors, singers, or dancers. It is what energizes politicians to withstand the pressures of harrowing election campaigns.

In the extreme this reflects our need for symbolic immortality that Ernest Becker studied so extensively. This is the deepest motivation of the quest for fame and extraordinary achievement. But as a matter of logic, only the few will attain symbolic immortality. If everybody could be famous, fame would cease to have any value; and by implication, we know that the vast majority of us will not make it into human consciousness at large.

From Immortality to Celebrity

In our age of global infotainment networks, fame has become both more complex and less stable. It is often not even based on extraordinary achievement. Paris Hilton is basically famous for being famous. She has no achievement worth speaking of, yet paparazzi can make small fortunes for photographs depicting her in some particularly compromising or scandalous situation. Other celebrities, like Beyoncé Knowles or the A-list couple Brad Pitt and Angelina Jolie, are valued not just for their talents and achievements but for the very fact of being famous.

Prima facie, it seems preposterous to think that celebrity has anything to do with the striving for symbolic immortality. Yet research on the cultural function of celebrity has shown that the social role of celebrity has taken over functions of religion.[16] Celebrities are invested with a special aura. Fans seek to touch or physically see celebrities in the same way as the faithful want to touch the relics of a saint or the hand of a high-ranking cleric.

Paradoxically celebrities *are* invested with very special powers even though it is of a somewhat more earthly sort. Early in the twentieth century, the fledgling film industry found out that the fame of an actor could become the central selling point of a movie. Now, a century later, Hollywood megastars can get paid $20 million, plus a percentage of profits, for the simple reason that their names are the crucial factor in determining a movie's success.

But striving for glory is not primarily motivated by material gain. Glory is primarily sought because as humans we seek to matter. We want to be significant, and ultimately, we want to be immortal.

The paradox of contemporary celebrity is that it has become more and more evanescent. The latest evictee of *Big Brother* or *Survivor* may well acquire great celebrity for the proverbial 15 minutes of fame and his or her final interview may be watched by millions. But chances are that their names will no longer be remembered soon thereafter.

Celebrities that remain popular for a long time require careful brand management. For actors this means that they need to continue getting star roles in successful movies. In sports the cruelty of time is topped only by the cruelty of the world of fashion models. Athletes know that the decline of their physical abilities guarantees relatively short careers, and models are unlikely to have careers that will outlast their midtwenties.

Depending on the sport, careers may be limited to the early twenties (female artistic gymnastics) to the early thirties (soccer, tennis, football), and there are very few instances in which athletes can continue into their forties (wrestling, boxing, car racing).

Very few actors and athletes achieve a status that allows their celebrity to outlast their careers in the way Michael Jordan is known a decade after the effective pinnacle of his career with the Chicago Bulls and half a decade after the de facto end of his career with the Washington Wizards. Another rare example is tennis champion Bjorn Borg who is still known and covered by the media decades after the end of his active career.

Celebrity, in anything, should be associated with evanescence rather than immortality, but it isn't. The age-old association between fame and immortality, illusory as it may be, retains its power over our minds.

The Problem with "Just Do It"

Is the myth of JDI indeed pernicious, then? If humans have always striven for glory, even though folk wisdom and art have always warned against the fickleness of taste and the short-lived nature of glory, it might well be argued that JDI is but one incarnation of a desire that has played a role during all periods of human history.

Doesn't Michael Jordan speak for all of us when, in the "Look into My Eyes" commercial, he says, "I will become what I know I am"? Furthermore, is the message of JDI not ultimately positive because it empowers us to try to become the best we can be? Does it not encourage the search for excellence—particularly if, as in "Look into My Eyes" and "Failure," the message is connected to the virtues of patience, resilience, and perseverance?

I believe it is a less clear-cut answer than many left-leaning critics want to make it out to be. Michael Jordan has inspired many youths to try to strive for more. Tiger Woods, Roger Federer, and Maria Sharapova are doing the same for many now. It has certainly been shown that in countries that have a first-rate tennis star, many youngsters are motivated to work hard at tennis. Sweden was the most spectacular instance. The phenomenal success of Bjorn Borg in the 1970s and early 1980s led to a whole series of first-rate Swedish players that played a leading role in international tennis during the 1980s and early 1990s.

I think that any attempt to demonize striving for fame and glory simply does not take into account one of the deepest layers of the human psyche. Existential psychology certainly shows that this striving is one of the more benign ways in which humans try to deal with the terror of mortality. The alternatives of religious and political fanaticism, self-righteous moralism, and bigotry certainly do more damage than the striving for fame, which at best produces true excellence and at worst transient celebrity devoid of valuable content.

The problem of JDI resides with the technological means that were both the condition of its success and the source of the noxious part of its influence. Ancient Greeks could read about mythological and historical heroes; so could ancient Romans, but still very few actually read about them until the invention of the printing press, which greatly increased the accessibility of books.

It is not a coincidence that the culture heroes of the past were bound to be just that. They needed to have done something that you could write about. Whether it was to have been a great political or military leader, a writer, scientist, or an explorer; these were feats that could be transmitted through words and turned into gripping narratives.

It is vastly more difficult to write about beauty or athletic feats at length in a way that grips the imagination. If we read a biography of Marilyn Monroe or of Pelé, what captures our minds and souls is the human drama, because there is a limit to how long you can write about an acting performance or a soccer game in ways that really get across the beauty and excitement of what those who actually see it experience.

The celebrity per se, the social role of those who are primarily famous for being famous, only became possible with mass media—the movie industry and even more through television. The reason, as most media analysts since Marshall McLuhan have pointed out, is that the human brain is singularly attuned and susceptible to direct visual impression.

The shift toward those whose physical beauty, charisma, or grace are their primary asset has been marked. Within a few decades the list of celebrities has been almost entirely taken up by people in the world of sports and the media. The *Forbes* Celebrity 100 list for 2008[17] is quite instructive because it ranks the most powerful celebrities according to four factors: pay, press rank, web rank, and television rank.

In the top ten there is only one writer, J. K. Rowling, who is flanked by The Police and Brad Pitt. You have to wait until number 75 to encounter the next figure who is not strictly a media person—that is, someone who is known to people primarily through his physical presence and its impact: Tom Clancy.

The significance of the shift toward people who are known for their very presence rather than for their deeds is as follows. As mentioned above, there are three factors that help us overcome the terror of mortality: emotionally significant attachments to spouses, parents, children, and friends (a factor not dealt with in this book); a worldview that provides us with an understanding of the world and our place in it, and provides us with meaning; and finally, self-esteem, which is derived from the feedback of our close attachments, our sense that we are living valuable lives as defined in our worldview, and our perception of our place in the world at large.

Feeling significant within a frame of reference that we deem to be valuable is important for our self-esteem. There are two factors that weigh into how we build self-esteem: The first is the nature of our worldview. If, for example, our worldview values achievement that creates value for many others, we will measure ourselves differently than if our worldview emphasizes living according to a religious standard.

The worldwide infotainment system is driven by its own economic logic, which in turn is largely quantitative. Newspapers, magazines, television shows, and websites thrive on readers, buyers, zappers, and hitters. As a result they are driven to write and broadcast about events and people who generate interest.

Given that consumers are largely drawn to reading, hearing, and seeing information, stories, gossip, and analyses about those whom they know, being known becomes an economic value in itself for the infotainment system. This in turn reinforces the tendency of the consumers to be drawn to those they know, increasing the value of being known per se.

Knowing about people whose physique is not remarkable requires us to remember a lot of information about what they have done and why those things are significant. Knowing the significance of a person's deed requires the effort of acquiring knowledge as opposed to that recognizing a beautiful face relies on an inborn capacity.

The result follows almost inevitably. The infotainment system, by its inner logic, is driven to seek out and develop celebrities standing out through their physical beauty and attractiveness, because this is what will keep the consumers interested.

This in turn feeds into human nature's deep-seated desire to be loved, the second factor that weighs into building self-esteem. We all want to be cared for and we have all experienced this in our lifetime. Evolution has programmed adults to love babies just for their being, and it is part of the painful losses of growing up that we need to earn love and esteem and that the guaranteed love of infancy can no longer be taken for granted.

Celebrities represent just this fantasy of being loved just for their being. This is why we endow them with magical qualities. They have the aura to attract attention, fascination, and love from everybody that we crave by nature, even if in the process of maturation we have come to eliminate this as a goal that can actually be achieved. Turning into a celebrity has therefore become today's mass-media culture symbol of the transformation of the self.

German philosopher Walter Benjamin many years ago proposed an interesting explanation why we are obsessed with the authenticity of a work of art.[18] His argument was that we seek sacred objects that order our universe into a hierarchy, and works of art achieved the status of such sacred objects, particularly since the nineteenth century when art was elevated into a substitute for religion.

With the advent of photography and the possibility for mass reproduction of works of art, the obsession over the original set in. Even though we can see extremely good reproductions of the *Mona Lisa*, millions of visitors flock to the Louvre every year to see the original in a proceeding that calls to mind the Islamic Hajj, Jews praying at the Western Wall, or Christian pilgrimages to the holy places of Jesus's birth, suffering, and death. Benjamin suggested that our culture has endowed the original work with what he calls an aura, an almost mystical power of sacred objects.

During the same period, when art replaced religion for the educated middle classes in Europe, the artist replaced God. With the advent of romanticism in the second half of the eighteenth century, the modern concept of the genius was born. Romanticism was obsessed with the process of artistic creation. Nothing seemed more magical, more special, and almost sanctified than the creation of a great work of art. The artist was endowed with the quality that had been exclusively God's for millennia of theology: the ability to create something out of nothing, the miracle of *creation ex nihilo*.

My suggestion is that celebrities have become the auratic objects of a culture centered on and fueled by the infotainment system. In religious systems we have the function of the holy person: saints, prophets, and those touched by God who are beyond the natural order.

Touched by God has been replaced by the magical quality of being known, loved, and admired by the masses. And our culture has found a substitute to the question of how you achieve enlightenment, faith, or whatever it takes to achieve holiness with the question of what it takes to become a celebrity.

No phenomenon illustrates this dynamic more than the advent of reality television, which has become the single most powerful factor that has changed the landscape of television in the last decade. Reality shows have been the top rated programs on American television in most years since 2000, with *Survivor* and *American Idol* leading the charts. Since 2008 the four national broadcast networks, ABC, CBS, NBC, and Fox all plan to have at least one prime-time reality show a year.

Reality television focuses on the process of transformation itself; the process that turns an ordinary mortal into a demigod. This process is normally hidden from the spectator's eye. We are not privy to the process that has turned Brad Pitt, Angelina Jolie, George Clooney, and Scarlett Johansson into celebrities. We only see the end result of the human already transformed into a demigod. But our culture is obsessed with this transformation; we want to see the miracle happen.

The success of reality television is based on its symbolic significance: its focus is on the process of the magical transformation of a human being from the status of ordinary mortal to the status of demigod. Followed by countless cameras, we can watch the process of transubstantiation—the moment in which a human being is touched by grace.

This process touches on one of the deepest roots of our being. Let us return to one of the most basic insights of EEP: we all start in a state of grace. We are loved for our being and we are, as yet, before the advent of self-consciousness. We live before the fall, before the original sin of self-knowledge, in the paradise of timelessness; without knowledge of the passage of time and mortality.

The advent of self-consciousness forever expelled us from this paradise. We are doomed to self-consciousness and to the knowledge of death, and we will never return to the wholeness and innocence that we once knew. We will have to deal with the knowledge that love can be lost, that we are not alone on this earth, and that there are others who are more loved and admired than we are.

Being a celebrity is the way our culture has revived the fantasy of returning to paradise. Loved for just being who they are, celebrities have returned to the state of grace before the fall. They have finally overcome the incompleteness of unrequited desire, and because of their fame, they are immortal. Their memory will live on forever.

Never mind that most us are well aware that celebrity is far from being a magical quality bestowed on somebody to lift them to another plane. We maintain the sense that there is a way to return to the wholeness of unbounded love.

The Downside of JDI: The Reign of Fantasy

Here we finally come to the enormous downside of the myth of JDI. It has led to an incredible increase in the reign of fantasy. The human imagination is an invaluable tool. It allows us to envisage what does not yet exist; it allows us to develop scenarios for our personal and collective futures. It is at the foundation of innovation, art, and planning ahead.

But the human imagination is highly prone to an activity that we all know very well: fantasying. We often use the imagination to make a short-cut. When we do not know how to reach a goal, we can easily imagine that we are *now* where we would like to be. We can fantasize that the woman we desire is ours even though she doesn't show the slightest interest in us. We can fantasize about flying around the world in our Gulfstream 550 even though we don't have the slightest inkling about how to make the money it takes to buy one. Or we can fantasize about being renowned rock stars even though we have neither the talent nor the looks that are needed for it.

JDI may speak about finding the strength, patience, and resilience to become who we know we are. But the bottom line is *become legendary*. It is not worth investing in a goal as pedestrian as making a good career and living a meaningful life on a terrestrial scale. Immortality and ever-lasting fame; achievement like Tiger Woods's, Roger Federer's, or Maria Sharapova's; these are what we should strive for. Anything less is to settle for mediocrity.

Little or nothing is said about the painful process of finding out who we really are and what our gifts and limitations are.[19] The opposite is being sold: *no limits*.

Reality television illustrates how deep this message resonates and how little room the fantasies promoted by the infotainment system leave for the idea of objective self-knowledge.

Of course deep down we all know that there *are* limits and that JDI is a myth and reality television has integrated this knowledge into its genre. Consumers of shows like *American Idol* eagerly watch preliminary stages of the audition process in which candidates that do not have the slightest singing talent are publicly humiliated. This leaves the audience with the dubious but intense pleasure of seeing others undergo the painful process of having their fantasies shattered through a cruel confrontation with real-ity. But all this is covered up by the knowledge that at the end of the process one contestant will undergo the magic transformation from ordinary mor-tal to demigod, and thus the reign of fantasy is kept alive.

The more gifted Homo globalis indeed rarely indulges in the fantasy of being transformed magically into a celeb through reality shows. But mem-bers of the species certainly do aspire to climb on the ladder of the global

I-Commodity Market that will bring them glory through their chosen careers. (Even this desire has already been appropriated by reality television through shows like Donald Trump's *The Apprentice*.) Here, it might be argued, the myth of JDI is useful. Doesn't it encourage people to reach for the stars, to become the best they can be?

The problem is that there is a big difference between reaching for the stars and becoming the best you can be. For the overwhelming majority of us the best we can be is nowhere near the stars.

The catastrophic impact of JDI is in the denigration of the ordinary careers that once seemed perfectly respectable and constituted achievements that gave reasons for pride (e.g., the law, medicine, academia, architecture, or engineering). In addition, JDI promotes a myth that simply does not correspond to reality. It is simply not true that only talent, willpower, character, and courage determine who makes it to the top. Malcolm Gladwell has shown in detail to what extent circumstances of birth, parent's connections, the coincidence of meeting the right person at the right time, and sheer luck are the ultimate determinants of who will make it to the top and who won't.

The New York Times has published an extraordinary series of articles called "Class in America"[20] that dismantles another aspect of the myth of JDI. While the infotainment system keeps telling us that there are no limits to what can be achieved, and that everybody can make it, the facts show a dramatically different picture. Social mobility in the United States at the onset of the twenty-first century is substantially *lower* than it was half a century ago.

The prime factor that contributes to this decrease is that access to good higher education has become more expensive, prohibitively so for most of the population. If in the 1950s the G.I. Bill helped many to gain an education that allowed them entry into the middle class, this is no longer true.

And contrary to the myth that college dropouts like Gates and Zuckerberg can do as well as those who actually finish their degrees, higher education is crucial in determining access to the better-paying jobs and certainly entry into the new upper class. In fact, as Rothkopf shows in some detail and Reich confirms, the upper echelons are recruited from a small number of elite universities that provide both the title and the beginning of the network necessary to make it into the upper ends of the business hierarchy and the closely aligned top tiers of government. More than ever an MBA from Harvard, Stanford, Wharton, or INSEAD are requirements to even get a shot at the dream to make it to the top.

The two decades of JDI have indeed created enormous wealth for the very few. Never had there been as many billionaires (in 2008 their number crossed the threshold of one thousand worldwide), and never had the top

0.5 percent of the population made as much money as today. Never have the stars of the sports world and show business made such astronomical sums and held such enormous power to sell millions of albums and gross revenues in the billions for box-office hits or, as the leading sports stars, make dozens of millions of dollars a year just from advertising endorsements.

As modern cognitive psychology shows, the human mind is not well equipped to think in statistical terms, but the numbers say it all: All this is out of reach to 99.5 percent of the population in developed countries (never mind half of the earth's population that lives in abject poverty). But instead of integrating the statistics into our understanding of what we can or cannot achieve, the Homo globalis of the last two decades was more influenced by the myth of JDI than by the dry reality of the hard facts. And while many are doing well, they feel that the better they do, the more their goal is receding into distance.

In a global I-Commodity Market that values the achievement of the top 0.5 percent, Homo globalis mostly feels left out of the global rating system. No wonder that the commoditization of the self has left the overwhelming majority of the globally oriented with the feeling that their lives are missing the crucial ingredient of glory that helps humans to overcome the dread of mortality. And while humankind has always been eager for glory, this may be the first time that so many feel that they are so close to redemption that keeps eluding them, even if this redemption is illusory.

3

The Defeat of Mind

Relativism and Pop Spirituality

Before the age of Amazon.com, I did much of my book shopping on my trips to New York and London. I would systematically scout the sections that interested me, and these included, of course, philosophy and psychology. Through the 1990s I witnessed a rapid development. In the early 1990s a large Barnes & Noble would have bookcases about ten meters long that carried serious psychology titles followed by one bookcase of "self-help/self-improvement" books. Within a span of a few years the proportions had changed completely. There is hardly any psychology left, and the space is taken up by the "self-help/self-improvement" section that is often augmented with a lot of spirituality titles.

The situation in philosophy is not much better. Smaller bookstores don't even differentiate between serious philosophy and a category often called "religion/metaphysics/spirituality," and the vast majority of the titles belong to the latter hodgepodge of occultism, mysticism, and New Age thinking. This is also reflected in the publication of serious publishers who carry titles like the aforementioned *The Secret*, making a lot more money on them than they make, say, on a masterpiece like Scott Atran's *In Gods We Trust*, a riveting analysis of the evolutionary basis of religion.[1]

Some of these changes are due to the restructuring of the publishing business. Most traditional publishers have been bought up by infotainment giants run by executives who have no connection whatsoever to books. They see the bottom line of what sells, and they care more about the synergy between their various divisions. A title that stands a chance to be turned into a movie matters more to them than, say, discovering a major new novelist, historian, or physicist. As publishers will tell you, they don't have much of a choice: they live on bestsellers, and only by selling those, whatever their quality, can they stay financially afloat and publish the high-quality books that will sell in small numbers.

But the publishing business and bookstore chains cannot be held exclusively responsible for their readership's tastes. These tastes reflect a wide cultural trend. Companies, not just in America, pay enormous sums to what is nowadays called "motivational speakers," who advertise themselves as "electrifying" and "uplifting." I experience this when companies invite me to speak at their conventions; they mostly want to make sure that their executives will get a "feel-good" effect from my lecture. They are worried that my talk may require some intellectual effort to follow, and they anxiously ask whether there is a simple, positive bottom line to what I will say.

This is quite surprising given the audience. In the technology and finance sectors, all the executives I speak to have been to college. A high proportion of them have continued to acquire MBAs, and the research-intensive companies have a fair share of PhDs as well. Why then are they worried that my talk might be too complex? Why are they adamant to "uplift" their executives rather than inform them and provide them with food for thought? Actually, when they invite economists or experts in marketing, they do want actual information and not just a vague feel-good message. But when it comes to the human soul, their conception of what they want to provide sounds more like a form of mental massage than anything worth calling education or information. Companies wouldn't do this if there was not a genuine need for it. I think they are responding to the difficult predicament of Homo globalis.

Instability, Fluidity, the Pressure to Achieve, and the Need for Comfort

Members of Homo globalis go through frequent upheavals. Their careers often evolve through a variety of lateral moves. None of their typical occupations provides much in terms of stability.[2] Careers in technology, finance, management, and the media mostly evolve through a series of diagonal moves through different companies. Hence many need to make nerve-racking choices once every few years. They need to decide whether to stay or to move on; what options suit their careers best. Through the "just do it" (JDI) decades, those who didn't make such moves felt that they were left behind, that they didn't get the most out of their careers, and that they didn't move fast enough.[3]

These career moves generate a lot of excitement but offer very little support and comfort. No company or firm truly becomes a source of safety and rarely do those on the fast track feel that the company they now work in is bound to be their home for long. They become adept at adapting quickly to corporate cultures. They know that they will have to develop team spirit and to adjust to the company's values and style, but they mostly look at this adjustment as a game rather than an integral part of their identity.

The situation is even more precarious for the ever-growing number of entrepreneurs who run their own businesses, consultancies, practices, or clinics. They need to juggle between time allotted to networking and marketing themselves, doing the actual work, and looking out for changes in their environment that may impact their careers.

Most members of the creative class don't marry early, but once they do settle down, their lives are anything from quiet and stable. Sociologist Dalton Conley[4] has described in lucid and often humorous detail how their lives turn into complex multitasking operations that never rest. Conley is chair of the Sociology Department at New York University and his wife is a well-known designer. Both run successful and complex careers. Both are free to work at home a large part of the time—which means that there isn't a single moment where they feel completely free of the obligation to work. In addition, both are internationally connected and need to function in tune with a variety of time zones ranging from Europe to eastern standard time to the Far East.

They are highly conscious of the responsibilities involved in parenting. They want to be emotionally attuned to their children's needs and to spend quality time with them. They also want to provide them with enrichment ranging from music through sports to psychotherapy if they feel that there is a problem. Between their various professional responsibilities they drive the kids from yoga to pottery class and fix them dinner while trying to keep an eye on the never-ending stream of emails on their BlackBerrys or iPhones.

In the back of their minds there are the ever-present questions that we dealt with in Chapter 1: "Am I doing well enough?" "Is my career sufficiently spectacular?" And finally, they are bothered by what Conley calls the "economic red-shift effect." They make more and more money and feel that they never get to the point where it's quite enough to be comfortable; partially because life in global cities is so strongly attuned to the wealthy, and partially because they feel that their achievement is overshadowed by the masters of the global I-Commodity Market.

Amid all this fluidity, uncertainty, and competition, members of Homo globalis often feel that they are losing their moorings. Many of them feel anxious, even when things are going well, and they rarely feel a true sense of satisfaction with their lives. An ever-growing number of them seek pharmaceutical help; they don't feel that they have the time, energy, and sometimes the money to invest more deeply in a process of self-reflection. Given the relative ease by which even family doctors prescribe the ever popular SSRIs (selective serotonin reuptake inhibitors: antidepressant drugs like Prozac, Paxil, and so on that are used for severe anxiety disorders), many feel that they might as well opt for the quick fix, if it works.[5] But it often doesn't. SSRIs are quite effective in dealing with major depressive disorders, severe anxiety disorders, and obsessive-compulsive disorders. But their effectiveness in mild depression and the anxiety quite naturally associated with a lifestyle that provides little security is highly questionable.

In all this instability, it is quite understandable that many of those involved in the global race are hungry for belief systems that provide some assurance that their lives will not go wrong. It is this need for assurance that has generated the huge demand for the pop spiritualities that are flooding the market.[6]

My hypothesis is that these spiritualities are meant to provide the assurance that achievement and spiritual well-being necessarily go together. Logically this means that the following assumptions need to be combined: The first is the assumption that there are indeed no limits to what you can become. This is the assumption that the self can be designed at will. The second assumption is that humans who apply these various magical techniques do not really turn themselves into something or somebody else. They become who they were to begin with—the true self.

The problem is that these two assumptions are diametrically opposed to each other. If the self can be shaped at will, how is it possible that the designed self is also the true self?

This contradiction can be resolved only with a third assumption that is not always fully spelled out: it is the assumption of the self as the source of deep, unadulterated truths. According to this view, we only wish the wrong things as long as we are disconnected from our deep, true self, because in our deepest selves we know who we are. Hence, once we connect to our true selves, we connect to a source of knowledge that is infallible. Behind the confusions and the false starts that characterize the lives of actual people as we know them, there is another realm; the realm of the pure, true self that cannot possibly be wrong.

It is this assumption of the self as a source of deep, infallible knowledge that allows squaring the circle. Yes, there are no limits to who we can become.

There are no limits because deep inside there is an awesome power of unlimited potential: our deep spiritual self. Once this self is unleashed, we can become the tycoons, singers, writers, and filmmakers that we really are; we will shed the excess weight that has nothing to do with our true self. The true self is an infallible guide to the good life and unlimited fulfillment. If we are confused, this is only because we are disconnected from its power.

The idea that there is a true self, fully fledged, buried inside is a power-ful cultural fantasy. Almost everybody at times feels that the actual lives we lead cannot possibly be all that there is. Most of us feel at times that we are like butterflies locked into a cocoon, and that the day will come in which our powerful, unlimited, "butterfly self" will burst out of the cocoon and fulfill its endless potential.

The allure of pop spirituality derives its power from this fantasy. It is very difficult for humans to resist the idea that we are really much more valuable, gifted, good, and potentially successful than we are in our real lives. Belief systems that tell us that this is indeed true—and that we just need to connect to this deep self to become the success stories we hope to be—must indeed have a powerful allure, particularly if we need to cope with the fluidity and uncertainty typical of many lives today.

The Supermarket of New Spiritualities

Homo globalis often does not have the comfort of metaphysical consola-tion provided by the established religions. In Europe most of the popula-tion is not attached to any religion. In the United States, the situation is more complex. While the absolute majority of U.S. citizens say that religion plays a very important role in their lives, there are strong indications that the religious landscape of Americans has changed dramatically. Ever-larger numbers report that they do not adhere to the faith in which they have been brought up.[7]

Furthermore there are indications that the higher the educational level, the less likely they are to belong to one of the traditionally established religions. They are, as Richard Florida says, more likely to seek spiritual fulfillment in much more individualized ways. They seek introspection, meditational practice, and spiritual community in forms of religious orga-nization that are of more recent vintage.[8]

This shouldn't be surprising. Isn't it to be expected that a group charac-terized by tolerance, creativity, and openness to the world is bound to seek forms of spirituality that transcend the classic religions with their emphasis on unique truth and their tendency to deny the validity of other religions? Awareness of global interconnectedness does not mix well with religious histories that are connected to concepts like inquisition, jihad, crusade, or other forms of interreligious competition and warfare.

Where does Homo globalis seek solace and comfort? The sales num-bers make it very clear that most members of the species don't seek out books, sources of information, or lectures by professionals who bring them empirically well-supported information (most of these books hardly sell).

Many are likely to seek out the pastures of pop spirituality in its various new forms.

Some of the authors and speakers who take them under their guidance have good academic credentials; others come from backgrounds ranging from sales to engineering and from marketing to law. Most of them do not even try to provide systematic empirical evidence for their claims. This would, in any case, be quite impossible for many of these doctrines that claim sources of "knowledge" that are of quite a different sort.

The first category is composed of people whose authority is based on their personal experience and transformation. A good example is Eckhart Tolle, whose *The Power of Now* was a huge success. He went through a prolonged crisis during which he was obviously depressed and had lost orientation. He tells the story how he began to embrace his suffering and pain, and he describes the final stages of his transformation with the following words:

> A time came when, for a while, I was left with nothing on the physical plane. I had no relationships, no job, no home, no socially defined identity. I spent almost two years sitting on park benches in a state of the most intense joy.
>
> But even the most beautiful experiences come and go. More fundamental, perhaps, than any experience is the undercurrent of peace that has never left me since then. Sometimes it is very strong, almost palpable, and others can feel it too. At other times, it is somewhere in the background, like a distant melody.
>
> Later, people would occasionally come up to me and say: "I want what you have. Can you give it to me, or show me how to get it?" and I would say: "You have it already. You just can't feel it because your mind is making too much noise." That answer later grew into the book that you are holding in your hands.
>
> Before I knew it, I had an external identity again. I had become a spiritual teacher.[9]

Tolle's narrative is, of course, structured around an age-old narrative blueprint. Spiritual and religious authorities such as the Buddha, Martin Luther, and Hassidic teacher Rabbi Nahman of Bratslav have described periods of intense mental suffering that led up to their experience of enlightenment. This paradigm is well entrenched in a large number of cultures. Let us call it "authority through personal experience."

A second paradigm is no less venerable in its historical lineage. It is recourse to a source of ancient knowledge that is infallible, because it is based on either revelation from a divine source or mystical intuition of a timeless truth. This is the basic justification of the great monotheistic religions and a variety of other spiritual traditions.

The model of the authority of ancient knowledge is problematic nowadays for a number of reasons. For most of human history there was indeed very little well-grounded knowledge of the universe and there was even less systematic knowledge about history and about other cultures. Hence it was much easier for a religion to claim that it was based on the one, true prophet or seer who had received divine revelation. The difficulty of this model became insuperable in the nineteenth century with the advent of modern philology and history. Given the encompassing extant knowledge on the history of religion, we have known for quite some time that almost every major culture and countless tribal traditions have claimed exclusive possession of the truth about the universe. Given that these claims are mutually exclusive and contradict each other, this casts great doubt on the viability of such knowledge claims, as only one of them can be true, if any at all.

Another problem of the paradigm of ancient knowledge is that modernity has evolved a powerful alternative narrative of the direction of history. Certainly in the last four hundred years there are powerful reasons to think that the enterprise of generating human knowledge is progressive. The nineteenth century possessed far more knowledge about all aspects of the universe than any time before that; and the twentieth century, with its powerful network of knowledge-generating institutions like universities, scientific journals, and vast research facilities, has led to a veritable explosion of knowledge in all domains. Modernity presented a powerful alternative to the model of ancient knowledge: the story of human history as progress—at least in the domains of knowledge and technology.

Hence the model of ancient knowledge is under duress from these two fronts. But it finds ways of dealing with these problems. I will take my example from the budding domain of popular Kabbalistic preachers, not because I think it is worse than others but because I think its strategies are representative of contemporary pop spiritualities. Rabbi Michael Laitman is one of the New Age gurus who have been building empires on their combination of contemporary language and "ancient knowledge." His rhetoric is interesting not because it is unique but because it is rather characteristic of the new religious entrepreneurs catering to the endless hunger for meaning. In trying to establish why Kabbalah is relevant today he first set out to undermine the status of the natural sciences: "A fundamental concept of Quantum Theory is the Uncertainty Principle, which maintains that the *observer* affects the observed event. Hence, the key question is, 'what do the measurements actually measure?' This principle implies that the concept of an 'objective process' becomes irrelevant. Moreover, beyond the measured results, an 'objective reality' simply cannot exist."[10]

The first move is to say that science is incapable of providing us with absolute truth. Quantum physics is one of the New Age gurus' favorite ploys to undermine the unsuspecting reader's belief in science. Heisenberg's uncertainty principle is invoked to justify anything from the idea that "there is no objective reality" to the claim that "science undermines its own foundations."

The next move is that the author claims that, as a result, the authority of science is diminished: "Acknowledging the above has significantly diminished the predominance of natural science in general and physics in particular. Instead, it positioned science as a tool that uncovers a limited part of reality, rather than the absolute truth. The actual reality is hidden from us; we cannot discover it by means of scientific research."[11]

At this point I am always wondering whether authors like Laitman actually believe their own arguments or whether they make cynical use of them. Quantum physics has never claimed that its results undermine science. If anything it has argued that certain common sense notions that we have about the nature of physical reality and the relationship between observer and observed must be discarded once we investigate the smallest constituents of matter accessible to research nowadays.

There is indeed no reason whatsoever for physicists to feel uncomfortable about their discipline. Quantum physics is spectacularly successful. Its predictions are born out to an amazing degree, and our understanding of how matter works has increased enormously over the last century. Yes, it is becoming progressively more difficult for the layperson to understand contemporary physics, but this has absolutely nothing to do with the validity of physics. If anything, we can say that modern physics has become immensely sophisticated in dealing with the complexity of the interrelationship between experiment and nature, observation, and experimental result.

If indeed modern physics implies that we humans cannot understand reality except as it is in interaction with us, this should lead us to expect that nobody is in possession of absolute truth. But quite surprisingly, it turns out that we got the inference wrong. Laitman tells us that there *is* an absolute truth, and it has been known for thousands of years. In fact this ancient knowledge is so comprehensive that it includes pretty much all the wisdom humanity has ever come up with: "This is the background for the appearance of the wisdom of the Kabbalah, which offers humanity a new perspective, a scientific worldview that Kabbalists discovered thousands of years ago. The Kabbalistic perception of the world includes premises that other religions accept on faith, coupled with a scientific approach. Kabbalah develops tools within us that welcome us into a comprehensive reality and provide means to research it."

In a leap that is completely devoid of any logic, we are now urged to believe that science's complex understanding of the notion of reality undermines modern science, but not an ancient system "discovered thousands of years ago"—for some reason Kabbalistic gurus tend to claim that Kabbalah has been in existence at least since 1800 BCE.

Never mind that there is an impressive body of historical and philological research that shows the exact provenance of Kabbalistic thought. It is not, as Laitman or Rabbi Philip Berg, who founded and turned Kabbalah Centre International into an empire, claim, several thousand years old; however, it is part and parcel of the Gnostic movement that emerged around two thousand years ago. But its period of flourishing was from the twelfth to the sixteenth century, first in Spain, and later in the city of Safed, Israel, where several of the most influential Kabbalistic authors resided.[12]

And never mind that it is based on a cosmological model that has been completely discarded by modern science. Mathematical physics became possible once the idea was *discarded* that symbolic relations have any physical reality.[13] But Laitman glosses elegantly over these little inconveniences and grandly proclaims that the Kabbalists are in possession of a wisdom that surpasses anything that the human race has ever produced.

The Anti-Intellectualist Argument

My own environment is primarily composed of left-leaning liberals and I often found myself in situations I had difficulty to handle.[14] Since Rabbi Berg had founded his Kabbalah center and turned it into an empire, many friends and acquaintances from the center started studying it. They soon shared with great conviction that "Kabbalah—the world's oldest body of spiritual wisdom—contains the long-hidden keys to the secrets of the universe as well as the keys to the mysteries of the human heart and soul. Kabbalistic teachings explain the complexities of the material and the nonmaterial universe, as well as the physical and metaphysical nature of all humanity. Kabbalah shows in detail, how to navigate that vast terrain in order to remove every form of chaos, pain, and suffering."[15] This was quoted from the home page of the "Kabbalah Centre International," followed by the assertion that Kabbalah had been around for thousands of years.

I happen to have studied the history of Kabbalah to some extent, and I find it very instructive.[16] The oldest extant Kabbalist texts are indeed close to two thousand years old, and they seem have been written within the same context that had produced the Gnostic religions that were among the early sources of Christianity. The real flourishing of Kabbalah began in the twelfth and thirteenth centuries, and its most famous text, the *Zohar*, was written toward the end of the thirteenth century by one Moshe de Leon (1240–1305), according to most modern scholars. In accordance with a frequent practice of the time, he did not claim authorship but claimed that the work was dictated to him by one of the great figures of Talmudic history, Rabbi Shimon bar Yochai (fl. 135–170 CE), to give the work more authority. While de Leon's authorship cannot be ascertained completely, linguistic evidence that it is a medieval text is overwhelming. Unsurprisingly, contemporary salespeople of Kabbalah as "the world's oldest spiritual wisdom" make no reference to modern philological and historical research.

When I asked whether my acquaintances from the center had any interest in historical studies about the development of Kabbalah, most of them would tell me disdainfully that such studies did not capture the spirit of Kabbalah and that it was something to be "lived, not learnt."

At this point I expect a rather common objection, which I have heard quite often from those who felt that their Kabbalah classes had provided them with new meaning and a better understanding of their lives. "Why are you so stingy and obsessive? You simply have never *experienced* the power of Kabbalah! You have never participated in the ritual in which a Kabbalah class relives the moment when God gave us the Torah! You have a problem, because you are simply not open to spiritual experience!"

I often point out to them that mystical experience is quite a universal phenomenon. It raises very interesting questions about the human mind and its ability to dismantle the differentiation of the "I" from the non-"self." It is not necessary to deny the spiritual power of mystical experience to question its ability to inform us about the ultimate reality of the external world. I also tell them that I don't quite see why such experience should teach us anything about the external world any more than hallucinations or other seemingly extrasensory experiences do. Mystical experience has been a source of meaning and comfort in many cultures that differ widely. Shamans have relied on it in tribes ranging from Africa to Siberia, and interpretations of mystical experiences have ranged from their being the result of communication with ancestral spirits to indications that the very idea of the self is illusory in Buddhism.[17] Hence there is no way you can reasonably argue that mystical experience provides access to the nature of the universe. It is an experience that needs to be explained through a reasonable theory of the world, because in itself it can lead to any number of contradictory conclusions about reality.[18]

I have mostly encountered slightly annoyed gazes at best and angry responses at worst when I dare voice such arguments. There seems to be a very powerful mechanism at work: when it comes to religious experience in the widest sense, many simply want to shut off their critical faculties.

They want to be charmed rather than merge thought and experience. And hence they argue that dry intellectuality is opposed to what Rabbi Berg calls "lived experience."

My most authentic reaction would have been to tell them that they were being indoctrinated and that they should at least get a minimal understanding of the actual origins and metaphysical structure of Kabbalistic thought before becoming enthusiastic about it. In my experience, intellectual and cultural history is the best way to gain a clear perspective on a system of thought—which is why religions have never liked philological and historical analyses of the origins of sacred texts. Because these acquaintances from the center were highly intelligent and educated, I thought they might want to know how the concepts they were studying had evolved.

I thought that it might be important to know that the original Kabbalistic notions were based on a conception of analogy of microcosm and macrocosm, a cosmological conception that was discarded with the ascent of modern mathematical physics. It was also based on the idea of structural similarity between God's body (original Kabbalistic thought was based on the idea that God had some form of mystical body) and the human body. I thought it would be interesting for them to understand the complex interrelation between mysticism as a form of resistance against religious establishment and the idea of mystical *gnosis* and *unio mystica*. If I dared saying something of the sort, I was mostly looked at as something of a party pooper at best and devoid of tact and respect for spiritual experience at worst.

Representatives of religious orthodoxies often make similar, intellectually irresponsible "arguments." Acquaintances once took me to a lecture in which an ultraorthodox rabbi tried to demonstrate "scientifically" that (a) God existed and (b) evolutionary theory was untrue. His proofs for the existence of God were half-baked versions of arguments that have been used during the history of philosophy to this purpose, even though they were stripped of their original context, subtlety, and elegance. His "disproof" of the theory of evolution was based on total ignorance of both biology and evolutionary theory.

When I started to challenge him on all counts, the people present felt that I was exceedingly rude—whereas I thought that what he was doing was immoral to the highest extent, as he was basically capitalizing on his audience's ignorance, a tactic that Richard Dawkins has exposed in detail in his *The God Delusion*.[19] The scene ended by my being convinced gently by the Rabbi's followers that I should leave the hall before they would use other means to shut me up. Daring to ask critical questions was simply not in the cards.

Nowadays such discussion is more often than not disqualified as cerebral, and people who cherish it are bound to find themselves accused of lack of spiritual sensitivity. Basically we are told to shut up, to keep our useless and dry knowledge to ourselves, and to leave the clients of pop spirituality in their happy universe in which spirituality has become an excuse for buying into any concoction that makes them feel well, never mind its incoherence or inconsistency with established knowledge.

The argument that rapture and analytic thought do not mix, which I have heard many times, doesn't hold water. If this were true, authentic connoisseurs of art would enjoy it less than those who don't have a clue about art history. Those who have the ability to understand classical music in depth and understand the complex compositional techniques used by the great composers would pay the price of never enjoying Bach, Beethoven, or Mahler as deeply as they did when they understood very little about music. In both cases the opposite is true. The more you know about the history of art or music, the more you can enjoy its greatest achievements.

The same holds for religion. If the anti-intellectualist argument were valid, the Pope, who is generally chosen, among other things, for his intellectual ability and theological knowledge, should feel less religious fervor than those of his flock who know very little about Catholic theology. The opposite is true as is certainly borne out by Pope John Paul II and Pope Benedict XVI. The same holds true for the present Dalai Lama and the list of religious authorities who are intellectual heavyweights that do not shy away from difficult philosophical questions.

Hence the idea that critical thought and the experience of meaning are inconsistent should make us suspicious rather than convince us. In any field that I know from music through visual art and film, to philosophy, physics, or psychology, greater understanding always leads to an *increase* in pleasure and meaning that can be derived from its creations and ideas. A body of ideas that loses its power when it is analyzed in depth has something to hide: it is mostly incoherence, with a lack of logic, and lack of evidence.

Pop Spirituality: Fusing the Sacred and the Desire for Success

If Kabbalah and many other belief systems popularized nowadays primarily address the need for spiritual comfort, one of the most popular forms of pop spirituality sells a new mix: the combination between spirituality and worldly success. I first came across this phenomenon when I saw friends and acquaintances whom I highly value and respect read books like Robin Sharma's *The Monk Who Sold His Ferrari*.[20] One of them, a successful businessman with a brilliant mind, told me that he was reading the book very slowly "because it takes time to let all these deep insights sink in." Another acquaintance, a respected financial analyst, was marking all the sections that seemed particularly deep to him.

Skeptical as I am, I said to myself that as an observer and critic of contemporary culture I needed to have a look at what the buzz was about. Reading the book I didn't know whether to be angry or to laugh. It's a dreadfully written "fable" that makes neither psychological nor philosophical or spiritual sense. It is a completely unbelievable story of a top-notch lawyer who has a heart attack because of his work-hard-play-harder lifestyle. He disappears and returns looking twenty years younger after he has spent time with a mysterious group in the East: people who live very long lives are all incredibly fit and healthy and look decades younger than they are.

Its message is basically very trivial: don't let yourself be driven by pressure, think about what is really essential to you, and take good care of your health (one of the central "gains" of the book's hero is that he loses a lot of weight, never mind that his hair grows back, too). Sharma covers this up by the book's imagery and metaphors that are a hodgepodge of Eastern sounding philosophical "wisdom" not based on any actually existing Eastern tradition. I was truly shocked, and I started to wonder what on earth these intelligent people had been doing with this book and how they could possibly have felt that there was something deep and enduring there.

Thinking that maybe I had missed out on something, I looked for more material by Sharma, after all, as he says "one idea discovered in one book can change the way you see the world." Here is a brief selection of such gems that will change your life:

- Being great at what you do isn't just something you do for the organization you work for—it's a gift you give yourself.
- As you live your hours, so you create your years. As you live your days, so you craft your life.
- The most successful people on the planet have failed more than ordinary ones.
- Yes, reach for the mountaintop. But enjoy the climb as well.
- Great achievement often happens when our backs are up against the wall.
- Do a little each day to get you to your goals and over time you'll get there.
- Blaming others is excusing yourself.
- Every challenge is nothing more than a chance to make things better.
- Aging only happens to people who lose their lust for getting better and disconnect from their natural base of curiosity.[21]

These quotes have the advantage that they are less obfuscating than Sharma's philosophical fable. They are brief, to the point, commonsensical platitudes that have been sold over and over by many self-help writers, and you wonder why anybody should flock to hear such simplistic "wisdom" and why its salesman has become a guru.

But the numbers speak for themselves: the market for this merchandise is huge and growing. Books like Rhonda Byrne's *The Secret*, condemned by the serious critics around the globe as irrational, shallow, quite simply false and morally repugnant, or the books of Esther and Jerry Hicks, who claim to gain their "knowledge" from a number of spirits collectively called Abraham, sell millions of copies.[22]

The Secret, described as one of the most amazing publishing phenomena of recent years, is certainly admirable as a feat of marketing. The book's design creates an association to a book from the Middle Ages, riding on the success of Dan Brown's *The Da Vinci Code*, which had proved that there was an enormous appetite for anything that reminds readers of ancient knowledge. Its basic thesis is that there is a secret that had been known to great thinkers such as Plato, Goethe, and Einstein but had been kept away from the masses.

This secret is the "law of attraction." The universe is built in a way that when you think hard enough of something that you want, the universe will send it to you. As critics have pointed out, most of the examples of what can be achieved just by wishing them are quite mundane and reflect middle-class worries such as weight loss, a new car, or a nice vacation.

Byrne claims that she was let into this secret in a difficult period of her life. She doesn't show how she knows that Plato, Goethe, and Einstein "knew" or believed in the law of attraction, and she finds it very difficult to demonstrate this. It is true that some of the thinkers that she mentions at the book's beginning had quite a few abstruse beliefs, but the law of attraction is not among them, as can be verified easily by delving into intellectual history or, for lack of time, into relevant Wikipedia entries.

She then proceeds to buttress the secret's validity by quoting 24 "authorities" extensively. Research journalists have taken the trouble to check out these "authorities."[23] All but two of them are motivational speakers of some sort. Two are actually physicists, even though not ones held in esteem by the scientific community. When these physicists were interviewed, they disassociated themselves explicitly from *The Secret's* major claim—that is, the law of attraction. One of them says that he mostly spoke about his view of quantum physics, but all this material had been edited out.

The Secret relies on both models of validation mentioned at the beginning of this chapter: it is a combination between the validation by personal experience and ancient knowledge but doesn't even bother to go through

THE DEFEAT OF MIND   6|

the type of moves Rabbi Laitman makes to argue for its thesis. It rests content to mention some great historical figures without bothering to give a single reference (which would have been impossible, given the blatant historical falsity of the claims) and then to move on to the dubious authorities for confirmation.

Background research showed that Rhonda Byrne's inspiration for *The Secret* came primarily from an old book by Wallace D. Wattles, *The Science of Getting Rich*, which she was handed by one of her children when the reality-television show she was producing was losing its ratings. She then contacted a couple that had been making tons of money through selling, basically, the law of attraction. Esther Hicks claimed to get her "knowledge" through spirits she was in contact with and whom she collectively called "Abraham." We needn't be concerned about the legal tussles that emerged between the Hickses and Byrne later.

What matters is that the book is not only completely unfounded in its claims. As critics have pointed out, its thesis is also morally despicable. Since all that happens to us is supposedly a function of our positive or negative thoughts, the millions who died through either political persecution, genocide, or starvation must have brought this on themselves and are therefore responsible for their own demise.[24]

At this point the following objection is conceivable: "Why are you so harsh against people like Byrne, Esther and Jerry Hicks, or Sharma? After all, they make people feel good, they give them some optimism, and that can't be a bad thing. Aren't you just being plain elitist when you thunder against their shallowness and the lack of foundation of some of their claims? What's so bad about a little feel-good effect?"

The answer is very simple. I have no doubt that all those who turn to these sellers of spiritual snake oil suffer from genuine distress of some sort. Sometimes the problem may be no more specific than dissatisfaction with life. But sometimes the problems are very real: experiencing economic hardship; children who are in trouble, or experiencing real health problems.

Those who suffer from real problems need real help. The price these people pay for a little feel-good experience is much higher than defenders of pop spirituality admit. First, because they may forgo actual help they need. Illness is to be taken very seriously and it needs to be treated according to the best knowledge we have. Positive thinking does not cure cancer, and research studies—funded by millions of dollars—have shown conclusively that prayer is of no help either.

The second price they pay is that of shattered hope. To take an example I have studied extensively,[25] a growing number of midlifers do not find work; either they have no pension or their pensions are simply not enough to make ends meet. We are faced with the despair of huge numbers of people who have sent their resumes to hundreds of companies without ever being invited to interviews.

If Byrne, Sharma, and company were right, we would just have to teach all these people to think positively and they would be flooded with work opportunities. But wishing for money hard enough does not bring you either money or a job, even if Oprah Winfrey endorses *The Secret*. My objections against many forms of pop spirituality are therefore not just based on my distaste for baseless claims about "deep knowledge," but I believe that they are morally dubious to say the least. When false hopes are raised and then shattered by reality, the resulting despair is even more difficult to bear.

The Strange Conservative-Liberal Alliance That Produced Political Correctness

The attraction of occultism has always been strong. New Age thinking and fusion spirituality are not new either. They emerged in the late nineteenth century fueled by charismatic figures like the legendary and charismatic Madame Blavatsky, who claimed to have mystical access to truths that were basically a blend of various spiritual traditions. Serious academics ranging from William James to Carl Gustav Jung were strongly attracted to the wave of occultism that flooded Europe and the United States during this time. The phenomenal success of the flat, uninteresting, and morally repugnant *The Secret* is only the newest edition of the human tendency to fall for those who promise us that we can have everything we want quite simply if we just get this one thing right.

The reason the current flood of pop spirituality needs special attention is that there has never been an age in which there was as much knowledge and as much easy access to this knowledge. For most of human history there was not too much systematic knowledge about nature, history, economics, the human mind, or any other aspect of the universe, and the extant knowledge was difficult and expensive to come by. For millennia only few could read; and even in the last four centuries since the scientific revolution of the seventeenth century, you needed access to expensive books, schools, and universities to learn.

This is no longer true. The Internet has made it possible for anybody with a computer and a broadband connection to access enormous troves of knowledge. The National Institutes of Health (NIH) has an excellent website providing surfers with up-to-date and easily understandable medical information. Wikipedia, one of the marvels of the human ability to produce results through users' collaborative insights, offers free information that is mostly quite reliable with links reaching out through cyberspace for those who want to delve more deeply into their subject matter.

The global creative class is sociologically and culturally different from any previous class in two respects: they are highly educated; they have at least undergraduate education, and a large percentage has postgraduate education as well. They have been taught how to evaluate knowledge critically and they have no problem investigating whether a source of information is reliable or not. They have access to knowledge to a degree never before possible in the history of humanity through the Internet and have a higher degree of awareness of global interconnectedness than any previous generation.

Given all these assets, you might expect them to show a high degree of awareness of history and science in formulating their worldviews. You might think that they are not bound to be gullible by knowledge claims that are spurious to say the least and sometimes downright absurd. You might hope that they apply the critical tools they have received during their education to prevent their worldviews from being parochial, irrational, or based on ignorance. Yet it seems that many have little interest in applying these tools to their worldviews.

What is the basis for the tendency to bury critical acumen when it comes to formulating our worldviews? What are the reasons for the current anti-intellectualism when it comes to questions of faith? Why should highly educated people want to sell their minds to those who sell them solace at the lowest intellectual price?

There is, of course, no simple answer to this question, and reality is much more multifaceted than any simple theory about the matter could allow. Let me therefore first define the domain of my subject matter. I am certainly not addressing the fundamentalist backlash that has preoccupied so many, particularly in the United States. Most members of the global creative class are not amenable to this type of attack on reason and science; few find the aggressive intolerance, the condemnation of gays, and the broadside attacks on abortion congenial. They tend to be highly tolerant; they don't like aggressive partisanship, nor do they like repressive conservatism.

In fact it may precisely be the penchant for tolerance that gets members of Homo globalis caught up in a facile relativism. They would like a world in which everybody gets along with everybody and people don't kill and don't die for questions of belief. Mostly liberal in outlook, they abhor the idea of the state's intrusion on the individual's freedom of thought and prescribed lifestyle.

Their problem is rather how to preserve the space of freedom that they have come to cherish, and the solution that many of them advocate is the avoidance of trenchant argument. Multiculturalism was supposed to be the deus ex machina that will solve most illnesses of modern society. Wolves and sheep would finally dwell together; devout Muslims would coexist with Evangelical born-again Christians; and Rastafarians would sing together with atheists, and Buddhists would dance with Hindus. Religious strife was supposed to be out and harmony and understanding was in, as the title song of the musical *Hair* predicted for the Age of Aquarius.

I want to make clear that I have no intention of joining conservative writers who see the sixties as the root of all evil and as the beginning of disintegration of the social order and the uprooting of traditions. I believe that the sixties are responsible for many highly important developments that have produced a lot of good in the Western world, ranging from the beginnings of the feminist movement to gay liberation.

The current anti-intellectualism does not have its roots simply in the 1960s. In many ways the opposite is true. The 1960s and 1970s were characterized by trenchant intellectual debate in the political sphere. If anything, the 1980s marked the onset of the more strident forms of anti-intellectualism that has dominated Western culture for the last decades.[26]

While it is "in" for liberals and conservatives to accuse each other of the current ills of society and culture, I think that current anti-intellectualism has its sources in both camps, which interacted with each other in a strange dance of synergy that has led our culture to its current level of intellectual shallowness.

On the conservative side, the United States witnessed an upsurge of disdain for incisive intellectual debate that started with the rise of Christian fundamentalism in the 1970s. The election of Ronald Reagan in the 1980s marked the breakthrough of this disdain for trenchant debate into the public sphere. Reagan himself, while being a savvy politician gifted with great communication skills, made it very clear that he had little use for eggheads, either in his administration or in the general cultural scene.

In doing so, Reagan plugged into the powerful anti-intellectual strand of American culture that has been described in Richard Hofstadter's magisterial classic *Anti-Intellectualism in American Life* (1963), a book that repays reading to this very day. I do not have the space to present Hofstadter's intricate historical analysis here. Let it be said that America has always valued the man of action (and generally the emphasis was indeed on men) over the man of thought. The "talkers" were always looked down upon by the "doers" to some extent.

In parallel, the American religious scene was dominated by puritan forms of Protestantism. Emphasis on the faith in the simple heart and disdain for those who valued complex thought has always been a powerful strand in American culture. It was counterbalanced by the forces that put great emphasis on sophistication and learning that led to the establishment of the great American universities. It was exercised by the Founding Fathers with their willingness to embrace complex thought in formulating the foundations of the fledgling federation.

The Reagan era more than anything else led to the powerful surge of the combination of the American love for business unfettered by intrusions and regulations and the emphasis on simple faith as opposed to complex argument. It initiated the deregulation of the financial markets that, for more than two decades, had been seen as the wellspring feeding the growth of the American economy—and now has turned out to be the root of the greatest economic disaster since the Great Depression.

Ever since, the Republican Party's reliance on the religious-conservative base has only increased and it has come to a climax in the two terms of G. W. Bush, who, both for political reasons and, so it seems, out of sincere belief, drove anti-intellectualism to new heights. Since his tendency to read sermons rather than intelligence briefings before making critical decisions has been well documented by a number of chroniclers of his administration, there is no need to retell the facts. Susan Jacoby has shown in detail the extent to which Bush's policies quite explicitly rejected the idea of fact-based argument, because they sincerely believed that since they would *create* the facts, there was no need to study them.

But liberals have also contributed their share to the anti-intellectualism of the last decades. Both in Europe and in the United States the liberal Left developed a hefty dose of disdain and even hatred for the Western intellectual tradition, and this hatred of everything the West stood for, took many forms.[27]

The first was the unequivocal condemnation of all the West stood for as an expression of imperialism, colonialism, and repressiveness. Many Marxist intellectuals reveled in formulations that attacked the Western tradition as the root of all evil: everything from male dominance to capitalist exploitation was somehow connected to the West. From Herbert Marcuse and Norman Brown to the later Jean-Paul Sartre and Felix Guattari, the all-out attack on Western culture was on. For some, the primal sin had already been committed by Plato through his putting reason over feeling. For others, the bourgeoisie and capitalism were the roots of all evil because they had commoditized everything from the self to art.

Many of them clung to the belief that Communism was the alternative that would bring salvation to humanity and clung to this belief despite the growing flow of information about the atrocities of Stalinism.

Others again thought that all the categories of Western thought needed to be debunked as ruses hiding class interests or gender inequality. "Subversion" became the intellectual's greatest virtue and many academics in the humanities and social sciences outdid each other to dismantle the ruse of the Western lie that it was spreading freedom.[28]

This was not enough for liberals: the idea that the West had produced anything of quality was seen as a form of domination. The canon of Western works that had been taught at universities was now disqualified as nothing but a collection of the works of dead white males. The very act of arguing that Shakespeare, Tolstoy, Stendhal, Thomas Mann, and so on were great writers was seen as just another ploy to enforce the supremacy of the "dead white males." Arguing for intrinsic standards of quality in art or science was denounced as another base tactics to keep some group (blacks, women, Muslims, gays, lesbians—anything but white heterosexual males) out of sharing the limelight of cultural hegemony.

This was the birth of identity politics. Trenchant argument and rational analysis was supplanted by a new form of competition. Groups competed with each other for the dubious honor of being the most oppressed, disadvantaged, and traumatized. Were black women worse off than gays and lesbians, or were women in general the group whose suffering and oppression was the cause that beat all others in scope and importance?

Every year brought a new fad of uncovering another form of oppression and abuse. The 1980s imported the idea that all psychopathology was due to sexual abuse, and the whole of society was accused of covering up the horrors of an underground male abuse of women.[29] A whole psychotherapeutic movement emerged that claimed to help patients recover repressed memories—and if they didn't remember without help, hypnosis was used to "recover" these memories, leading to countless cases of charges based on nothing but hypnotic suggestion sold as pure unadulterated truth.

Students who went through their education during this period ended up with a combination of bombastic terms like phallo-logo-centrism, deconstruction of forms of governmentality, and the like combined with a vague feeling that it was wrong to look at arguments critically because it might hurt some oppressed person or group's feelings.

Between the conservative emphasis on unadulterated faith and the liberal attack on rational thought as an invention of white Western males, the ground for the ideology of political correctness was set. Conservatives cherished this because they needed to accommodate the growing number of religious denominations, Evangelical sects, and new churches. For political reasons, they did not want to criticize any new form of religious belief since it strengthened the growing tide of the "moral majority" that they hoped would return America to its roots and excise the un-American implantations of welfare, big government, and liberal atheism. The more extreme fringes of liberals loved it because it served their crusade against the West as the root of all evil.

This unholy—and unintended—alliance generated the anti-intellectualism of the last decades and a blooming buzzing confusion among those who tried to make sense of their lives and times. Students that came of age during these years mostly came to the conclusion that anything that was not in the domains of mathematical sciences and management was simply not amenable to critical thought and inquiry. Most of all anything that touched on questions of faith and belief was supposed to be completely off limits for rational discussion. Beliefs had to be respected just because somebody held them and because touching on such belief might be offensive. Hence anything went: The belief that God would take the believers of certain Evangelical sects physically to heaven only to return them to earth for eternal life was just fine, and so was the belief that extraterrestrials had brought some enormous wisdom that L. Ron Hubbard distributed to the Church of Scientology. The belief that the Jewish conquest of the West Bank was the onset of the Messianic period went hand in hand with the belief of other Evangelical sects in the apocalypse.

The defeat of mind was now all but complete. The unavoidable consequence of the idea that questions of worldviews could not be discussed reasonably is a facile relativism that claims that there is simply no difference between carefully argued positions and beliefs that are held just because they seem right at the moment or because they charm us or provide us with comfort.

Part III of this book will address the question how we can maintain worldviews that satisfy our need for meaning without numbing our critical faculties. I think that Homo globalis has a strong interest in moving toward worldviews that have stronger intellectual foundations. Pop spirituality rarely leads to what we all need: a relatively stable worldview that provides us with meanings that withstand criticism. Those who succumb to the allure of the quick fix promised by pop spiritualities are likely to be disappointed: whatever the charm of a comforting worldview may be, in the end, it cannot provide a stable foundation for our understanding of us, our lives, and our world. After the honeymoon with Kabbalah, Indian astrology, or the teachings of the latest self-help guru is over, we only find ourselves facing the emptiness that we have sought to escape.

Part II

From the "I" Commodity to the Drama of Individuality

4

The Drama of Individuality

The core idea of liberalism is that society should foster and must not interfere with the flourishing of the individual. John Stuart Mill's classic, and to this day unsurpassed, defense of liberalism is based on one, central notion: individuals must have the right to make up their mind on the most basic questions of life and to live according to their understanding and preferences as they have evolved.

It has since turned out that for liberalism to work, quite a few conditions must be fulfilled: a society without institutions that provide individuals with the tools to choose and foster the value of free choice in its citizens is likely to undermine liberty.[1]

Yet it is becoming clearer that three recent developments in the Free World have undermined the core values of liberalism. The first is the obsession with quantifying the individual's value that we have analyzed in Chapters 1 and 2 and the attempt to formulate all value in economic terms. The result of this deification of the economic bottom line was that the process of developing a worldview and of the personality's evolution was no longer seen as a value in itself. Only the spectacular result, measurable in terms of the "I" commodity counted.

The second recent danger to liberalism has been the prevalence of the politics of identity. The individual's true self is supposedly defined by belonging to a religion, race, culture, gender, or sexual minority, particularly if this group had been disadvantaged in the past or present. The politics of identity has also fed into the third obstacle to liberalism, the devaluation of thought that we have analyzed in Chapter 3: if I am X (Jewish, Muslim, black, gay, a woman), I am supposed to accept the package deal of beliefs, values, and attitudes that supposedly define my group, and to fight for them, sometimes to the death.

Indian Nobel Prize laureate in economy Amartya Sen has become one of the most outspoken critics of reducing individuality to group identity.[2] He has made a powerful case for reflective individualism: every individual belongs to a variety of groups (you can be Muslim, a lawyer, a lover of classical music, an Indian, heterosexual, an activist for gay rights, a connoisseur of Italian cuisine, etc.). It is up to the individual to determine which of these identities is more or less central in shaping a life. Identity must not be reduced to a single group that is supposed to determine one's politics, values, and way of life.

Liberalism depends on the idea that the process of individual development is in itself a value; that the arduous task of becoming an individual with character and with a worldview must be celebrated. If all we want is a highly functioning individual (a highly traded "I" commodity), or someone with blind allegiance to a group (Jew, gay, black), but no longer value working on the conflicts and tensions involved in the process of development, a fundamental tenet of liberalism is undermined. The process of going through illusions and disillusionment, building hopes and revaluing them, acquiring beliefs and discarding them in the light of criticism, and thus acquiring self-knowledge must be an intrinsic value if a liberal society is to flourish.

One of the enduring legacies of European romanticism was that it was fascinated by the complexities of individual development. From Rousseau's *Confessions* to Goethe's *Wilhelm Meister*, and from Stuart Mill's *Autobiography* to Søren Kierkegaard's *Either/Or*, the celebration of *Selbstwerdung*, the evolution of the individual became a central theme of romanticism.

This theme was developed further in psychodynamic psychology and existential thought. It added to the celebration of individual development the examination of the conflict between desire and reality and between fantasy and self-knowledge. It showed that this process is poignant because the individuals cannot choose the base materials of their lives (gender, culture, language, etc.) and shape them into lives experienced as truly their own. It showed how difficult it is to acquire some objective self-knowledge and yet maintain passions that make life worth living. The task of Part II is to delineate some of the core ideas of the existentialist understanding of the process of becoming a person.

Modernity and the Crisis of Meaning

In his great diagnosis of modernity, Max Weber[3] characterized its essence as the "disenchantment of the world." The essence of the scientific revolution of the seventeenth century was that modern natural science no longer made use of symbolic relations to explain the world. In the sixteenth century an explanation of the sort "there are seven planets because the human body has seven orifices" was perfectly acceptable. The macrocosm and the microcosm were correlated through a nexus of meaning and the human species had a special place in the fabric of the cosmos (literally "order").

The Copernican revolution and the advent of mathematical physics destroyed the fabric of the anthropocentric cosmos forever. Modern humanity no longer had a privileged place in the world and the meaning of our lives could no longer be derived from the symbolic network that connected the universe's creator, the structure of the cosmos and human nature.

The existential question that arose became: if the universe is indifferent to us, how can we know that we are leading lives of significance? How can we still feel that we have a vocation in this world now that the literal meaning of "vocation" (being called on by God) could no longer be grounded in the new cosmology?

Weber's reconstruction of the nature of modernity connects the disenchantment of the world with the advent of the Protestant work ethic. In a disenchanted world, the question of what it meant to live a meaningful life had become deeply problematic and the idea that humans can have a vocation became difficult to maintain as it originated with the notion of being called by God to do something. The Protestant work ethic answered this question by giving capitalism a theological grounding. Weber brilliantly connects this to the theological notion of vocation, which originally quite literally meant to be called on to do something, usually by God himself. The meaning of life was reformulated correspondingly: financial success became a measure of the human being's intrinsic value. The new Protestant work ethic linked salvation and riches. There was no longer any need to feel guilty about being rich. The opposite was true and it was a new indication that God has given you a special place in the universe. This provided the theological background the process of ever-growing rationalization through which the Western world began its ascent toward world domination by optimizing all aspects of life from engineering through commerce and warfare.

The age of the golden calf at the end of the twentieth century therefore has deep roots in the advent of modernity. To some extent the global I-Commodity Market is a radicalized version of the Protestant work ethic; it now defines the state of grace through the self's rating. But as we have seen financial success and a high rating on some global rating scale have turned out to be a very shaky foundation for the sense of leading a life of significance.

Existentialist thought, starting with Kierkegaard and Fyodor Dostoyevsky and culminating in the work of Martin Heidegger, Karl Jaspers, and Jean-Paul Sartre in the twentieth century set out to address precisely this conundrum. How can we experience meaning in a universe that is basically indifferent to us?

Existentialism's answer was that indeed human freedom and human finitude are sources of deep anxiety. While existentialism is certainly not a light-hearted and optimistic view of human existence, it is not nihilist. Its great claim was that meaning is generated in the attempt to face the tragic structure of our existence: knowing that we will die, we can find our freedom by assuming responsibility for our lives and identities without denying the tension generated between our biological nature and the self-awareness that forces us to ask what it means to live a meaningful life.

It is not surprising that existentialism lost much of its cultural impact during the age of the golden calf, which celebrated the illusion of omnipotence. In arguing for the value of existentialism's core ideas, I critique the conception of life that states that the good life is bereft of tension and conflict, that our goal must be to normalize our lives and design them along the lines of the one-dimensional icons of the "good life" fed to us by the infotainment system.

Hence the basic thesis of Part II of this book is that the ideology of "just do it" (JDI) has made it almost impossible to feel that we live meaningful lives because its essence was to deny that human life inevitably faces what the German philosopher-psychiatrist Karl Jaspers called "boundary situations."[4] He defined these as the inevitable failures vis-à-vis the immutable limitations of human existence, most of all death.[5]

Instead, I will argue, it is precisely our dealing with the limitations and tragedies of our individual and collective identities that provides us with meaning. In a universe that is not attuned to our needs and desires, each of us is faced with the task of forming the raw materials of our existence into a life that we truly experience as our own and that is recognized as being of value by those close to us and by the worldview of the culture we live in. Thus the theological notion of vocation is given a new interpretation: when the solutions we find to our personal conflicts and tragedies become valuable for others, we can feel that our lives are truly meaningful.

Romanticism: Life and Individuality as Art

European romanticism had argued since the late eighteenth century that rationality and efficiency could not possibly be a sufficient source of meaning.[6] Its solution was to put the source of meaning into the creative self. In doing so, romanticism transformed the notion of art from being just a type of craft to being the pinnacle of humanity.

Because our culture is essentially postromantic, it is at times difficult to realize how historically recent is the exalted status of art. Johann Sebastian Bach, who died in mid-eighteenth century, still understood his profession as a craft; he prided himself for his exquisite technique. If he had been asked whether his compositions reflected his individuality and creativity, he would not have understood the question. He didn't mind writing some of his greatest compositions on themes that had been sent to him by others, and his *Art of the Fugue* was meant to be a tour de force of fugal technique and not an expression of his personal voice. During his time artists were still producers of beautiful products commissioned by those who paid for it, and their standing was not very different from that of other craftsmen who provided services and goods.

Rousseau's *Confessions*,[7] one of the founding documents of European romanticism, told a very different type of narrative. The development of individuality was no longer toward a cosmic truth but toward authenticity and a connection with an *inner* truth to which the individual needed to be true to live a life truly worth living. The enemy of true individuality was no longer paganism; the struggle was to overcome the social pressures toward conformity that prevents us from living a life that is truly our own.

Within the span of half a century after Bach's death, Western culture completely changed its understanding of art and its place in culture. Romanticism became obsessed with the notion of genius and with the process of artistic creation. The truly great artist was a demigod, somebody who shared God's privilege of *creatio ex nihilo*.

Creativity now became an end in itself.[8] The good life was one in which an individual came to full fruition. The criteria for such fruition were no longer universal nor determined by a catalogue of virtues predefined by an external authority like religion or the social order, but the internal coherence of character. Friedrich Nietzsche put this new cultural command in a nutshell:

> *One Thing is Needful.*—To "give style" to one's character—a great and rare art. It is practiced by those who survey all the strengths and weaknesses of their nature and then fit them into an artistic plan until everyone of them appears as art and reason and even weaknesses delight the eye . . . In the end, when the work is finished, it becomes evident how the constraint of a single taste governed and formed everything large and small. Whether this taste was good or bad is less important than one might suppose, if only it was a single taste.[9]

Romanticism turned all of us into artists. Living a life worth living now meant to be the author of one's life. Nietzsche formulated the criterion for judging this creation: it had to be a life with inner, aesthetic coherence. Like all artistic creation, this required judicious use of our aesthetic faculties.

Yet there is one central difference between the creation of other works of art and that of living a life. An artist can choose his theme, his motif, and his technique. He can pick from a variety of genres and apply his creativity to this. As opposed to that, in living our lives we cannot choose our base materials.[10]

We are not self-created. Our physical existence is the result of an act of sexual intercourse between a man and a woman whom we did not choose to be our parents. Our minds are the result of a multiplicity of influences none of which we control. Our genetic inheritance evolves into mental abilities, temperamental traits, and an emotional disposition that is the biological basis of all we will ever think, feel, and experience. Our perspective onto the world is invariably shaped by the language that constitutes the base materials of our minds, the culture that determines our basic outlook on life, and the social class into which we are born. Our character is indelibly shaped by the impact of the personalities of our parents and educators.

By the time our sense of individuality begins to evolve, the basic parameters of our lives are set; we have been dealt a deck of cards that can no longer be changed. This is where the drama of individuality begins. Even though, metaphysically and logically, we could not be the offspring of someone other than our parents,[11] we can feel that we were born into an environment that is recalcitrant rather than nourishing to the development of our personal idiom.

Individuals can find themselves in conflict with their families, their culture, or their religion. A naturally inquisitive child may find that questions about the nature and authority of the family's religious belief are judged as heretic and morally unacceptable. Another conflict that can be very painful is if youngsters find out that they are homosexual and neither their families nor their cultures accept this sexual orientation as legitimate.

Our basic desire to be individuals often rebels against having to live under constraints and limitations we have not chosen. The project of becoming the authors of our lives is an attempt to recreate the aspects of reality that are unbearably fateful, sometimes in fantasy, sometimes in reality. Some people approach this project consciously and deliberately. The self and its life course are shaped in the fashion of a work of art. More often, though, the forces of fate; the desire for authorship; and the multiple layers of pain, desire, anxiety, and rage interact in ways the individual cannot fully decipher.

The effectiveness of the project of becoming the author of our lives varies greatly. For some individuals the project of reshaping their selves leads along roads opposed to social norms. They choose lifestyles that require a conscious choice most of the time, since they are not in the mainstream of society. They sometimes cross the boundaries of religious and political views deemed acceptable by their culture of origin; they create lifestyles and endorse values that require living in conflict with all they have been taught. Sometimes, after painful struggles, they recreate their selves and their lives to their satisfaction and thus restore their sense of authorship. They lead rich and rewarding lives, they have close and meaningful personal relationships, and they find various ways to express their creativity. Nevertheless the wounds of fate and the insecurity involved in the project of self-creation always leave their mark on a person's life.

Of course the romantic narrative of the individual as author of their lives has its limitations. Many of us, much of the time, do not necessarily feel that we have created our lives; we feel that we were guided by cultural norms, family expectations, and the need to fit into society. Nevertheless this narrative captures something profound about the human condition. We are the only known animal that has self-consciousness. We do not just exist, but we have a relationship to our selves and our lives. Our identity is not simply a given; it is also the result of our decisions, and thus, to some extent of our making.

Existentialism and the Structure of Human Existence

German philosopher Martin Heidegger in his epochal *Being and Time* used a poignant term for the fact that we haven't chosen any of the basic parameters of our existence:[12] we choose neither our parents, nor our bodies and biological sex, nor the culture that formed our minds, nor the level of our talents, which determine much of the course of our lives. He calls this feature of our existence "thrownness." We are thrown into existence (we haven't chosen to be born, after all, even if we welcome this fact now). The basic metaphysical structure of our existence is therefore that we have not had any say with respect to any of our most basic parameters.

This sets the stage for the drama of human existence and human individuality. Humans are endowed with two abilities that, to the best of our knowledge, are unique in the animal kingdom. The first is that we have self-consciousness. We know that we exist, we have a conception of ourselves, and we have an attitude toward who we are. The second is that we are endowed with an imagination fertile and active enough to be able to imagine that things could have been different.

Another of the great twentieth century existential philosophers, Jean-Paul Sartre, turned this tension into the foundation of his philosophical masterpiece *Being and Nothingness*. On the one hand we are just biological organisms. Sartre says that we are *en-soi*, an in-itself; something that just *is*.

But we are also *pour-soi*, a for-itself. We have self-consciousness, and this changes our whole existence. We are capable of transcending the constraints imposed by the parameters of our existence that we have no control over by using our imagination to go beyond these limitations even though we are not free to change them at will.

The essence of the existentialist understanding of the human condition is that it is basically tragic, because there is no way we can escape the basic tension between Heidegger's "thrownness" or "facticity" (the fact that we cannot choose the basic parameters of our lives) and the freedom of self-consciousness. We can neither escape the freedom bestowed on us by the realization that our lives are of our making nor erase the facticity of our history; we cannot change the basic parameters of our identity.

Hence the basic thesis of Part II of this book regards the true drama of individuality as the tension between facticity and freedom. We cannot break away from this tension. The myth of "just do it" is profoundly misleading because it assumes that we can shape our selves at will. But human beings are by nature historical and we cannot escape our historicity. Hence a life well lived is not one of fantastic self-creation; it is to accept the tension that is built into our existence and to live it as fully and creatively as we can.

This project is by no means simple. We are like bricoleurs—artists who can never start their work from scratch by putting a new canvas on the frame or put a new, empty page into our typewriter. Our raw materials are given and a large portion of the work that is our life is always already there; we can only continue on the basis of our histories. Because we need to build our lives on base materials we have not chosen, the creation of our lives never starts from scratch. Our existential situation is that of an artist who can never buy the materials for his creation according to a preconceived plan; but like the bricoleur, we must take the materials found in our backyards and try to turn them into the creation that is our life. It is our life's task to turn this story into a work that we truly experience our self; to become the authors of our lives, even though we didn't start the story with our choices.

Facticity and Self-Consciousness

Milan Kundera has given one of the most poignant literary expressions to the tension between facticity and self-consciousness in his seminal novel *The Unbearable Lightness of Being*.[13] With the brushstroke of the grandmaster,

Kundera characterizes each of the four protagonists by a basic existential tension that they cannot escape, what Kundera has called a character's "existential equation."[14] *The Unbearable Lightness of Being* is one of the few instances of a philosophical novel that succeeds both as literature and as philosophy and its philosophical thesis is powerful: human beings are shaped by an existential equation that they can neither choose nor escape. All we can do is live this equation as best as we can.

Tereza, one of the novel's protagonists, grows up with a mother who hates her, because Tereza's pregnancy made her marry a man who turns out to be a disappointment. She feels that the attractiveness of her own body was just an ephemeral commodity that has vanished with age and she is determined not to let Tereza feel that she is special and truly an individual.

It becomes Tereza's deepest wish to get away from the existence to which her mother is condemned and with which her mother wants to bind her: an existence in which she is but pure flesh, with no soul, and no individuality. For Tereza, books and culture are the only ways to sense the possibility of an existence less brutish than what she sees in her small-town environment.

When Tomas, a neurosurgeon from Prague, arrives in town to perform an operation, a series of coincidences make Tereza feel that this is the man who is destined to help her escape her dreary existence. Without any previous arrangement she moves to Prague, knocks at Tomas's door, only to faint, because she is running a high fever.

Tereza's existential equation is the tension between body and soul. In the terms of existentialist philosophy we might redescribe this as the tension between our biological nature, symbolized by Tereza's mother, and self-consciousness, exemplified by Tereza's indelible striving for individuality and freedom.

Tomas's existential equation is the conflict between lightness and heaviness. Having lost contact with his son, because he was incapable of fighting with his wife about how to bring him up, he decides never again to have demanding emotional relationships. Seemingly he completely opts for a life of lightness, limiting his relationships to women to what he calls "erotic friendships." Yet when Tereza faints on his doorstep, he feels as if a baby was delivered to his doorstep and that fate has entrusted him with a responsibility that he cannot refuse, and heaviness finds its way back into his life. At a later stage he will pay a great price for his unwillingness to retract an article in which he criticizes the Czech Communist regime—the conflict between lightness and heaviness never lets go.

Throughout the novel we see how Tereza's attempt to solve her existential equation fails. In the most intimate moments her stomach suddenly gurgles, making her feel ashamed and uncomfortable. And while Tomas indeed helps her to escape her small-town existence, he revives her suffering because he is neither able nor willing to stop sleeping with other women, thus making Tereza feel once again that she is reduced to being flesh among flesh.

Kundera's novel implies that Tereza's problem is not unique. The opposite is true because it expresses the tension between our bodily nature and self-consciousness, which determines the course of a lifetime. Tomas cannot resolve the tension between lightness and heaviness any more than Tereza: while he cannot stop his philandering, his love for Tereza remains overwhelming. And while he does not want to be involved politically, he ends up losing his position as a surgeon because he is not willing to compromise on his principles.

Kundera shows that there is no way to solve our existential equation. After trials, tribulations, and tragedies, Tomas and Tereza seem to finally have found a way out of their respective existential equations. Living in a small village in the countryside, Tomas finally feels that he can be faithful to Tereza, and she finally feels confirmed in her individuality—and then they die in a car accident. *Our existential equation is who we are.* The fulfilled life is not one in which the existential equation is solved, but a life in which the existential equation is lived out fruitfully and creatively. The resolution of this equation can only mean death.

Homo Globalis's Struggle for Authorship

Homo globalis is more likely to encounter the difficulties of dealing with conflicting strands of identity than humans ever were. It has become a truism that a growing proportion of humans live with what are now called hyphenated identities. The complexities of these identities are often remarkable. If in the past it was often enough to link two terms like "African-American," "French-Muslim," or "Polish-Jewish" to describe an identity, this is often no longer enough. The best-known example is President Barack Obama. Part of his lineage is Kenyan and half Muslim; on his mother's side, the family is of Caucasian American descent and Christian.

Behind the seemingly simple term "hyphenated identity" there is mostly a complex drama. Obama's life exemplifies the complex structure of the project of individuality in full. The facts of his life are too well known now to require detailed recounting.[15] Born to a white American mother and a black Kenyan father who divorced when he was aged two, he grew up in Hawaii and Indonesia.

Returning to the United States, he experienced the complexity of race relations often painfully. He writes that he needed to be laid-back, so people wouldn't be afraid of him. Always a man of burning ambition, he succeeded in channeling this raw power through the elite institutions of American academia. He was elected the first black president of the prestigious *Harvard Law Review*, and then he combined his job as a law professor at the University of Chicago with his activity as a community organizer. He continued to live the various conflicting strands of his identity through the writing of his autobiography *Dreams from My Father*. He already knew then that his life would be about bridging different social and political groups, and he renounced the "natural" option of a star student at Harvard who had the option to embark on a lucrative career in a major law firm. But Obama clearly felt that his existential equation was about bridging conflict and resolving identity issues, and thus began his slow ascent through public service to elected office—first in Illinois and then in the U.S. Senate.

Now that Obama has become president of the United States, asking why he "didn't grow up" and get a partnership in a leading law firm with the perks and income attached seems preposterous. But we need to remember that in 1995, when he wrote his autobiography, Barack Obama had no idea that he would reach the most exalted political office in the United States. He *did* know that his life's task was to mediate between conflicting identities, groups, and ideals and that this gave him the sense that he truly was living *his* life.

He has integrated the various strands of his complex background into a powerful identity: complex and multifaceted and yet unified and unmistakably individual. He is both cosmopolitan and American; both black and white. He has a clearly defined worldview and yet is open to many forms of social, cultural, and religious experience other than his own. If he had not succeeded in the ongoing process of building bridges between opposites, the American people would not have entrusted him with the task of being commander in chief, and we can only hope that he will continue his ongoing existential task on the worldwide scale assigned to him by his office.

There are many examples of people who were faced with a conflict between their basic, inborn character structures and the circumstances into which they were born.[16] Some of them poignantly show how conflict can turn into the cornerstone of their individuality. Somali activist and writer Ayaan Ali Hirsi was born with a rebellious temperament into a traditional society, and this strain has determined the rest of her life. Even though she broke out of the confines of traditional Muslim society, the past will forever stay with her.

She was born the daughter of a leading figure in the Somali Revolution who was incarcerated for his political activity when she was a child. Her father opposed the practice of female genital mutilation traditionally performed in sub-Saharan Muslim society, but her grandmother performed the operation on her when she was five years old. Through a variety of trials and tribulations, Ayaan Hirsi fled her family to avoid an arranged marriage and received refugee status in the Netherlands, became a Dutch citizen, and eventually was elected to the Dutch parliament.[17]

For several years after her flight to the West, Hirsi remained a believing Muslim, endorsing, for example, Ayatollah Ruholla Khomeini's fatwa condemning Salman Rushdie to death for writing *The Satanic Verses*. Through prolonged internal conflict, she renounced Islam after coming to the conclusion that Osama bin Laden had indeed found ways to justify the terror act of 9/11 using the Qur'an, and became an atheist and outspoken critic of Islam.

She wrote the script for a short film called *Submission*, directed by Theo van Gogh, which attacked the role assigned to women in Islam. Van Gogh was murdered by a Muslim fanatic, who pinned a message to Van Gogh's body that Ayaan Hirsi was to be next. After the Dutch government withdrew the funding of her personal protection, Ayaan Hirsi Ali, fearing for her life, left the Netherlands, and is now a fellow of the American Enterprise Institute and lives in Washington, DC. She has published an autobiography and is currently working on a novel that describes the Prophet Muhammad's visit to the New York Public Library and his encounter with the great Enlightenment philosophers.

Some may ask, "But doesn't she know that she will be the target of Islamic reprisals when she publishes this book? Doesn't she learn from experience? Can't she grow up?" But what would it mean for Ayaan Hirsi Ali to grow up? The mutilation of her body will stay with her forever, and so will the memories of living in a society that tried to force her to live in a way that did violence to her. She will forever know what it is to be a refugee, and the experience of living under the threat of being killed by religious zealots is a normal occurrence for her anyway.

Sure, there are many respectable writers who think that Hirsi is overstating her case; that her attack on Islam is too radical and will only be taken seriously by the converted. There are those who call her an Enlightenment fundamentalist, and think that her philosophical position is naïve.

Yet there is no doubt that Ayaan Hirsi Ali's existential equation is set. Her past and its clash with her fiercely independent and outspoken temperament are burned into her soul for as long as she lives. For her to live a rich and fulfilled life does not mean to move beyond the conflicts and rifts in her identity. It is to live them to the fullest.

A third example is American writer Philip Roth, who was born into a traditional Jewish family. His father, a first-generation American of Polish-Galician descent, worked very hard to give his family a decent life and his children the head start that he had not had. Selling insurance policies, he made it possible for his son to get an academic education. He not only raised his children to be proud Americans but also taught them that loyalty to the Jewish people, their history, and their values must never be abandoned or forgotten. Roth was grateful to his father and respected him—and he has given moving testimony both to his father's strength and decency of character and to the filial love he experienced toward him.

Roth went to college during the economic boom after World War II. He grew into the generation that was no longer shaped by the Great Depression. The values of being a decent provider and a good family man were giving way to the idea of creative self-expression. Young Roth felt stifled by the environment of the decent, hardworking people who strove for middle-class status and were proud of achieving it. Already in the collection of short stories that gained the public's attention, *Goodbye Columbus*, Roth's description of his parents' generation is packed with often aggressive irony, and already then, the Jewish community of his parents felt that he was devoid of loyalty because he portrayed them as narrow-minded and limited rather than decent and hardworking.

In 1969 Roth published *Portnoy's Complaint*, the novel that would catapult him into the forefront of the American literary scene. The novel is a monologue of its protagonist, Alexander Portnoy, during the first sessions of his psychoanalytic treatment. Portnoy recounts how overwhelmed he felt by his overbearing mother and how his budding sexuality drove him crazy. He describes how he is torn between his high ethical values embodied in his career as a civil rights attorney and his insatiable desire for women, and the impossibility to experience such desire (or at least to consummate it) within the context of durable relations—particularly with Jewish women. Portnoy feels condemned to live between the poles of insatiable desire and unbearable guilt.

The novel is highly explicit in its sexual imagery, hilariously funny, and totally irreverent with respect to Roth's Jewish upbringing. Besides being an instant success, it also provoked outrage among many members of the American Jewish community who felt that Roth was betraying them through the portrayal of his parent's generation.

Roth was 36 years old when *Portnoy's Complaint* was published. During the years that followed, there was no sign that the themes that had plagued Portnoy were about to abate. Nathan Zuckerman, Roth's fictional alter ego through nine novels, would speak endlessly about the problems that Carnovsky (the fictional counterpart of *Portnoy's Complaint*) caused him: his trouble in committing to women, the traps of literary fame, and his continuous struggle with the endlessness of desire.

In the standard views of personal maturation you would expect Roth to finally overcome these themes and to move on. But he didn't. To date, Roth has published nine Zuckerman novels, the latest being preoccupied with the ravages of aging and the humiliations inflicted by physical limitations of age.

Some may wonder, "Is this man never going to grow up? Isn't he finally going to leave the conflicts of his past behind? Why can't Roth become more balanced and mellow, both as a writer and as a human being? Why does he have to live like a hermit in his small house in Connecticut, maintaining a rigorous writing schedule interrupted only by a swim and rarely by phone conversations with close friends like literary critic Harold Bloom?"

I believe that this expectation is based on the mistaken idea that a life well lived is a life in which an individual's existential equation is solved; in which the themes and conflicts that have shaped him are outgrown and life mellows into the peace and harmony that pop spirituality promises us.

An existentialist view of life suggests something very different. A life well lived is a life in which an individual's existential equation is most fully lived. Of course we hope that people learn from their mistakes; we hope that they find ways to live the conflicts and tensions that define them in ways that are creative rather than destructive, and that such creativity enhances both their well-being and their contribution to the world.

Individuality, History, and Culture

At this point I anticipate a very reasonable objection. You have relentlessly attacked the "just do it" mentality, one might point out, but Barack Obama, Ayaan Hirsi Ali, and Philip Roth have, each in their unique way, lived their existential equation in a way that led to extraordinary achievement. How do these examples square with the claim that the overwhelming majority of us will not turn our pains, conflicts, and rifts into such achievements?

This is certainly true, and my message is definitely not that living our existential equation to the fullest is a recipe for success; and success is not the issue here. Obama, Hirsi, and Roth exemplify the drama of individuality writ large. Like all human beings, they were born into specific historical, physical, economic, and cultural realities that determined their bodies and their minds. None of them had easy lives. They experienced the tension between facticity and freedom sharply, and it presented them with dilemmas, pains, and difficulties beyond what most people encounter. Each in his or her own way gained literal and metaphorical authorship over his or her life and formed it into a creation that could be fully embraced. Nevertheless their past neither was buried nor ceased to determine the course of their lives.

Our self's basic structure is, among other factors, determined by the culture we are born in. Yet, in the modern world, we have access to other cultural paradigms, and to some extent we choose what cultural tradition will be central to our lives. This doesn't mean that our culture of origin disappears or ceases to play a role. It is by bearing the tension between the facticity of our upbringing and the desire we feel to turn our lives into our creation, to integrate cultural paradigms that we have encountered and toward which we feel an affinity, that we can live our lives fully.

This is well reflected in a story Lord John Alderdice, originally from Belfast, told me in the context of the World Federation of Scientists Permanent Monitoring Panel on Terrorism in Sicily. Alderdice, a psychiatrist by training, received his peerage in honor of his crucial contribution to peacemaking in Northern Ireland well before the Good Friday Agreement, while he was still leader of the Alliance Party and before becoming the first speaker of the Northern Ireland Assembly.

When he was a child, he was wondering how his Protestant community could possibly protect themselves against Catholics. His father then told him, "Imagine that our house is locked, and that you can't get out, and that there is a cage with a lion in it. In two weeks this cage will be opened, and there's nothing you can do about that. Don't you think it's a good idea to start talking to the lion?" Of course this advice is frightening. Can you ever know for sure that the lion is not going to eat you? The one thing you know for sure is that the lion is here and that he will come out of his cage.

Alderdice's first step was to study psychiatry. He felt that he needed to understand the irrational layers of the mind that caused so much suffering in the country of his birth. He then continued with training in psychoanalytic therapy to deepen his understanding of how the layers of the mind shaped through trauma, loss, and rage can be addressed. The insight that he gained through his training guided Alderdice through the arduous process of, ultimately successful, peacemaking in Northern Ireland. Alderdice could certainly choose a more comfortable and peaceful lifestyle now. Instead he is now applying this lesson in various parts of the world, traveling to areas ridden by seemingly irresolvable conflicts.

The result is not always an easy life. Women who have seen family members suffer greatly and have become nurses to alleviate such suffering often work very hard; they are faced with illness and death daily through their jobs. Men who have suffered from violence and decided to join the security forces to minimize the harm inflicted by crime not only encounter a great deal of frustration and hardship but also experience satisfaction when they succeed in achieving their mission. Those who, like Obama, Hirsi, and Alderdice, try to make the world a better place by drawing on their difficult early experiences take much risk in doing so.

What all these examples show is the complex relationship between individuality and culture. None of us can generate a sense of living a life of significance without a cultural background and a worldview that defines what is meaningful and what is not. This is most obvious in politics, the activity of managing, regulating, and leading a human collective bound by a common framework. But it is no less true for the seemingly solitary activity of writing fiction. Philip Roth has made it his task to continue the tradition of the European novel. The very definition of writing as a valuable activity is bound to a culture that has emerged from a long-held tradition that came to fruition in European romanticism.

Homo globalis needs to find a way to integrate the various cultural traditions that shape its life. People like Obama, Hirsi, Roth, and Alderdice demonstrate that this requires a complex negotiation between different cultural contexts and their integration into a life that is both experienced as truly individual and yet recognized as valuable by a cultural framework. In the case of Obama, he merged different continents, races, and religions into an identity that Americans recognized as truly American, while the rest of the world can see him as truly a citizen of the world; Hirsi and Roth required a painful break with their past; and Alderdice merged his religious background with the universalist values of psychiatry and psychoanalysis into the vocation to bring peace first to his home country and now to conflictual areas all over the world. We will return to this tension between particular cultures and universalism in Part III.

The Tragic Sense of Life

The essence of the existentialist view of human life is that tragedy is inherent in the very structure of human individuality. Condemned to the tension between facticity and self-consciousness, we have no way of escaping it.

There are countless myths that try to capture this tragic tension. One of the most poignant is the biblical story of Adam and Eve's fall and expulsion from paradise because they eat the forbidden fruit of the tree of knowledge. As a result they suddenly experience shame and feel that they must cover themselves.

This myth is a powerful expression of the human condition: as babies we did not have self-consciousness, and hence could not experience shame. It is with the advent of self-consciousness that our relationship to ourselves becomes tragically complex. On the one hand, we just *are* in our facticity (Sartre's *en-soi*). On the other hand, we have an image of ourselves; we feel demands on what or how we should be, and we feel shame when we fall short.

The biographies of artists are particularly suited to understand the deep structure of individuality, because writers like Roth, Sartre, and Simone de Beauvoir make their struggle the subject-matter of their writing. But artists just make this struggle explicit; business, art, science, and politics are other ways of playing out the drama of human individuality no less than the way we rear (or do not rear) a family, serve (or not serve) our countries, or any other aspect of our lives.

This is beautifully expressed in a story told by Ástor Piazzolla, the composer and bandonion player who revolutionized tango by integrating it with elements of classical music and jazz. Piazzolla, born in Argentina, grew up in New York, where he was exposed early to both jazz and classical music, particularly Bach. His father, missing his home country, bought a bandonion for his son in a flea market, and throughout his teens Ástor would play tango in various dance halls for a living.

Arthur Rubinstein, one of the great classical pianists of the twentieth century, lived in Buenos Aires at the time, and advised Piazzolla to start studying classical music, which he did for a number of years, writing score after score of classical music, symphonies, chamber music, and solo compositions.

At age 32 Piazzolla won a scholarship to study composition under legendary composer, conductor, and teacher Nadia Boulanger. Here is how he describes his first, fateful encounter with her:[18]

> When I met her, I showed her my kilos of symphonies and sonatas. She started to read them and suddenly came out with a horrible sentence: "It's very well written." And stopped, with a big period, round like a soccer ball. After a long while, she said: "Here you are like Stravinsky, like Bartók, like Ravel, but you know what happens? I can't find Piazzolla in this." And she began to investigate my private life: what I did, what I did and did not play, if I was single, married, or living with someone, she was like an FBI agent! And I was very ashamed to tell her that I was a tango musician. Finally I said, "I play in a *night club*." I didn't want to say *cabaret*. And she answered, "Night club, *mais oui*, but that is a cabaret, isn't it?" "Yes," I answered, and thought, "I'll hit this woman in the head with a radio . . ." It wasn't easy to lie to her. She kept asking: "You say that you are not pianist. What instrument do you play, then?" And I didn't want to tell her that I was a bandoneon player, because I thought, "Then she will throw me from the fourth floor." Finally, I confessed and she asked me to play some bars of a tango of my own. She suddenly opened her eyes, took my hand and told me: "You idiot, that's Piazzolla!" And I took all the music I composed, ten years of my life, and sent it to hell in two seconds.

I am inevitably moved by this story, because it compresses the complexity of the human search for authorship in a nutshell. Piazzolla for years tried to be someone other than he was. He had encountered classical music; he decided that he had to be a classical musician, and put enormous energies into achieving this goal.

But he was denying an essential element in his basic musical idiom in the tunes and rhythms that had shaped his basic musical sensibilities, which sterilized his compositions, even though his gifts were evident. Nadia Boulanger's sensibilities were legendary. The list of her students sounds like a who's who list of twentieth century music, such as Leonard Bernstein, Charlie Parker, Burt Bacharach, and Daniel Barenboim, and she had an incredible knack for bringing out the best of talented composers.

Later in life, Piazzolla would say that he was just a night-club player; this statement of identity was a way to preserve the insight he had gained from Boulanger that tango was essential to his musical sensibility. This did not prevent him from developing tango into completely new direction, integrating complex baroque structures into his compositions as well as jazz elements. He would end up collaborating with leading classical quartets and performing at the Carnegie Hall. His music is played and recorded to this very day by leading artists like cellist Yo-Yo Ma.

As long as Piazzolla tried to resolve the basic tension of his existential equation, he could not find his unique voice. Trying to become a classical musician and denying his grounding in tango deprived him of the source of his originality. Only when he understood that he would forever be a tango musician deeply steeped in classical music, he would gradually evolve into a master who wrote hauntingly beautiful and at the same time daringly experimental compositions.

In his twenties Piazzolla had lost his true voice, his originality, because he had tried to be somebody else. He wanted to shape himself along the model of the great classical composers of his time: Stravinsky, Ravel, Strauss. He didn't lack talent as a composer. The problem was that the idiom of classical music did not connect to the cultural material that had shaped his sensibilities and basic musical idiom.

Nadia Boulanger did something tremendous for him: she helped him to realize that he could never become a full-fledged composer if he remained disconnected from the musical traditions that had shaped him. This was the moment when Piazzolla ceased to shape himself along the image of composers that he admired. He began the process of active self-acceptance, the process in which self-knowledge is used to start shaping individuality that is truly ours and not a persona externally imposed on our natural propensities. As we will see in the next chapter, the outcome of this process of active self-acceptance is not far removed from the fantasy of a true self that effortlessly bursts to the fore. The difference is that active self-acceptance is an arduous process that requires discipline and the ability to withstand mental pain.

5

From "Just Do It" to Active Self-Acceptance

The myth of "just do it" (JDI) is based on a deep and pervasive philosophical mistake. It is the image of freedom as an absence of limitations. This image is fed by the tendency of our culture to see youth as the only truly valuable period. Youth is seen by our culture as the time of maximal freedom in which there are plenty of open possibilities and very few limitations.[1] As a result the suggestion that there is true freedom later in life either is experienced as a cheap and inauthentic attempt to provide comfort or is quite simply wrong given the awareness of our growing physical limitations. This has horrendous psychological consequences. Insurmountable limitations become a reason for terrible self-loathing, which in turn often makes it impossible to actualize genuine potential.

The myth of JDI is supposed to encourage us to do what we really want. But for many it can be paralyzing. When faced with larger-than-life stories of magical changes (lawyers who become chefs, managers who turn into successful entrepreneurs overnight, housewives who suddenly become famous writers, etc.), real-life human beings can become paralyzed. They often come to think that the ability to change is reserved for this special class of human beings who develop large-scale visions out of nowhere.

The goal of this chapter is to present a conception of freedom very different from that of freedom as lack of limitations. I will call it the conception of freedom as *active self-acceptance* or the ability to gain freedom by facing what Karl Jaspers, the great German existential philosopher and psychiatrist, calls failure vis-à-vis boundary situations.[2] One of Jaspers most interesting claims is that we are thrown back into our freedom precisely when we face insurmountable difficulty, the boundary of what humans can do. One of the built-in boundary situations in human life is that there is a core that we simply cannot change. Karl Jaspers calls this our "being *thus and no other*"[3] (*Sosein* in the German original. I will use this term for brevity and precision).

As Jaspers points out, a person's *Sosein* cannot be defined except as the core that resists any attempt to change. Yet this sense of an unchangeable core need not be a reason for distress. It can also be one of the greatest sources of pride, joy, and a sense of individuality. Frank Sinatra's unfailingly popular song "My Way" is an expression of the need to feel that there is a consistent self that is expressed through a lifetime of actions and results in a coherent life. The human desire to leave a mark[4] would not make any sense if there wasn't a consistent self that leaves this mark. Hence a person's relation to her *Sosein* can be the source of both endless suffering and a sense of achievement and meaning.

A realistic relationship to our *Sosein* requires that we gradually achieve self-knowledge, which can be very painful, and parting with cherished fantasies that we have entertained about who we are or who we can be. And yes, it means to accept our limitations. But like in sports, achieving the maximum that we are capable of often requires us to part with other possibilities. We need to know what we will *not* be able to do to fully realize our potential.[5] Misconceptions and illusions we have had about ourselves must give way to the accumulated evidence of who we are and how we have lived.

Active Self-Acceptance

Yet the point of this chapter is not to have us resign to be who we are. In his Nobel lecture Saul Bellow complained (with some justification) that therapeutic culture does not leave any room for a positive notion of character. He related this to "the psychoanalytic conception of character—that it is an ugly, rigid formation, something to be resigned to, nothing to be embraced with joy."[6]

Bellow's work shows how lucid contemplation can allow us to see a flawed character's lovability. Perhaps this is most pronounced in the masterpiece that placed him in the pantheon of leading American writers: *Herzog*, his novel about midlife (written in midlife).[7] Its protagonist, Moses Herzog, goes to pieces when his marriage falls apart. His magnum opus, a history of romantic thought, forever remains a monstrous manuscript that he cannot end.

We come to know Herzog with all his shortcomings. We see how his intellectual apparel does not help him deal with real-life situations. Yet, like Ramona, the woman who tries to lure him back into life because she finds him an attractive and endearing man, the reader cannot help liking Herzog's character. This is one of the achievements great writers are capable of: to paint characters without hiding their shortcomings and yet let their humanity shine through.

Passively accepting one's limitations rarely leads from self-hatred to self-acceptance and certainly not to transformation. In any case I have never seen such instances whether in midlife or at any other age. Real change often requires something like a metaphysical realization about what it means to be free, as Jaspers emphasized time and again.

The freedom I am talking about is impressively revealed in Rembrandt's self-portraits. He drew himself throughout his lifetime, and his more than ninety self-portraits span more than four decades of his career.[8] As art historians have pointed out,[9] Rembrandt's self-portraits served as marketing tools through part of his life, but during his fifties he turned them into a form of self-examination. At that time Rembrandt had experienced the rise to fame and the fall from grace, and he had been pushed to the outer circles of society.

In his later self-portraits we often see him quite disheveled, the ravages of age quite visible; his gaze, somewhat wary, is that of a man who has known the hardships of life and has pierced the veil of illusions. Nevertheless the paintings are neither grim nor pessimistic. Instead they emanate still luminosity and mesmerizing beauty. They are not depressing but induce a state of contemplation and pleasure.

It is sometimes easy to forget that these paintings are creations that required protracted activity. Rembrandt needed to contemplate himself in a detached and objective manner while making decisions about how to compose the paintings. After all, the most important goal of painting, certainly in the seventeenth century, was the creation of beauty.

By rendering himself on the canvas, Rembrandt combined the lucidity of self-knowledge and self-perception with the creation of art that was to stand the test of centuries. While showing himself as he really was, Rembrandt also exercised his art at its best: his mastery of light and color and his talent for composition. By painting his likeness unsparingly, he expressed and asserted his identity as a great artist.

Self-acceptance as expressed in Rembrandt's self-portraits is not a passive subjugation to reality. It is an active expression of the mind's ability to see, understand, and shape this understanding into creations of value. I suggest that we call this *active self-acceptance*. It is active for two reasons. First, the mind is not a passive receptacle or mirror of reality.[10] It needs to construe representations actively. The process of painting a self-portrait highlights this complex creation dramatically.

The second reason for my choice of terms is that the result of active self-acceptance is not equivalent to simply acquiescing in who we are. It is to accept the existential call to be what we can be and is thus—as Jaspers suggests—the beginning of self-transformation. It requires doing the hard work that Friedrich Nietzsche has summarized in *The Gay Science* as giving style to our character: to see our strengths and weaknesses clearly to make our lives into a coherent creation.[11]

Karl Jaspers: Lucidity and Self-Knowledge as Conditions for Freedom

Active self-acceptance requires us to be fearless in our questions and to face the answers that we will find inside ourselves. This may sound like advice that is easy to give but difficult to implement. Let us therefore look at the life of a philosopher who early in life encountered illness and the possibility of death.

Karl Jaspers was born in 1883[12] to a well-to-do family in northern Germany. He grew up in the Protestant faith. He was a balanced and fairly happy youth until the age of twenty, when he began to suffer from persistent respiratory symptoms. His doctor was evasive and didn't divulge the diagnosis. Young Jaspers insisted that his doctor tell him exactly what the illness and its implications were.

The answer was shattering. He had an incurable lung disease. There was a good chance that he would not live for long. In any case he was to refrain from physical exertion of any form. He could not work more than seven hours a day and he was condemned to the following ritual: every day he had to lie down for an hour and warm his lungs, and then he was to try to cough out the substances that had accumulated in his lungs for half an hour.

Most people, certainly at such a young age, would have broken down. Jaspers's reaction was rather amazing: he reflected and built a plan to make the most of the remainder of his days. In a moving letter to his parents, which he never sent and that has survived as part of his diary, he wrote that he intended to live a fruitful life as long as it lasted. Because he did not think he was sufficiently gifted for a scientific or philosophical career, he decided to study medicine so he would at least get a decent grasp of one scientific discipline.

He specialized in psychiatry, partially because no other medical discipline was consistent with his physical limitations and also because of his instinctive interest in psychology. When he was thirty years old, the prestigious publisher Springer commissioned a textbook of psychiatry from him, which was published in 1913 and was immediately recognized as a classic masterpiece. Throughout his life Jaspers would update the *General Psychopathology*, which is reprinted and read to this very day. Nevertheless there was a certain quality of loneliness in his life, which came to the fore in a beautiful piece he wrote on the topic in 1915.

In his midtwenties Jaspers met a young Jewish woman named Gertrude Mayer who, like him, had met illness and death early in her life. They felt a deep affinity and married. This experience of how intimate communication and love could relieve loneliness became one of the defining experiences in Jaspers's life and played a great role in his future writings.

Jaspers was characterized by an impressive ability to look at human reality with a lucidity that at times may seem merciless. From his early psychiatric writings through his later portrayals of August Strindberg and Nietzsche and finally to his harsh diagnoses of the reality of the German Bundesrepublik after World War II, he shows himself as a keen observer with a tremendous grasp of human reality.

Toward 1920 Jaspers felt drawn more and more to philosophy, began publishing extensively in this domain, and was accorded a professorship in this field at the prestigious university of Heidelberg. During the 1920s he wrote his philosophical masterpiece *Philosophie* in three volumes. It is not possible to summarize all aspects of his huge work here, so I will focus on the aspects most relevant to the idea of active self-acceptance.

Jaspers has attempted to elucidate the basic structure of human existence. His early experience with incurable disease found expression in his concept of the boundary situation, which he defined as the encounter with an insuperable limit at which we necessarily fail. Paradigmatic boundary situations are illness and death. Boundary situations and the intrinsic failure built into them confront us with the basic limitations of our existence. Jaspers saw the existential failure characteristic of boundary situations as the source of philosophical inquiry and the human awareness of freedom.

For him the encounter with a boundary situation was essential to human life, and he showed that human beings could find their freedom through this encounter. In being thrown back to the failure intrinsic to human existence, as in finitude, illness, and death, human beings can also experience the freedom to choose how to deal with these problems. We can choose between love and hate; between facing reality and avoiding it; and between dignity in facing pain and cowardice in avoiding it.

Thus Jaspers turned his experience of encountering the boundary situation of the threat of death and the limitation by illness into the foundation of a systematic philosophy. Soon enough he encountered such boundary situations again. During the rise of the Nazi regime in Germany, Jaspers showed great courage in trying to defend Jewish colleagues at the university and never thought of cooperating with the regime. As a result he was stripped of his professorship in 1937.

Because his wife was Jewish and because he had opposed the regime, they knew that they were in substantial danger. They decided that they would not fall into the hands of the Nazis alive and carried cyanide capsules with them at all times. They survived the Holocaust, and after the liberation of Germany, Jaspers was chosen by the American administration to help in rebuilding the university given his impeccable behavior during the war.

Nevertheless Jaspers felt that he could not impose on his wife to live in a country that had threatened her life, so he accepted a professorship at Basel University, Switzerland, where he continued teaching until 1961. He became one of the leading figures of German intellectual life and the first to tackle the question of how Germany should deal with its responsibility and guilt for the Nazi period. Jaspers died in 1969, aged 86, after having published 34 books on a wide range of topics.

Jaspers encountered severe limitations quite early. Many would have chosen to live their lives in bitterness and with a sense that they had been stripped of most of the pleasures of life.

Jaspers found his freedom by facing his limitations, including the possibility of an early death. Instead of panicking, denying the truth, and haggling with fate, he faced the facts calmly. He found the freedom to compose a life plan in a situation that had seemingly deprived him of all freedom. He also turned his suffering into one of the sources for his immense philosophical achievement, and his interpretation of human freedom became an inspiration for many readers.

Jaspers at no time tried to glorify suffering. He never turned his own ordeal into a source of pride or melodrama. He simply faced it as a condition that he had not chosen and that had no deep meaning. Throughout his later life, he refused to be turned into a hero on account of his refusal to cooperate with the Nazi regime. He felt that he had just tried to live decently in a period of horror and to live according to his principles.

As opposed to other existentialist philosophers like Albert Camus, he felt distaste for the heroic attitude. Jaspers's most salient character trait was his search for lucidity. He thought that all you could do was to face reality as clearly as possible. Human freedom consisted in accepting limitations with dignity, not in turning it into drama.

Jaspers's emphasis on the necessity of failure in boundary situations is profoundly opposed to the current Zeitgeist with its endless hope to solve all existential problems through technical means. While he certainly cherished scientific progress, he was deeply suspicious toward scientism, the belief that the language and practice of science can change or abolish the basic structures of human existence. He would have looked at the current antiaging craze with dismay. He would have welcomed any medical advance that improves life expectancy and quality. But he would have said that no scientific advance liberates us from the need to face finitude and death.

Jaspers wrote this many decades before intervention in human genetics was anything but science fiction. But his thoughts are at least as relevant today as they were in the first half of the twentieth century. Death continues to be the inevitable horizon of our lives. No amount of medication, rejuvenating cosmetics, or plastic surgery will change this. Let us now turn to an example of some of the central tenets of Jaspers's thought.

Daniel: "I Don't Want to Be Who I Am"

I, that am rudely stamp'd, and want love's majesty
To strut before a wanton ambling nymph;
I that am curtail'd of this fair proportion,
Cheated of feature by dissembling nature,
Deformed, unfinish'd, sent before my time
Into this breathing world scarce half made up,
And that so lamely and unfashionable
That dogs bark at me as I halt by them;
Why, I, in this weak piping time of peace,
Have no delight to pass away the time,
Unless to spy my shadow in the sun
And descant on mine own deformity:
And therefore since I cannot prove a lover,
To entertain these fair well-spoken days,
I am determined to prove a villain
And hate the idle pleasures of these days.

—Shakespeare, *Richard III*, 1.1.16–31

Daniel sat down in his chair and looked around with the air of a connoisseur. He immediately identified the paintings on the wall I had received from my father, an art collector, and then threw somewhat disapproving glances on the mess that inevitably characterizes my consulting room. He himself was dressed impeccably, far more formally than what is generally the case in Israel.[13]

He was on a sabbatical. An art historian, he had a professorship at a major French university. He said "I don't really think I deserve this professorship. Let me make it clear: when it comes to the numbers, I fit the role. I've published enough to count as a professor. I'm not even a bad lecturer. My students moderately enjoy my classes, and, I guess, they probably even learn something."

I wondered, "So why do you feel you don't deserve the professorship?"

"I haven't really done anything exceptional. Well, in a sense I do deserve it. I perfectly fit the stereotype of the professor who has written enough to get his appointment but has not produced anything of real value." His tone of voice was difficult to classify. To some extent he sounded infinitely bored in a blasé manner. Whatever he said implied that he kept an ironic distance from everything, even his own self-irony. He certainly didn't come across as somebody who was suffering, except maybe from mortal ennui.

I inquired what I might help him with. "Well" he said, "there is this *really* bothersome problem I have. I obsessively cheat on my wife."

I pointed out that his mode of expression didn't seem to express much suffering, trying to see whether I could get behind his tone of self-irony.

"Oh, of course. Shrinks think that if you don't express feelings you are not authentic. You would like me to express some sadness or preferably rage. Then you would feel that we are really in touch. How could I forget? Any particular affect that would please you in particular, doctor—oh, sorry, professor?"

The facts as he related them to me over the next month, briefly, were as follows. Daniel had grown up in a middle class French family with social ambitions. His father, a lawyer, never quite made enough money to make it into the *haute bourgeoisie*, and his lifelong ambition to be distinguished was never really fulfilled. Together with his wife he embarked on the project of making up for the lack of money with cultural snobbery. Daniel and his sister were trained to consume only highbrow culture and to be condescending to those whose tastes were less distinguished, and they would be subject to periodical surprise exams in which they were supposed to identify pieces of classical music or some Renaissance or impressionist painting. He remembered that he was constantly torn between the terror of not knowing one of the works he was supposed to identify and the pride that he almost invariably knew the answer.

He was not supposed to like doing "ordinary" things like playing football—and he taught himself early on not to like what he wasn't supposed to. He remembered fleeting moments in which he desired to have a childhood like all the other kids at school, but they were, well, fleeting. He would quickly revert to his snobbish ways. "Even my hairstyle was remindful of a nineteenth-century aristocratic brat."

"Do you know Sartre's *Les Mots*—'The Words,' his autobiography? Well, of course you do. You're supposed to be very cultivated yourself, aren't you? So you remember that Sartre realized very early on that his mother would go into states of rapture whenever he wrote something. And that's how he became a writer, an eternal pleaser, just out to receive his mother's attention. And in fact he would live with her from the 1940s onwards, and she would take care of his household."

"Well, that's my story. They were enthralled by my cultural sensitivity. So what better thing could I do than become an art historian? The only difference is that as opposed to Sartre I was pleasing *both* my parents. Actually, I'm quite surprised that I didn't become homosexual. I think they would have *loved* it. It would have fitted their view of a *cultivé* intellectual dandy more than just being an ordinary straight guy. Unfortunately I couldn't fulfill that part of their fantasy. Sexuality, it seems, is in the end determined by biology more than anything else, so I slept with women instead."

With his somewhat feminine, very striking looks; his tall and thin but muscular frame; and his great intelligence, he was a success story with women. Until his early thirties he had an endless number of affairs, always taking care not to be touched in depth by any of the women.

Until he met his wife. She was not just beautiful and intelligent; she was warm, gentle, and caring. To top it all she came from a wealthy family. He was struck by her. She touched something inside him; she seemed to be able to reach out behind his *blasé* façade, and rather soon he married her.

"To this day I wonder. I think, to the extent that I'm capable of loving, I love her. But then sometimes I think that I married her because she rounded the image of who I was supposed to be. After all, the one wish my parents could never fulfill was that of being rich. By marrying Marie, I automatically got a wonderful mansion in one of the best areas of Paris, which we outfitted in the most *tasteful* way. Soon after that I got my university appointment, and so the image was complete. We became this absolutely ravishing couple who had it all, soon including two *wonderful* children."

I asked him what he expected from working with me, and why he had chosen to come and see me in particular. "Oh, a while ago I was working on Picasso, and this colleague of mine told me that you had an interesting analysis of his deeper motivations in one of your books. Frankly, I thought your analysis was really unoriginal; at least you had the decency to admit that you based it on other people's work. But then I came across this case of yours of a philandering man, and I thought that you seemed to have a good angle on him. I'm not sure I can expect much from working with you. I need to go back to Paris in about half a year and I doubt that much can be done in this respect."

I felt torn. Daniel had told his story in his usual bored tone, barricading himself behind irony all the time. But in reality, the story was of a man who was one big fraud. That's the way he saw it. He was nothing but a walking façade, a pleaser who was nothing but *persona*, all effective acting from his professional life to his marriage.

But I couldn't help thinking that this man lived in hell. I perfectly understood his reference to Sartre. In *Les Mots*, Sartre, one of the great writers and philosophers of the twentieth century, writes his own story as that of a pathetic little child who has his way with words, because it pleases his mother, and in middle age comes to the conclusion that all this dealing with words was nothing but a ruse. Daniel's self-hatred, hidden behind his bored façade, was acidic. Daniel had managed to touch me with his story despite the distance from which he was telling it.

But could I help him, given the little time that he was still going to stay here?

I gave it a try, and Daniel came to share more of his deep disdain and hatred for himself with me in the months to come.

"I have been turned into . . . you know those poodles that are being done up in all of these absurd hairstyles? That are turned into show animals, trained to beg for treats exactly the right way, and then fed? That's what they did to me. That's what I became. What's worse: I've become a *willing* poodle. I learned the tricks and I perform them well to this very day; I get the applause and go to my next show; a bit like a whore."

"Wouldn't gigolo be the more appropriate term?" I asked.

He paused for a moment, and then broke into a bitter grin. "That's the best thing you've said until now, professor. That's exactly what I am. After all I'm a kept man. My lifestyle is made possible by the fact that I'm fucking the woman that keeps me."

We paused for a while, and his last sentence sank in.

Then a thought went through my mind. "If that's true, it's really strange that you keep fucking other women for free."

Daniel looked at me with an intensity I had never seen in him. He seemed shaken and relieved at the same time. "I never told you, but in a sense I make sure that they don't get the value for the money that they don't pay. With the other women I'm actually a pretty lousy lover. I get what I want, and I don't really give a damn if they enjoy it. My escapades are probably the one thing I do without being a pleaser." And then, pensively, he continued, "And that may be the reason why I don't stop my affairs. At least there I'm a bad dog who mounts females and not a poodle."

His mode of existence had now become much clearer. His insight that he felt like a willing rape victim, a man who had sacrificed any authenticity for the sake of reaping his parents' applause, and who had turned this into a way of life crystallized in the ensuing weeks. He lived with the fantasy that one day he would change completely; sometimes he jokingly told me, "I should put on Nike sneakers and 'just do it'; just become somebody different." And while he did not really believe in this possibility, he often ruefully said that he wondered whether the stories of magical transformation that he read about in the popular press were true and whether this could happen to him as well.

His way of communicating with me changed, too. He no longer played the role of the eternally bored playboy or gigolo as we now called it. At some point he said, "For you this must certainly be very satisfying. You've succeeded in getting through to me. I'm not quite sure whether I like the result, though. I frankly don't know what to do with myself now. I'm 48 years old, and I have never lived a single authentic moment in my whole life, yet I don't know anything else. I have nowhere to go."

I told him, "I'll take a risk, and tell you what I think, even though I don't know whether it's true. Donald Winnicott, a British psychoanalyst, had a beautiful saying, 'Sometimes the false self is what the true self would have been if it could come to the fore.' I wonder whether that isn't your story. Couldn't it be that you really love the history of art, even though you acquired that love for the wrong reason, in the same way as Sartre went into writing for the wrong reason, but truly was a great writer? Or in the way Mozart became a musician because his father trained him from earliest childhood; this does not change the fact he may have been one of the most gifted musicians humankind has ever produced? And couldn't it be that you love your wife, even though you're not sure that you didn't marry her for the wrong reasons?"

The dialogue with Daniel seemed productive, but not long before his sabbatical was coming to an end he said, "I still feel that I have lived the life of a gigolo or a poodle. I am not the person I would like to be. Yes, my parents pushed me in a certain direction; but if I had had more character, I could have resisted. Or, if I couldn't do so in childhood, I might have done it later, in early adulthood, but I didn't. I'm just not a strong person. I go for the easy way."

"I can't change my biography. I can neither wipe it out nor just declare my life to have been a success. You shrinks seem to think that there are insights that change a human being. I don't think so. Or do you think that after what you said I should now feel great about myself? Is what you told me supposed to comfort me? Am I supposed to love myself and my life? Do you really think it is that simple?"

We seemed to be stuck. Daniel had a point. While my hypothesis made sense to him, this changed nothing about the way he felt about his life. Yes, it might be that his choices happened to fit his temperament and his abilities. But they had largely been made out of his desire to please his parents. That's why he hated himself and his life, and in the final analysis, this hatred was his real problem.

There wasn't much time left. Daniel was about to leave Israel, and we only had a few sessions left. I thought a lot about Daniel before our next session and decided that I needed to take his objection seriously. So at the beginning of the next meeting I told him the following:

> Daniel, I've thought a lot about what you told me last time, and I've come to the conclusion that I agree with a lot of what you said. The perspective I proposed on your life cannot induce change in itself. Let me make clear that I was not and am not trying to sell you cheap comfort. And I'm also not trying to rewrite history. I understand why you accuse yourself for having been pliable and a pleaser, even if your choices fit your abilities and temperament.
>
> I also understand your association with Sartre. Yes, in Sartre's terms you might say that you made an originary choice. You chose to be the highly cultured son your parents wanted and you made a career out of it. My question to you is, "Do you think Sartre's self-loathing was the only way to deal with the facts of his life?" Would it not, for example, have been possible for him to relate to his own choices with some more humor? Isn't the expectation to make every choice out of our deepest being rather unrealistic? Isn't it possible to laugh at the human condition instead of hating it? Never mind the possibility of going one step further and feeling some warmth for humans and for you as a specimen of this weird species. . . . Is hatred and loathing really the only way to deal with this?" I would say that's a *choice*. And if it's a choice, I think you have to take responsibility for it.
>
> The bottom line of what I'm saying is, however we understand your existential stance toward your life, it is not something that can or will change through understanding itself. In the end, Daniel, you will have to make a choice—and that's your sole responsibility. I can advise; I can be there for dialogue. But the choice will be yours.[14]

Daniel listened attentively, and kept silent for a few minutes after I had finished. Then he grinned. "I like that a bit more. What you're saying is that your help just goes so far. Once we have mapped the corner in which I'm staying, the rest is really my decision. We're lucky; we've come to the decisive moment shortly before I leave. If I understand you correctly, now it's all up to me anyway."

"There is just one thing I would like to add," I said. "Sometimes acceptance of who we are opens the possibility of becoming who we can be; because as long as we rage against what we are, transformation is simply not possible."

In the two years that followed, I had irregular contact with Daniel. Sometimes we had sessions on the phone. Twice we happened to be in the same city at the same time and we met.

The process that Daniel underwent in those two years was remarkable. At the beginning he went through a mild depression. Everything felt bland and pointless. I asked whether he could speak about his feelings to his wife.

For the first time after 15 years of marriage, he spoke to her about his sense of being a fake and of being a terrible husband. To his surprise his wife told him that she knew about his feelings, and that she had known his character weaknesses from the outset. "I just happen to love who you are, difficult as this may be for you to believe."

Daniel was totally shocked by Marie's words. It took him months to start believing them. It took him some more time to realize that he truly loved and cherished Marie, even though he had considered himself incapable of genuine love. This changed his whole outlook on his marriage. He no longer felt that he was nothing but a gigolo who had married for the money his parents never had. He realized that there was no point in loathing himself for the marriage. From that moment on, he stopped his extramarital affairs.

After more than a year, Daniel moved on to the next stage. For more than a decade he had listlessly repeated the same courses. He now asked his department for a reshuffle, and he took on some new courses. He spent the summer preparing them meticulously. For the first time in his life, he would go over each lecture time and again, considering every concept, every term, making sure that he was getting across to the students exactly what he meant to say. He discovered the pleasure of finding out that there were better ways of conceptualizing major topics, and by the end of the summer he realized that he was working toward a new conception in his field of expertise and began jotting down notes for a book. The last I heard from him two years later was when he sent me a copy of the new book, which was hailed by his profession as a breakthrough.

The Paradox of Self-Knowledge: Pain and Liberation

British psychoanalyst Wilfred Bion used to think that the process of psychic growth is primarily a function of the ability to bear psychic pain.[15] While this has some validity, it seems to me that it is only half the truth. Let me explain this through an analogy. After workouts, we are supposed to do stretching exercises. Everyone who has done them knows the dynamics of the process. When we stretch a muscle, we get to the point of pain. If we shy away from it, the muscle will not be stretched. If we try violently to go beyond the muscle's limits, our body reflexively mobilizes its defenses against injury and blocks movement. The resulting symptoms are back pain and other ways in which our body immobilizes itself.

The process of stretching is fruitful when we can bear the pain calmly and allow the muscle to expand gradually. The result of good stretching is not just pain. It is that our body feels lighter and more limber. If we stretch consistently, in time our well-being increases. We become capable of moving in ways previously not possible. Bearing pain is not a goal in itself when we stretch. It is a means toward the goal of increasing both fitness and well-being.

Daniel's view of his own character was not true self-knowledge. It was closer to the act of trying to stretch a muscle violently, a rather futile exercise. Instead of increasing his ability to actualize his potential, it immobilized him. He was stuck in a position of existential back pain, so to speak, in which he sometimes indulged in fantasies of total transformation that he did not really believe in. Whenever he encountered memories of his pliability and the way in which he had formed himself to please his parents, he would fall into blinding self-hatred. He saw one aspect of his character but was incapable of seeing anything else. He could see the pliability, but he could not see his capacity for love. Hence he mistook his love for both his wife and his profession as expressions of his weakness.

He could not perform the psychic work that Jaspers took upon himself both in his youth and throughout his life. Jaspers never took his limitations to be a gift. He sometimes said that the only thing he could do was to work, and was profoundly aware of the narrowness of existence that his illness had forced on him.[16] Jaspers seems to have been endowed with an exceptional ability to bear psychic pain without distorting his view of reality. In his life as well as in his philosophy he found freedom in the meaning he gave to unalterable facts of boundary situations.

Jaspers's creative expression of his existential pain made it easier for him to bear his limitations. Through his philosophical work, suffering turned from a brute fact to a source of insight. For most of his life Daniel was not capable of this transformation of pain into meaning. Unlike Jaspers, he could not say, "Yes, I have indeed been pliable. But I was fortunate enough to bend in a direction that allowed me to develop my true interests and talents. So while I may not like the way I developed, I can still cherish the results of this process." The pain and the hatred blinded him toward some of the most positive aspects of his personality, which he could start cherishing only in the years after our therapeutic journey.

In my experience, the process that Daniel underwent is in no way unique.[17] The crucial step is to accept that to become the author of our lives, we need to accept that we haven't chosen the base materials of who we are. We can only choose to shape them with clear view of our strength and weaknesses, as Nietzsche says. This process, like stretching, involves pain and requires discipline. The next chapter will examine what this kind of active self-acceptance requires.

Paring Down Life
to the Essentials

An Epicurean Proposal

Members of the global creative class live in great confusion about what today's life cycle is supposed to look like. The wunderkind myth creates the panicky feeling that by thirty there should at least be clear indications about what your great achievement should be like, and that by forty you should understand that what you haven't achieved by now, you will no longer achieve. From that moment onward it will only be downward.

But then again we are supposed to "just do it." Why, in fact should we not "just do it" after forty, or even after fifty? After all recent neurophysiologic research shows that those who have been mentally active for the first half of their lives, have brains that are flexible, adaptive, and store vast experiential knowledge that can be a huge asset.

But here comes the paradox: life expectancy has risen dramatically in the last century. Today's forty-year-olds can realistically expect to have more lifetime ahead than they have already lived. This should counteract the panic of time running out. But the fact is that those on the fast track mostly feel at their forties that they are running out of time, and when they reach fifty, most of them feel that the rest of their lives are nothing but a gradual process of decline.

Professionally, they feel, they will no longer achieve anything they haven't done before. If anything, they may only lose the positions they hold. Personally there isn't much to look forward to either. In sports they will never be as good as they were; they will jog more slowly (if at all, and if they don't have to go for a knee replacement); they will play tennis less well and will have to take it easier when skiing.

Then there is, of course, the specter that haunts us all: our value on the market of sexual attractiveness starts to decline in the thirties and then takes a plunge that ends only with death. While we can at least dream about higher professional achievements, nobody in their right minds expect to have the physical fitness and sexual attractiveness of the twenties again.

This problem is not new. All cultures and all ages have sought the wellspring of youth and mourned the price of aging. But something has changed. More traditional cultures had roles for those at midlife and the elderly. The generation that had ended its fertility cycle had an important social function. It was the keeper of tradition and of a culture's knowledge. It had wisdom that needed to be imparted to the young.

In our culture the notion of the wisdom of age has acquired the ring of a quaint, antiquated adage. How exactly are elders supposed to contribute with their wisdom? Many have hardly mastered basic computing skills. They do not understand how contemporary markets work. At best they know the tastes of their own generation. So there are some cases like Warren Buffett and George Soros who in their seventies are still authorities on how the financial markets work. The Police did another tour that had a nine-figure gross, even though Sting and his friends are in their sixties. But these are the exception, not the rule.

So much for the myth. The reality is that in many fields the second half of life leads to enduring achievements and to a deepening of creativity. When it comes to the positions with the highest responsibility, we still tend to seek out experienced men and women. Obama, with all his tremendous ability and appeal, seemed at the lower end of the spectrum even for those of us who endorsed him enthusiastically. The average age of CEOs of leading companies is in the midfifties, and the pinnacle of military careers is never reached before fifty.

Yet, it might be argued, these are examples of linear careers. Is it possible for people to reach significant new venues and achievements, to find new meaning later in life? Or do the choices we have made in our twenties nail us down for the rest of our lives?

This chapter intends to show that significant new meaning can be generated at many junctures in life. Yet a proviso is in order: such meaning never reflects the myth of "just do it." The examples that I will show are instances of evolutionary changes rather than cases of reinvention of the self.

One of the most poignant examples is the life of Elliot Jacques. Paradoxically this is the man whose seminal paper "Death and the Midlife Crisis"[1] introduced the very notion of the midlife crisis that we have come to take for granted. Jacques was 48 years old when he published the paper in which he argued that the resolution of the midlife crisis consisted in accepting mortality.[2]

Jacques's thesis was primarily based on the analysis of the life work of a large number of artists. He claimed that a very distinct development was to be observed when they reached midlife (the onset of which he took to be age 35). They moved from a jubilant, ebulliently optimistic view of life to what he called "sculpted creativity." He interpreted this transformation to be a reflection of the integration of mortality-awareness into their psyche and their creativity, and the resulting works were autumnal, darker, and more realistic in a deep sense.

After this paper Jacques embarked on a journey that turned him into one of the leading thinkers in the domain of organizational development. He published another 12 books. Together with his wife Kathryn Cason, he founded a company that disseminated his ideas and consulted with major for-profit and nonprofit organizations. He died in 2003 at age 87, soon after completing one of his most ambitious theoretical works.[3]

It would be tempting to say that Jacques's life disproves his theory of the midlife crisis and its resolution. After all the second half of his life was a protracted burst of creativity that came to final fruition rather late in life when he wrote books like *Requisite Organization* and *Social Power and the CEO*.[4] On the face of it there is very little death acceptance in his later life.

But I believe that such a conclusion would be simplistic. It is certainly true that Jacques placing the midlife crisis at age 35 does not fit with the current conception in which midlife is generally considered as an extended period covering, roughly, the two decades between ages forty and sixty. The question that arises is, are there psychological determinants that can increase the likelihood that career changes will be made fruitfully and lead to satisfaction both in life in general and in work?

Between Acceptance and Denial of Death

If we want to understand the existential panic of today's members of the global creative class, we must address the central topic of modern existential psychology and our dealing with death and mortality. On the one hand, I believe that there is something essentially right about Jacques's idea that facing mortality is one of the crucial developmental tasks at midlife. On the other hand, any discussion of awareness and acceptance of mortality today must relate to Ernest Becker's thesis that denial of death is one of the deepest motivations of the human species, which we have discussed in earlier chapters. A form of this denial is what Becker calls "the heroic attitude." We try to create works that will immortalize us, or at least be part of a group that claims that it will survive into the eons.

How does Jacques's hypothesis that acceptance of mortality is the outcome of successfully negotiated midlife crises relate to Becker's well-established hypothesis that in a deep sense human nature is adverse to the full realization of our mortality?

I want to try to bridge the two theses dialectically. As I have argued in the past, the human psyche is endowed with an imaginative core that refuses to accept that the world does not suit our deepest needs and desires.

> Even though it is not metaphysically possible for any of us to have been other than we are, we can dis-identify with all we are. We can dissociate ourselves from our bodies, our families, our biographies. We can imagine ourselves as being very different from what we are. The result is that we feel that there is an inner, self, the "I" which is more essential to who we are than the accidental characteristics of birth and history which have determined our actual fates.
>
> This imaginative creation of a self hidden from the outside world and untouched by the fate of the body is one of the paradigmatic strategies of what I will call the *ontological protest of subjectivity* . . . We can refuse to accept that we are who we ostensibly are by saying "I have the freedom and the power to shape myself and external reality according to my desire." The centrifugal strategy is exemplified by the cultural narratives of the transformations from rags to riches, from wimp to sculpture of muscle, from misfit to famous artist.[5]

The concept of the ontological protest of subjectivity is in tune with Becker's thesis of the denial of death. British psychoanalyst Donald Winnicott[6] assumes that even in health the human psyche does not fully accept that the world is external and governed by laws not under our control. Along with Becker, it assumes that the human protest against our temporality and finitude is the source of all specifically human creation. Since we can imagine that the world could be different, we create new worlds in science, technology, politics, and art.

This is where we reconnect to Jacques's thesis. Experience shows that there are shadings in the acceptance of mortality. Total denial of aging and death often takes obvious forms ranging from excessive preoccupation with health and looks to large scale cultural phenomena like the huge industry of so-called antiaging medicine and the lucrative boom in cosmetic surgery. We can also agree with Jacques that successful midlife transitions often lead from a more jubilant type of creativity in early adulthood to a more reflective and sculpted creativity at midlife and after.

Nevertheless mortality-acceptance is not an either-or affair, and the question is not whether we have fully worked through the depressive position and thus come to accept mortality in full. We might rather want to follow Donald Winnicott when he argues that even in health there is a core that can never quite accept that we have not created the world. In saying so Winnicott certainly did not mean to imply that there is no difference between the psychotic who claims that he is the godlike creator of the world, and healthy psychological functioning. In the latter case we consciously accept the world's externality, while unconsciously preserving what Winnicott called the intermediary realm in which the distinction of subjective and objective is kept in dialectical suspense.

I would therefore like to suggest the following amendment to Jacques's thesis. There is indeed a certain change to be observed when, at midlife, mortality becomes more salient. Yet along with Becker we need to refrain from saying that this simply means that death becomes an accepted fact. The ontological protest of subjectivity never quite lets us acquiesce in mortality.

The first suggestion is to refrain from talking about successful resolution of the midlife crisis, and instead speak of well-negotiated midlife crises instead. This difference is not just semantic; it implies that mortality acceptance is not an either-or affair but moves on a continuum between manic denial and the ability of calm contemplation.

Before continuing it is important to qualify the next thesis. I believe that it is unreasonable to assume that there is a single model that is likely to cover the great variety of existential situations that can be encountered at midlife. Jacques originally built his thesis on a very particular group, creative artists, who exemplify Becker's heroic attitude in its purest form. In what follows I will focus primarily on a similar group; people who at midlife have made creative achievement the center of their lives.

Here, then, is my second suggestion: Jacques's notion of sculpted creativity must be rethought taking into account Becker's notion of the heroic attitude.[7] The creativity that characterizes adult life from the midthirties onward is not of necessity more sober or less ambitious. The lives of the two founders of modern depth-psychology, Sigmund Freud and Carl Jung, proved the opposite.[8] While neither was devoid of ambition before midlife, both of them began building the grand edifice of their definitive work from midlife onward—in both cases arguably as a way of dealing with the midlife crisis as Becker has documented in some detail.[9] The same holds true of many other domains: in politics, business, the arts, and in many academic disciplines (even though more typically in the social sciences and the humanities), there are many examples for people who initiated their major projects from midlife onward.

In fact it may not be unreasonable to hypothesize that at midlife the need to create something that will create a lasting legacy acquires urgency, because the reality of death becomes more tangible. As a result, life as a whole, in many cases, becomes more focused. Anything that detracts from the central goal of creating a lasting legacy is called into question.

Midlife can initiate a process in which one asks, what am I really good at? What gives my life the most meaning? On what do I have to focus to leave a creation that has some lasting value?

This creation need not be a work that is distinct from life itself. The analogy between living a life and creating a work of art has been suggested by Michel Foucault,[10] who lived a truly philosophical life. Every aspect of Foucault's life—his writing, teaching, political engagement, and even his sexuality—served as a definition of philosophy as the process of finding out that we always have a little more freedom than we think.[11]

Foucault complemented this idea with his poignant definition of madness as *manque à oeuvre*. The state of madness is one in which a human being no longer feels that she has the possibility to link between desire and reality; no possibility of creating a life that she experiences in any way as her own creation. Madness is the most extreme expression of the sense of fatedness. There is no option but to create an alternative reality that is purely internal and divorced from actual life.

It is indeed often useful to look at a person's life as that person's central creation. The existential experience of having created a life that truly expresses a person's sense of individuality can be called the "sense of authorship."[12] The analogy to art is quite strong: an artist endorses a work as truly her own by signing it. This act shows that the creation indeed expresses the fulfillment of the artist's creative urge and her individuality. A sense of authorship over one's life, similarly, reflects the feeling that we have left a stamp on our own life, so to speak; that we accept it as our creation. Neither the sense of authorship nor the sense of having lived life as a work of art can be taken for granted. Many suffer from the experience that the raw materials of their lives simply don't allow the creation of a life that is experienced as satisfying. They suffer from a sense of fatedness instead—a sense that life has dealt them cards that cannot be played.

At midlife the urge to create an oeuvre (not necessarily beyond living a life well lived) often necessitates a process that has affinity to Jacques's notion of sculpted creativity. Sustained creation requires discipline; if during earlier periods of life we may harbor more of the illusion that we can be anything, do anything, and experience everything, midlife often heightens the feeling that there is not enough time left in life to waste. Life needs to be organized around a central theme, the creation experienced as the center, the critical mass around which everything else is organized. Life needs to be pared down to the essentials.

This model bears an interesting analogy to a philosophical school that was very influential in Hellenic and Roman culture: Epicureanism. As opposed to the stereotype that associates this school with gluttonous hedonism, the historical teachings of this school were very different.

Epicurus and his disciples[13] argued that freedom can only be achieved if we are relatively independent of the external world and its vagaries. Striving for freedom requires that we ask ourselves which of our needs and desires are truly essential to us and which are not. Once we have come to the conclusion that many of the things we strive for, like riches, fame, and power, are not essential at all, we can restructure our lives around the needs that are essential. Besides food, shelter, and sex, Epicurus put great emphasis on friendship, and Epicurean communities nurtured this kind of relationship with great care.

A central tenet of Epicureanism is its emphasis that the fear of death is irrational because death is not an event in our lives, and hence not to be feared—a thesis that stands in an interesting tension with Becker's hypothesis of the denial of death. The essence of freedom for Epicurus is the ability to pare life down to essentials. This process takes a particularly interesting form when creation becomes the center of a refocused life—reflecting both the acceptance that time is limited and the desire to leave behind works that will survive their creator. I will try to show how this illustrates the dialectics between Jacques's view of sculpted creativity at midlife and Becker's hypothesis of the denial of death.

Charles Handy: From Manager and Professor to Business Philosopher

As an exemplification of this dynamic we will now turn to the life of Charles Handy, who is in many ways similar to Elliot Jacques. In 2001 Charles Handy was voted number two in the *Thinker's 50* list of leading business thinkers in the world. He became a household name for many when he published *The Age of Unreason* in 1989. He is a particularly instructive example for us because he has documented his midlife transition in *The Elephant and the Flea*.[14] He has done so in his wonderful, down-to-earth, witty style devoid of pomp that does not even vaguely resemble magical transformation tales that are so common in the business literature.

Handy describes the first half of his life as a series of learning experiences. He was the son of an Irish parish priest who took over his dioceses when Handy was two years old and would stay there until his retirement forty years later.

Handy is very refreshing in describing some important junctures in his life as coincidences rather than planned decisions. In high school, he studied Greek just to keep company to a friend, a decision that later led to his receiving a scholarship for classics at Oxford, which was of crucial importance given his family's financial limitations.

After finishing his degree Handy did not really know how to make a living. Hence, aged 23, he accepted a position at Royal Dutch Shell without knowing anything about the oil business, business management, and certainly not about the Far East where he was first stationed. He learned about management and organizations on the job and doesn't hesitate in pointing out the funny aspects of this process.

Soon his ability as a teacher and mentor was recognized by the company, so he started a teaching career that led him to MIT and then back to London in 1967, where at the age of 35 he cofounded and was a professor of the London School of Management.

The death of Handy's father became a turning point. In his early forties, Handy was in demand, doing well, teaching, meeting people, being invited to fancy business lunches, and doing a lot of consulting; in brief, he was "a success," as he writes.[15]

His description of his father's funeral, devoid of sentimentality, is nevertheless moving. He had always been somewhat disappointed by his father, who had turned down larger urban dioceses and stuck to his country position. He was greatly surprised when hundreds of people turned out for the funeral, even though his father's death had not been well publicized. He wondered how many of the people he now saw at the dozens of occasions at which he was lecturing would be at *his* funeral and began to realize that his father, in many ways, had left more of a mark than his son had ever realized.

Briefly he considered going to a theological seminary. Returning to London he consulted with several bishops and expressed gratitude for their comments that he would serve God better "as a business professor than in a dog-collar."[16]

Nevertheless Handy felt that it was time for a change. He moved from business school to becoming the warden of Windsor Castle, founded by the Church of England and members of the Royal Family. It was devoted to seminars for leaders on wide ethical and religious issues. Handy felt that he was reconnecting to his upbringing and that he was focusing his life on issues of meaning and value.

But he soon started to feel uncomfortable because he was accountable to the center's board and, as he said, he was never very good at working under bosses. He writes,

I was unhappy and stressed . . . [and] that took me to the psychotherapist in the first place. I discovered only then that I needed him to explain to me that my problems might be because I had not fully understood what sort of person I was. "Know Yourself" was the maxim of the ancient Greeks, inscribed over the temple of Apollo at Delphi. I now believe that is difficult to do until you have gone through the process of knowing who you are not. That takes time, but in my mid-forties I was nearly there, having crossed several roles and careers off my list.[17]

Handy didn't like working in organizations even though he had become an authority in understanding them. He had started his career as a manager, but at heart he was a man of the spirit and the intellect rather than a man of action. He gives great credit to his wife for encouraging him to leave his position even though he had no idea how he would make a living.

At age 49, Handy was unemployed, by choice, for the first time since age 23 and made the jump into becoming a freelance writer and lecturer. He describes the months after his fateful decision without idealizing them; they were difficult. Used to having his schedule filled for months ahead, he gazed at an empty appointment book, and the phone hardly rang. He had neither the business card nor the institutional affiliation that brought engagements. While he had hated the social occasions forced upon him by his former employers, it had been more comforting to be invited and hating it, than not to be invited at all. Finally, Handy had no financial assets worth speaking about; no inheritance, no accumulated capital, and no significant pension.

Why then did Handy decide to clean the slate and start a new life? He never thought that his previous occupations were wrong choices or hadn't helped him to gain knowledge of the world and of himself. But at midlife he felt that it was time to pare down his life to its essentials. He was later to tell people that the secret of the good life was to live a deep and enduring passion, and he felt that he was missing out on his calling.[18]

Handy's decision was neither impulsive nor devoid of inner logic. He had already published some books, most notably *Understanding Organizations*. He knew he could teach, he knew he could lecture, and he had amassed a wealth of experience as a manager and professor. Nevertheless his move was not easy. He describes himself as rather shy; calling people for the sake of making contact goes against the grain of his personality.

Handy by no means knew that he would become one of the most respected business thinkers of his time. He does not describe his developmental trajectory as an inevitable journey toward success. He even says that if his literary agent had not insisted on the title *The Age of Unreason* (his title had been *Changing*), his second career might not have taken the turn it did.

He just knew that he was not living the life he should be living. By clearing his schedule and moving to a purely self-generated mode of work, he sought to truly become Charles Handy. Deep inside he knew that his true vocation was philosophical and he was willing to take considerable risks to live this vocation. From then on, his creativity burgeoned: he has written 17 books from age 50 to 75 and is still going strong.

Handy created a special oeuvre by combining a deep understanding of macro developments in the capitalist economy and society together with a deep concern for its spiritual substratum. Because he understands the economy well, he does not get lost in generalities of "connect to your spiritual energies" or "humankind needs to care more about mother earth." Together with his wife he embarked on several projects in which he identified both urgent issues and the concrete possibilities that ebullient hypercapitalism produces.

The relationship with his wife, Elizabeth Handy, plays a very important role in Handy's narrative of his midlife change. He makes very clear that he could not have done what he did without his wife's partnership. Elizabeth made her own midlife transition from being a couples' counselor to her true passion: portrait photography, in parallel with Charles. Several of their later books were cocreations of the couple.[19]

Handy narrates their central creation as their lives. *The Elephant and the Flea* is primarily a book about how to live right. Handy puts great emphasis on how to structure life: how to divide life into work that is paid, work that focuses on the home (family) and work that centers on developing the self and the mind. And the Handys have turned their lives into a creation that involves all these spheres.

The Psychodynamics of a Type of Midlife Change

The initial catalyst for midlife change can take many forms. Sometimes the event is external: a job may be threatened or lost, a spouse may raise the option of divorce, or a parent or close friend dies. Sometimes there is no identifiable external event but a change in inner constellation. One of the best-known phenomena is career burnout, the analogue of burnout in relationships, and the realization that a marriage no longer works.[20] Sometimes a round-number birthday (40, 45, or 50) generates the realization that death is coming inexorably closer.

The period of inception is always difficult because inevitably the realization that life no longer works is not accompanied by awareness of possible solutions. Hence the first signs of inception are sometimes symptoms rather than a conscious realization that a change is imminent. Depression and anxiety are the most common symptoms, followed by hypochondriac preoccupations, sudden obsessions with sports, the consideration of plastic surgery or other ways of dealing with aging by technical means, and so on.

In Handy's case the period of inception was initiated by his father's death, which is often one of the defining experiences of midlife. Parents, in a sense, continue to protect us against death awareness by their very existence. "It is not yet my turn" seems to be our, often unspoken assumption while they are still alive. We may be concerned about their health and well-being, and at times we are preoccupied by the knowledge that they will die at some point. But they are also the buffer between us and death, symbolically if not in actuality.

Handy's description of his reaction to his father's death is indeed instructive. He makes it fairly clear that his first reaction was one of guilt. He felt that he had not appreciated his father enough and experienced guilt about having judged him for not making more of his life than he could have. His first impulse of following his father's steps and becoming a priest is a nice exemplification of the mechanism described by Freud in "Mourning and Melancholia."[21] Because there is unresolved anger and guilt, we may try to keep the parent symbolically alive by identifying with him or her.

After this initial reaction, Handy continued to feel that he was not quite doing what he should. He has realized that teaching and writing about business per se were not quite right for him. While he had achieved a good understanding of the business world and had become an authority on various organizations, he did not feel that these fulfilled him. So as a first step, he quit teaching.

While Handy's development is unusual in its success and visibility, it is by no means unique. I have observed a number of developments in which substantial changes were made by people well into their sixties.[22] It is important to emphasize that in none of these cases was the transition miraculous. As in Handy's case, there was strong evidence of talents, inclinations, and passions. More than anything, these people felt the overwhelming need to become most truly who they felt they could be. They no longer wanted to invest energies in activities that did not serve what they felt was the essence of their lives.

As in Handy's case, some financial sacrifice was necessary. Some people made reasoned decisions, together with their spouses, about what in their lifestyle was essential and what they could do without.[23] Freedom at midlife often allows us to find out that much of what we had thought was absolutely essential ("How do you want me to do without my $20,000 membership in the golf-club?"), actually isn't.

Paring down life to the essentials requires us to ask what we want our lives to be *really* about. Questions at midlife can be quite radical: What are my deepest concerns? What matters to me? What is my place in the world? They touch on the essence of who we are and are correspondingly quite frightening. This is neither easy nor without risk. But we always need to remember that the risk of not living our lives fully carries a price tag that can be immeasurably high.

Here we come to the point where the proposed psychodynamic hypothesis is closely related to Elliot Jacques's thesis about resolving the midlife crisis and his idea that sculpted creativity characterizes midlife. Handy began to sculpt his life in the way Michelangelo describes the process of sculpture: chipping away the superfluous pieces. He pared it down to the essentials.

For Handy, the central theme was to find meaning in an increasingly capitalist world. Handy had realized that increased competition in a global capitalist economy was forcing organizations to rid themselves of any excess weight and to cut down the core of fully employed workers to the absolute minimum. Handy's prediction,[24] which turned out to be right on target, was that this would dramatically change the structure of employment in developed economies. A much larger proportion of workers would have to think of themselves as self-employed and learn how to market themselves.

Handy did not end with this prediction, though. He presented very interesting thoughts on how what he called "the portfolio life"[25] could and should be lived. His main argument was that it was a mistake to see work exclusively as defined by financial remuneration. Instead he took self-development through reading, study, and other means to be an essential ingredient of work; the same goes for investment in family, home, and a central relationship, mostly marriage.

Generativity, Creativity, and Flow

There are interesting analogies between Handy's biography and Jacques's. Both truly found their mature and unique voices in their late forties when each of them, in their respective ways, realized what their deepest talent was and turned it into a vocation in the deep sense. Jacques left England for Canada, distanced himself from organized psychoanalysis, and focused exclusively on organizational theory and consulting. For Jacques, paring down life to the essentials meant both more writing and widening his contact with the external world by building a company that disseminated his ideas. Handy, as we saw, quit organizations to focus on social philosophy.

Paradoxically, the process of heightening focus at midlife may be due no less to the denial of death than to acceptance of mortality, as Jacques would claim. Questions then remain: What is life's central theme? What is the activity or role that constitutes the organizing factor of a person's life? What is the life domain through which a person feels that her individuality is expressed and through which she can contribute to the world most effectively and meaningfully?

The biographies of Freud and Jung are instructive. Freud at age forty underwent a strong crisis following his father's death in 1896. A variety of hysterical symptoms made life quite difficult for him. His attempt to cure himself went through delving into the dark sides of the unconscious, thus initiating an almost uninterrupted period of creativity until Freud's death in 1939.

Jung's midlife transformation took a similar direction. After an intense friendship and collaboration with Freud, he came to the conclusion that he could no longer continue being Freud's disciple and that he needed to carve his own way. The break with Freud initiated a protracted crisis in which Jung went through what Henri Ellenberger has called a creative illness, which initiated Jung's most dramatic period of creativity and his emergence as a truly independent and seminal thinker.[26]

We can see a distinctive pattern here: an event at midlife triggers mortality awareness. The result is a move in the direction of increased individuality. Life becomes more focused on independent creation even though this focus entails a price: protracted isolation for Freud and Jung; financial insecurity for Handy; and the separation from psychoanalysis for Jacques.

Becker's theory leads to the following interpretation: the event that increases mortality awareness leads to an increased need for some type of defense that strengthens the human denial of death.

For a particular group of people the most effective defense is immersion in a process of creation that is fed by the hope that its result will outlive its creator. I am focusing here on thinkers whose main work is writing, but of course there are many other examples: the creation can be a business, a political movement, or a building. The focus of life on creation in Becker's view is a direct result of the increased need to feel that we do not simply disappear with death.

Becker's idea of the denial of death can also be used to shed new light on Erik Erikson's notion of *generativity*, which he took to be midlife's defining feature.[27] Listening to oneself at midlife often leads to growing concern for society and the world we live in. Handy's mature reflections on the spiritual needs of the age generated some of his most important work and earned him the distinction of generally being regarded as a business philosopher.

Handy widened his concerns to a truly global scale. What makes Handy stand out in the landscape of leading business thinkers is his preoccupation with the dimension of meaning. On the one hand he argued that those who will really make a difference are driven by true passion—a thesis that is not unique, but Handy gives it an interesting slant. He defines himself as a "reluctant capitalist,"[28] and is very preoccupied by the spiritual dimension in work. He has consistently argued that disregarding this dimension has not only personal but also large-scale implications.

Looking at the notion of generativity from Becker's point of view creates an interesting angle. Redirecting focus from the self's immediate needs to its place in and contribution to the world at large can serve our need to deny death. Focusing on the world that we will leave behind, we implicitly take the stance that our actions now will leave a mark beyond our personal deaths. This can be done in many ways, such as mobilizing ecological causes, improving the educational system, and creating a creative legacy that will contribute to culture and knowledge.[29]

How does this relate to Jacques's thesis that the resolution of the midlife crisis entails acceptance of death and finitude? The answer is complex. On the one hand the two theses seem to contradict each other—and to some extent they do. Becker sees the focus on creation as a heroic gesture of defiance against the fate of finitude. It is as if the creator says, "I know that I will die, but I will fight to my very last breath against this fate. I will create works that outlive me and will beat death!"

On the other hand the process of paring life down to the essentials seems to be based on an acceptance of death: "I know that I will die, and I am aware more keenly than ever that my time on earth is limited, and I cannot waste it on anything inessential. I must focus and concentrate on the task that is uniquely mine, because I have hardly enough time to do what I feel I'm meant to do."

As suggested at the beginning of this chapter, I don't think we need to decide which of these interpretations is right. They stand in dialectical tension to each other, and the psyche, as Winnicott has argued, indeed has the propensity to live with such tensions well.

I would like to add one final element to this model. The process of concentrated, sustained creation is likely to engender the state of mind that Mihaly Csikszentmihalyi has called "flow."[30] By this he means total immersion in an activity in which a person is highly skilled and in which he experiences meaning and value. Through ongoing research for more than thirty years, Csikszentmihalyi has come to the conclusion that flow is the state that is most highly correlated with a general feeling of happiness.

Phenomenologically flow is primarily characterized by a lack of self-consciousness. Reemerging from a flow experience, we are likely to say something like "I wasn't aware of myself for hours!" Flow therefore counteracts two aspects of the human condition that Becker most strongly associates with existential terror: self-consciousness and awareness of time.

Paring life down to the essentials and focusing on creation serves two functions: it liberates us from awareness of self and time and it allows us to be immersed in an activity that we experience as intrinsically meaningful. Along with Jacques we can say that it allows us to symbolically come to terms with our mortality, while at the same time, it sustains our defenses against mortality awareness.

Yet it also requires the often painful process of attaining self-knowledge and of committing to a central theme that can provide us with meaning. This process, as in the case of Charles Handy is very different from the myth of a full-fledged true self bursting into the world scene. It often involves trial, error, and learning about oneself. Along the way we often need to let go of many illusions.

Most of all, we need to drop the mistaken notion that freedom consists of a lack of limitations. Paring life down to the essentials requires the commitment to a few central themes that will be the major source of meaning in our lives. Such commitment means that we accept that there will be many things we won't do in our lives. For some of us this means that we would have to renounce riches; for others, it means that we would have to renounce fame; others, like Jacques, would have to take great responsibility upon themselves, as Jacques did in running his company and consulting with organizations, which can often mean less peace of mind.

The model of paring down life to the essentials is no more likely to be suitable for all than any other. Not all of us feel that we need a central theme around which we organize our lives. Some of us feel fine with a less-active life conception that is more dispersed between many interests, loves, and activities. Nevertheless it is interesting and intriguing in that it goes against the grain of our increasingly global consumerist culture. It is a model that in the midst of surging concerns about natural and human ecology may prove to be important for this troubled time in human history.

Putting our lives into focus requires a stable meaning system that puts order into our values. We cannot center our lives around a theme without having a worldview that tells us what is important, truly valuable, and what is nothing but a distraction that must not tie up our energies. We must therefore turn to the question how Homo globalis can develop worldviews that withstand critical scrutiny and thus provide an existential mooring required to live a rich and meaningful life.

Part III

Reclaiming Our Minds

7

Escaping the Platonic Cave

In Part II, I have developed an existentialist conception of human individuality, and have tried to show the tension between facticity and self-consciousness and between desire and self-knowledge as the defining element of our existence. But the creation of a life and self-knowledge cannot emerge in a vacuum. The existentialist interpretation of human lives often loses track of the simple fact that the deepest source of meaning is being embedded in a web of human relations.[1]

These human relations are structured by the meanings, narratives, and practices of a culture. From the rituals of love through those of professional interaction, artistic production, and appreciation to those of the production and transmission of knowledge, human lives are structured by cultural meaning systems without which nothing in our lives would make sense.

These cultural meaning systems are, in turn, integrated into worldviews that connect our understanding of the universe, our interpretation of social relations, and the value that we assign to activities, achievements, and our place in society. A life experienced as significant must be accepted as valuable in our culture. In fact the very definition of what we do and who we are depends on a cultural network that constitutes the roles, functions, and activities that define our identity.

As we saw in Chapter 3, during the age of the golden calf our culture largely lost connection with the idea that worldviews can be more or less rational and compelling. Our culture has retreated to the principle of political correctness that all beliefs need to be respected just because some ethnic, religious, or national group holds them. The task of Part III is to give an outline of a position beyond political correctness that allows for trenchant debate between worldviews—and also for dialogue.

The Existential Necessity of Worldviews

The value of our actions and our being depends on a cultural worldview that assigns meaning to actions. The very same action can be highly positive in one frame of reference and a deadly sin in another. Killing one's sister because she has slept with a man without being married to him is an act of honor in sub-Saharan, traditional Muslim societies and is simply homicide in Western culture.[2]

The culture that provides us with meaning is of profound existential importance to us. It protects us from the abject terror of death awareness. Hence we need to defend this worldview as one of our most precious assets, which we sometimes do guard quite ruthlessly, particularly when we feel a threat to our lives and self-esteem. We will go into this in detail later. For the time being, it may be enough to remember your reaction to 9/11.

On September 11, 2001, America experienced an unprecedented surge in patriotism, and George W. Bush's abysmal approval ratings skyrocketed overnight. In fact, most of the Western world rallied around America and New York in those days, as the whole of the Free World felt violated by terrorism of unprecedented magnitude. Our fundamental worldview was under attack, and we felt the need to defend it.

While we all intuitively know of the importance of having a worldview, existential psychology has buttressed this intuition with powerful empirical evidence. It turns out that one of the prime sources of existential safety is indeed a more or less integrated worldview. In fact existential psychology shows that our need for a worldview that provides us with meaning is so overpowering that we will do almost anything to defend it.

Let me retrace the steps through which experimental existential psychology (EEP) has validated the importance of worldviews to the human psyche.[3] It has been shown in hundreds of experiments conducted in dozens of countries that we indeed use the worldview defense to avoid the awareness of one's own death (i.e., mortality or death salience). The classical design is to expose subjects to a stimulus that promotes mortality salience. It may be a video showing us deadly car accidents or reporting on bereaved families after 9/11. The experimental control group is exposed to a neutral stimulus like a video about a new trend in restaurants. After that, both groups are exposed to stimuli representing members of another racial, religious, ethnic, or political group.

Experimental existential psychology predicts that the group that has been exposed to the stimulus with death salience has a strong need to defend against emerging death anxiety. As a result it is in strong need of worldview defense. Since our worldviews are inevitably threatened by the very fact that there are competing worldviews, our increased need for worldview defense is likely to lead to a lower tolerance for diverging world-views and for others in general. Hence EEP predicts that the experimental death-salience group will show increased intolerance for other groups. Christians will become less tolerant toward Jews, Buddhists, or Muslims, and vice versa.

In a way quite rare in the social sciences that generally need to cope with rather ambiguous experimental results, the predictions of EEP work like a Swiss precision watch. Invariably, the group exposed to death thoughts becomes more judgmental, more stereotypical, and less accepting of otherness.

The explanation of this phenomenon is as follows: people deal with the intrusion of death thoughts by employing the proximal defense of repressing them. Because this does not work in the long run, the distal defense of strengthening one's worldview that protects us from death awareness is summoned.

These cultural frameworks can take many different forms. They range from the great world religions to small sects; from totalitarian political ideologies like Communism and fascism to the ideal of liberal democracy; from academia with its guiding value of striving for truth and rationality to the world of the arts; and from causes like saving the rainforests to Scientology's crusade against psychiatric drugs.

Each worldview and cultural system claims that it is of unique importance. Communism claimed to be the way to implement universal justice. The modern university system is based on the idea that the various sciences are the only rational and empirically proven ways to arrive at the truth. Since the nineteenth century the art world has, for many, replaced religion in providing objects of veneration and beauty.

But defending a worldview, or even arguing for it has become a somewhat awkward task for Homo globalis. Were not all worldviews supposed to be equal? The ideology of political correctness has inculcated us with the dogma that beliefs needed to be respected just because somebody holds them. Questioning or criticizing beliefs is not just tactless but really a sin.[4]

For the last three decades, intellectual discussion about anything but business or professional issues has been well nigh forbidden, which has left many of those who are globally oriented in a quandary about how to discuss worldviews. On the conservative end of the spectrum, a worldview has become something that is defended by breast-beating and insisting on one's adherence to values and to faith. On the liberal end, one is supposed to tread lightly and primarily make sure that one does not offend anybody's sensibilities.

Religion in particular is a very thorny issue. Conservatives expect religion to be respected per se and any criticism is countered with almost violent outrage. Liberals have become accustomed to the expectation that they need to respect the religious dabbling of many of their friends and acquaintances, a phase in which these friends tried out some New Age spirituality or other religious expressions, often talking starry eyed about half-digested ideas.

The last decades have made it difficult for Homo globalis to think critically about worldviews. Many members of Homo globalis feel constantly threatened by the nagging doubt about whether their lives and what they do really matter. The need to feel significant and valuable within a cultural worldview that we identify with is a universal human need. Self-esteem has several components. We need to feel appreciated by our peers and community by living up to our culture's requirements. Every society expects its adult members to be productive and to contribute to the society's survival, quality of life, and wealth. Every society expects its members to adhere to its standards of morals and honor. To belong to a society and a culture, we need to meet these basic demands.

Arnold: The Retreat from Reason

Arnold, in his early forties, felt that his life had become futile. He had failed in his latest business venture, he had gone through a painful divorce, and he felt that nothing worthwhile was ahead of him. You could tell by his look that something was wrong. In the past he had been a great basketball player, but now his tall frame was flabby and his clothing showed that he no longer cared about his appearance.

Arnold turned to psychoanalysis to alleviate his anxiety and pain. In the process he began to realize that he had been laboring under a strong sense of guilt because he was less religious than his parents and because he had not continued the family tradition of high academic achievement, particularly in the field of mathematics.

The beginning of change for Arnold came from an unexpected corner: he began to rethink his relationship to religion. He soon discovered that he had been unconsciously convinced since childhood that his lack of religious fervor reflected his inherent badness and lack of spiritual depth.

Could it not be, I asked, that he was less religious than his parents, because deep down he didn't believe in the idea that there was an external authority that had formulated all the wisdom needed for the good life?

As a result of the analytic work following this question, for the first time in his life, Arnold started reading philosophy seriously. He discovered Darwin and started thinking about the implications of evolutionary theory. He enrolled in several courses in evolutionary psychology and the philosophy of science and gradually understood what he had never thought would be possible: he was really an atheist.

His chronic sense of guilt gave way to a sense of liberation and renewal that led to the beginning of a new life cycle. He married a woman whose values were close to his, and he initiated a new business venture that reflected his true talents.

Arnold exemplifies a pattern that is quite ubiquitous in members of the global creative class. Most of them came of age in the 1980s and 1990s, during the heyday of unfettered capitalist ideology. In the 1980s they had heard that the gifted among them could be making seven-figure salaries in finance, and they were keen to enter the race quickly. In the 1990s the stories of huge early success multiplied, and this increased the urgency of entering the race for the big money ASAP.

They mostly invested their energies in acquiring the tools that would further their careers and would likely make money. The relentless cultural pressure to have a "spectacular life" has undermined the idea of investing in knowledge for its own sake. Academic institutions have trouble resisting this pressure and maintaining the ideal of a liberal education as the foundation for a well-rounded personality. The demand is for them to provide entry tickets to lucrative professions as quickly as possible instead.

Like Arnold, many found themselves cruising through their thirties with very few assets, allowing them to think more deeply about existential questions. Many of those who had been born into an organized religion just kept some form of attachment to it but didn't invest much in deepening their understanding of their own religion or any other worldview.

Homo globalis's vulnerability to the fluctuation in the value of the "I" commodity has strong links to the democratization of taste that we have analyzed in Part I. Without independent inner resources to assess the value of ideas, policies, cultural production, and ways of life, the mind is left with nothing but the popularity of cultural commodities and the ranking of the self.

These commodities then function as nothing but memes. This concept was introduced by Richard Dawkins, one of today's leading evolutionary biologists in analogy to the concept of the gene.[5] Memes are cultural entities like tunes, ideas, fashion items, or dance movements that can precisely replicate themselves from individual to individual. A meme's survival capacity in no way reflects its value for the individual whose mind is taken over by it. In this respect memes are quite like viruses: the HIV virus has shown remarkable resilience even though it is likely to kill its human host.

Ideas like creationism, the conspiracy of Zionists and Jews to take over the world, the racial superiority of Caucasians, the literal truth of the book of Revelation, slogans like Nike's "just do it," or McDonald's "what you see is what you get" are showing enormous resilience. Like viruses they spread through the globe and infect the carrier's mind with their content.

If we are to measure the value of ideas, concepts, theories, and beliefs by the number of people that hold them, the literal truth of the book of Revelation is more valuable than quantum physics; the stories of creation in the book of Genesis are more valuable than modern cosmology and evolutionary biology; and Britney Spears's video clips have more value than Bach's Mass in B Minor.

The step from the meme market to the rating of humans by their ranking on the global I-Commodity Market is almost inevitable, and our infotainment system thrives on this classification of humans. Millions hungrily listen to the latest wisdom uttered by Bono (which isn't so bad, given his good intentions), Tom Cruise (which is problematic given his fanatic belief in Scientology), or Madonna (which may not be noxious but is unlikely to enrich minds greatly).

The memes that circulate through the global infotainment system crowd out sophisticated ideas that require some effort to understand and digest. Any of the star preachers filling the airwaves and the Internet reach incomparably more minds than the ideas of scholars like Jared Diamond, Richard Dawkins, or Steven Weinberg.

Minds fed on intellectual junk, incapable of judging ideas on intellectual merit rather than popularity, are no more resistant to infection by noxious memes than a body fed on junk food and untrained by exercise is capable of dealing with physical exertion. And a person who has no measure of her value other than her rating on the global I-Commodity Market is necessarily doomed to enormous volatility in self-esteem and likely to have very little resilience in dealing with either the hardships or the successes and pleasures of life.

In the 1950s sociologist David Riesman in his classic *The Lonely Crowd*[6] lamented the disappearance of the inner-directed personality type guided by standards that provide them with a sense of value and meaning and described the emergence of the outer-directed mind that aims primarily to please and be popular with the environment. Erich Fromm called this personality the marketing personality.[7] The global I-Commodity Market has sharply increased this tendency because of the immediacy by which cultural junk-memes flood our mind, channeled by a rating-driven infotainment network.

But the price of such ignorance is high on an individual level too. Few Western individualists believe that immersion in philosophical, social, and psychological thought might be a suitable way to address their existential concerns. Moreover, as Susan Jacoby shows poignantly in *The Age of American Unreason*,[8] intellectual pursuit seems to be a highly unattractive option. Many are attracted to religions that have evolved in a very different cultural context, such as Buddhism and Hinduism for North Americans, and they often don't realize that picking up some terms like karma, samsara, or mindfulness is a far cry from truly understanding a religion (even though there are, of course, a few exceptions who seriously study them). Eastern philosophies are misconceived as putting emphasis on spirituality and religion as opposed to the Western emphasis on rational thought. This is blatantly untrue. Indian philosophy throughout its history was based on complex systems of logic and metaphysics no less developed than those of Western philosophy.[9] Worse, many are often completely unaware that the synthetic pop spiritualities analyzed in Chapter 3 are concoctions put together from sources that are mutually incompatible like Indian theology and Kabbalah.

When many members of the global creative class feel uneasy about whether their lives matter, despite the fact that they have fine lives in most tangible respects, they start asking questions about more fundamental and existential issues. The range of ages in which this happens varies considerably. I have worked with many people ranging from their thirties to sixties who began to ask themselves why they felt insecure and often empty despite their flourishing careers and even though their private lives were quite satisfying. Some were religious but had invested little thought on religion up to that point. Others were atheists but had hardly invested time or energy on philosophical issues. Like Arnold, they needed to embark on a sustained inquiry into philosophical issues to be able to formulate their new worldviews. Developing the ability to judge cultural creations and ideas is a dire necessity for the mental ecology of our species that is polluted by noxious memes and for the well-being of each and every individual. It is what can provide us with the strength and stamina to evolve a sense of self that goes beyond the "I" commodity.

Argumentation Phobia

One of the reasons members of the global creative class have shied away from tackling questions of basic worldview and questions of basic faith for decades rests on a pervasive philosophical confusion. Well meaning and tolerant, they want to avoid conflict, particularly conflict that has little chance to be resolved. Arguments about religious faith very rarely, if ever, lead to any productive outcome. None of the interlocutors are likely to change anything in their belief systems. At best, such discussion is arid, which often leads to deep hurt and anger. At worst, it ends in often fatal violence.

Such skepticism about the possibility of discussing basic worldviews rationally is based on strong empirical evidence. The relations between Christianity, Islam, and Judaism were mostly fought out on the battlefield rather than through civilized discussion, as a cursory look at the history of the world in the last 1,300 years shows.

The results of existential psychology do not provide a basis for believing that such discussion is likely to be more productive in the future than it was in the past. Quite to the contrary, experiments corroborating the basic tenets of existential psychology give every reason to believe that humans will continue to cling to their worldviews as ferociously as they have in the past.

As a result many think that for the sake of harmonious relations, such argument should be avoided altogether. But how can we live with the knowledge that billions of human beings believe in creeds that contradict the creeds of billions or hundreds of millions of others?

On a smaller scale, how are we to live with the fact that friends and acquaintances adopt belief systems that we deem to be irrational or quite simply wrong? How are we to relate to those who become infatuated with the latest fad of the pop spirituality market?

Many have dealt with these questions (or avoided dealing with them) by retreating into an often vaguely formulated form of relativism: "there is more than one truth"; "rational argument is limited, and there are different realms that cannot be discussed"; and "we now know that there are contradictory truths"; these are the types of thinking by which trenchant discussion is avoided.[10]

The negative impact of such relativism is its almost unavoidable logical implication. If deep and trenchant thought and discussion about worldviews, particularly religions, is useless, why even bother to think deeply about them? Maybe it is simply not worth putting energy into such questions.

In Chapter 3 we have seen the devaluation of thought that has become characteristic of much contemporary discourse on meaning. In particular, we have seen that the strong impact of the idea that truth about the soul, about the world, and about so-called metaphysical realms can be achieved through direct intuition, and that rational thought has almost no place in the search for meaning.

This devaluation of reason has further empowered relativism. Religions, cults, and pop spirituality have just become competitors on the meme market. Careful argument means little on the meme market, as persuasion through indoctrination is far more efficient. For the most part, the success of memes in replicating themselves depends not on the intrinsic quality and truth value of the ideas but on their ability to address the more primitive strata of the mind, as every advertiser and political campaigner knows.

The Rude Awakening

Well-meaning proponents of tolerance were in for a rude awakening. Two developments in the last decades cast great doubt on the assumption that the principle of tolerance would minimize conflicts based on religion—but now this principle seemed no longer to work.

The first factor involved both the United States and Europe. A series of events forced Western countries to rethink the principle of religious tolerance. In hindsight many realized that in 1989 there were already clear indications that political correctness and the anxious appeasement of the feelings of all forms of belief, no matter how extreme would not work forever. In 1988, Salman Rushdie published his *The Satanic Verses*, a complex work in the tradition of magical realism that was greeted by outrage in the Muslim world because it was perceived as presenting the Prophet Muhammad irreverently.[11] On February 14, 1989, Ayatollah Ruholla Khomeini issued a fatwa demanding Rushdie's execution, and Rushdie was to spend the next years living virtually underground.

It may not be that surprising that many politicians criticized Rushdie instead of condemning Khomeini's fatwa in unequivocal terms. Instead of standing up for the political and ethical principle of freedom of speech and the principle that any belief and any person is a legitimate subject matter of fictional treatment and even satire and ridicule, they tried a policy of appeasement. It was more surprising that some of Rushdie's fellow writers turned against him and accused him of insensitivity to Muslim feelings, and in one case, quite unintelligibly, connected this to Rushdie's desire for fame and money.[12]

In 1995 I was in London and made my traditional visit to my favorite bookstore there, Dillons (now Waterstone's), off Gower Street. Browsing through the latest releases I realized that something strange was going on. A large number of people started to crowd in the entry floor, and quite a few of them seemed to be undercover security agents. When I asked one of the shop's employees what was going on, it turned out that Rushdie was being whisked in for a book signing of his latest novel, *The Moor's Last Sigh*. The book-signing had not been advertised anywhere to minimize the security risk, and it took place in a room that had no windows to protect Rushdie from possible attacks.

I felt quite lucky to have been there, and along with a surge of pride another wave of outrage went through my soul. Who were these people to interfere in the world of art? As a matter of principle I bought a copy of *The Satanic Verses* and had it signed by Rushdie, and the copy occupies a place of honor in my library to this day.

While the Rushdie affair provoked much outrage, little thought was given to the principle of uncritical toleration and its downside. It was only after the cataclysm of 9/11 that such rethinking began. The perpetrators of history's most lethal and dramatic act of terror had lived in the West for years, had studied at Western universities, and gained their flight training at American schools.

The plight of the principle of tolerance was to get worse after the murder of Dutch filmmaker Theo van Gogh in broad daylight in Amsterdam on November 2, 2004, and the subsequent threats on the life of Ayaan Ali Hirsi that ultimately led to her leaving the Netherlands for the United States. This exposed the shameful reality that European governments were not even capable of protecting elected parliamentarians from Muslim violence.

On March 11, 2004, 191 commuters were killed by four simultaneous bombs on trains in Madrid. On July 7, in London, four simultaneous bombs in the subway system and one on a bus killed 56 people. In both cases the acts of terror were perpetrated by Muslim radicals. The latter were particularly problematic in their implications because the perpetrators had been second-generation Muslims who had grown up in Britain.

The question now arose, could Western countries tolerate religious teachings that called for jihad against the West? Was every religious position to be respected as such? It seemed that the principle of religious tolerance had become self-undermining, because it allowed for positions that themselves attacked the idea of religious tolerance and the free society that makes it possible.

Politics was back, big time—and with a vengeance. Suddenly the all-but-unquestioned dogma that multiculturalism was the magic solution to all problems, that Western societies could integrate immigrants of different nationalities and religions, was becoming questionable. The harmony between ethnic groups and religions under a single political umbrella that had seemed the pinnacle of human achievement now seemed a relic of the past. We now faced the moment of truth. What were our values and how could they be defended?[13]

Members of Homo globalis instinctively have a cosmopolitan bent. They typically do not have much sympathy for nationalism, and they recoil from chauvinism. I believe that for most of them this is more than a knee-jerk posture of political correctness. A large percentage of them have hyphenated identities, ranging from African-American, Muslim-French, German citizens of Russian origins, and Asian-Americans to complex religious backgrounds in which one parent is Jewish, the other Catholic; one is Muslim, the other Protestant; and so on. Many of them have experienced the blessings of openness to immigration and multiculturalism in their lives by integrating into European, American, or Australian countries that gave them the opportunity to find their place in society and evolve in their own complex identities. Many others are children of immigrants who went through this process and have grown up in the knowledge that cultural openness and the weakening of nationalism is a precious asset that needs to be nurtured.

Hence the backlash against the United States (9/11), London (7/7), and Madrid and the French suburban riots were difficult to stomach. From the traditionally tolerant and secular Netherlands to Austria, a series of right-wing parties made strong gains in parliamentary elections. While many started seriously asking questions about how Western societies could defend their way of life, the retreat into right-wing nationalism left them distinctly uncomfortable. Further, it was understood that the powerful restrictions on immigration in the United States both substantially depleted the influx of gifted students from abroad, who bring in much-needed money to the American higher education system, and also created a shortage of qualified academics, particularly in the natural sciences.

The second factor was the growing power of the Christian Right in the United States and the growing political power of religion in America. Conservative religious groups in the United States tried to introduce religious teachings into the curriculum by arguing that the theory of intelligent design was a scientific competitor to the theory of evolution.[14] George W. Bush filled the U.S. Supreme Court with extremely conservative judges, and the specter of overturning *Roe v. Wade* became a tangible reality. The status quo based on mutual tolerance was endangered by a full takeover by those who called themselves the moral majority who were against many of the basic beliefs of most members of the creative class, like gay rights and the possibility of doing stem-cell research.

More frightening developments occurred. It turns out that a substantial proportion of the American electorate favored a highly biased Middle Eastern policy seemingly slanted in favor of Israel. But a closer look showed that this support of Israel was based on an eerie belief structure. A literal interpretation of the book of Revelation led them to believe that it was important that most Jews would live in Israel as a preparation for the grand war between Gog and Magog. In this war two-thirds of the Jews of Israel would be killed, and the remaining third would convert to Christianity thus heralding the second coming of Christ.

An astounding number of people in the Free World know very little if anything about the culture that has shaped the world they live in. Rushing toward success, many of them have never had the experience of truly immersing themselves in a culture that has created the language they speak, the political structure that provides them freedom and protection, and the science that allows them to make money. The very term "intellectual" has become somewhat old-fashioned. Sustained thought is taken to be useful in pragmatic contexts of business, research and development (R&D), marketing, or design, but not when it comes to core existential issues.

The currently sanctioned ignorance about Western culture, its history, complexity, and achievement has many enormous drawbacks. On a social level it leads to a stunning degree of ignorance documented by Susan Jacoby in *The Age of American Unreason*.[15] Many college-educated people do not have the basic knowledge that even allows for responsible citizenship—and worse, they do not think that such knowledge is necessary. Jacoby quotes the finding that 70 percent of Americans believe that it is not necessary to know anything about a country like Iraq—including its location on the globe—to make up one's mind on policy. The price of this ignorance has been all too palpable, when the U.S. electorate chose to reelect George W. Bush in 2004, to the detriment of the United States and the whole world.

Relativist tolerance turned out to be a double-edged sword. Political realities and social structures were being created that would undermine the very tolerance that had given place to all forms of belief. It turned out that a new pariah minority had been created in the United States. A *Newsweek* survey conducted in March 2007 showed that a full 62 percent of Americans said that they would not vote for an Atheist for president—way more than refused to vote for a Muslim or Jew. Not surprisingly, many atheists came to the conclusion that while America's constitution continued to uphold the separation of church and state, the reality was quite different: religion plays a huge role in the American polity. Atheism had become a sign of morally flawed character.

But most of all, after recovering from the shock of 9/11, the deleterious impact of the blatant anti-intellectualism of the second Bush's administration was keenly felt. The catastrophic impact of making policy decisions after reading religious sermons rather than studying intelligence reports and of marching into countries without any decent understanding of their cultural and religious structures became obvious. In-depth reporting from first-rate research journalists like Bob Woodward and Ron Suskind showed the extent to which the Bush administration had been both incapable and unwilling to come to terms with the actual complexity of reality rather than living in the near-delusional certainty that realities could be created and hence didn't need to be studied.[16]

Nevertheless a large proportion of Homo globalis didn't feel that they had the intellectual resources to deal with the large questions that had resurfaced: What is the relationship between religion and science? What place, if any, can be given to religion in primary, secondary, and higher education? Is religion a relic of archaic mental patterns inherited from our evolutionary past, or is it a valuable phenomenon that gives meaning to the overwhelming majority of humans? Is Western Civilization superior to others not only technologically but also in some deep sense?

But the most burning question was, could all worldviews indeed live together in the same polity? Is it indeed possible for humans to respect each other's worldviews no matter how deep the differences? If there are different perspectives on reality, how can we overcome the relativism that has played such a powerful role in thinking about ultimate existential concerns?[17]

Nonrelativist Pluralism

The first task of this chapter is to argue for a differentiation between relativism and pluralism. Pluralism not only has social and political meanings; it also holds an important place in epistemology and the philosophy of science.[18] In the pages that follow, I will summarize some important ideas of these fields in simple terms, which, as we shall see, will be of tremendous importance for our understanding of the difference between pluralism and relativism.[19]

A relatively simple example will do. Physics describes the material world as it functions on its most basic levels. The goal of physics is to find the most basic constituents of material reality and to describe the laws according to which they function. The story of physics in the last three centuries is certainly the most spectacular success story of the scientific endeavor, and humanity knows more about the structure and functioning of matter than ever before. Our ability to understand and predict phenomena ranging from the subatomic level to the laws governing solar systems and galaxies is positively stunning.

Economics is a discipline of great importance in our world. As we all know, and sorely experience, the ability of economics to explain and predict anything from financial markets to consumer behavior is relatively limited. Nevertheless, there is an impressive body of knowledge about the functioning of the ever more complex reality of the global economic system.

Opening any economics textbook, you will not find a single term, equation, or theory derived from physics. The concepts and theories of economics are on a totally different level than those of physics. Take one of the most basic concepts of economics: currency. Money, as we all know, cannot even be defined as a set of physical objects. It is an abstract quantity that can take many forms and follows rules and laws that are very different from those governing physical objects.

Does this mean that we need to stipulate a metaphysical realm that is radically different from that described by physics? Do we need to say that besides protons, electrons, and neutrons there are dollars, euros, pounds, yens, and Swiss francs? Or that there is an abstract entity called "money" that takes different forms? I wouldn't know of any economist who thinks so. All we say is that if we want to describe the world in economic terms, we must apply a different set of concepts to find interesting laws.

According to philosopher Nelson Goodman, there are different ways of carving up the world into entities. We can look at the same reality from the point of view of physics, and we get fundamental particles, forms of energy that are governed by one set of laws. When we look at the same reality from an economic point of view, we get currencies, various forms of equity and other financial instruments, gross domestic products and inflation rates. These entities or structures are governed by a very different set of laws, but this doesn't mean that we need to stipulate the existence of a different metaphysical realm unique to economics. Goodman calls these various ways of conceptualizing the world "Ways of Worldmaking."[20]

The same would happen if we look at other perspectives on the world: biology versus the history of art, chemistry versus sociology, or geology versus psychology. Each of these disciplines tries to formulate interesting laws about the world. To do so, each discipline carves up the world in different ways.

There is nothing mysterious about this. Think about the following: in designing a new car you have engineers, marketing specialists, and designers working together. They all conceptualize the car in very different terms. Engineers will talk about the mechanical structure, the weight, physical properties, and durability of the materials used. Marketers will talk about the image the car projects, its cost, and market price, whereas designers will talk about stylistic elements, the aesthetic properties of the materials and the car's overall stylistic statement.

Nobody would assume that this means the car that is finally produced is composed of the mechanical parts, the marketing parts, and the style parts. It is simply that you can describe the same car from a variety of perspectives. Of course you will need different concepts to describe these various aspects of the car; but they are not different *parts* of the car; just different aspects of the car, or different perspectives on it.

Philosophical pluralism is the thesis that the various perspectives that we use to describe reality (whether humans, cars, currencies, or financial markets) cannot be reduced into each other. There is no way to define stylistic or marketing properties in mechanical terms. Similarly, it is not possible to define economic terms in the language of physics, aesthetic terms in the language of chemistry, or psychological terms in the language of economics.

As a result we are left with a variety of languages to describe the world that are useful in different contexts but that are not reducible to each other. The position that endorses this multiplicity of languages is philosophical pluralism.

But pluralism does not entail relativism. Relativism asserts that contradictory positions can be equally true. A somewhat weaker version of relativism maintains that there is no way to argue for or against a thesis, a worldview, or a theory and that all worldviews are therefore equal in value.

You can be a pluralist and yet trenchantly criticize worldviews, theories, religious traditions, or art. While pluralism states that it makes little sense to criticize physics through economics or the other way round, there are powerful reasons why general relativity and quantum physics are preferable to classical mechanics and why evolutionary theory is a much more powerful theory than creationism.

A similar point holds true for the domain of values. One of the most important claims of Isaiah Berlin's lifework was that although values have objective validity, they can clash with each other.[21] We value liberty and equality, but by increasing one of them, we often limit the other. We value authenticity and loyalty, but the two can make conflicting demands on us, and there is no decision algorithm that gives us the perfect answer.

Worldviews are, among others, determined by the values that we deem to be overriding. European liberalism is willing to sacrifice some equality for the sake of safeguarding liberty, because the flourishing and autonomy of the individual is an overriding value for it. Social democrats are willing to sacrifice some liberty for the sake of maximizing equality. Berlin's value pluralism claims that there is no perfect solution for how to live because we will always have to make choices between competing values. But yet again, this does not mean that ethical and political worldviews cannot be discussed reasonably and that there are no better or worse social and political arrangements; value pluralism does not entail relativism.

Escaping the Platonic Cave

We are not condemned to live in worldviews that we accept uncritically on the basis of their popularity or packaging, and there are ways to live within worldviews that are more responsible. In a nutshell my argument will be that there are indeed ways to critically analyze worldviews. While we do not have the choice *not* to have a worldview, a frame of reference that provides us with meaning and a defense against the threat of insignificance, we do have a choice to invest careful thought in our worldview.

This chapter therefore argues for a more conservative approach to the quest for existential depth and enlightenment.[22] It is a plea to return to a classical view of the importance of intellectual investment in our worldviews, a conception that has all but disappeared during the last decades of frenzy. The great philosophical traditions of all high civilizations from China through India to Europe have argued that humans can liberate themselves from the shackles imposed on them by accident of birth to some extent. We are not condemned to live within the bounds of worldviews that we didn't choose but were implanted in our minds through early education.[23]

In the European tradition this idea has been put into a haunting image in Plato's dialogue *The Republic*. Socrates, the figure Plato uses to voice his views, tells the following myth to describe the human predicament:

> Make an image of our nature in its education and want of education, likening it to a condition of the following kind. See human beings as though they were in an underground cave-like dwelling with its entrance, a long one, open to the light across the whole width of the cave. They are in it from childhood with their legs and necks in bonds so that they are fixed, seeing on in front of them, unable because of the bond to turn their heads all the way around. Their light is from a fire burning far above and behind them. Between the fire and the prisoners there is a road above, along which see a wall, built like the partitions puppet-handlers set in front of the human beings and over which they show the puppets . . .
>
> They're like us . . . For in the first place, do you suppose such men would have seen anything of themselves and one another other than the shadows cast by the fire on the side of the cave facing them?
>
> Take a man who is released, and suddenly compelled to stand up, to turn his neck around, to walk and look up towards the light . . . What do you suppose he'd say if someone were to tell him that before he saw silly nothings, while now, because he is somewhat nearer to what *is* and more turned towards beings, he sees more correctly? . . . Don't you suppose he'd be at a loss and believe that what was seen before was truer than what is now shown?[24]

This parable of the cave is one of the most famous images in the history of Western philosophy. It is paralleled by many myths and stories in other cultures. The story of the Buddha's journey toward enlightenment is similar in that Siddhartha Gautama is originally shielded from the truth. Faced with the reality of human suffering, he goes through a transformation that leads him to realize that the way he has seen the world until now is illusory.

These philosophical parables emphasize that humans are prone to live in error, because the circumstances of our birth may not have given us the type of education that gives us access to the best thinking that humanity has produced. All philosophical traditions exhort us not to acquiesce to the limitations imposed on us by accident of birth and to make the painful effort of acquiring the knowledge necessary to live in a worldview as close to the truth as possible.

It is quite interesting to play with the question what metaphor Plato would have used for his parable in the present time. It is almost uncanny how much the physical arrangement of the cave parable resembles that of a cinema. Just replace the puppet players with the projection machine, and you get quite the same structure.

One of the most powerful contemporary artistic representations of the possibility that we live in a state of untruth is the Wachowski brothers' trilogy *The Matrix*. The metaphor for the cave is replaced by a computer-generated reality that looks exactly like our ordinary life. It is fed into the brains of countless human beings who, unbeknownst to them, are used as organic batteries powering a world that has been taken over by machines.

The trilogy's hero, Neo, played by Keanu Reeves, is bothered by strange phenomena until he is indeed approached from outside the Matrix by a group of humans who are trying to fight the rule of the intelligent machines.

The Matrix was not primarily meant to be a philosophical work. The Wachowski brothers quite explicitly say that their prime inspiration was taken from Hong Kong kung fu movies and from Japanese comics. Nevertheless the script makes quite explicit allusions to Plato's allegory of the cave and several religious traditions, and its power partially derives from the human feeling that indeed we may often live in a state of delusion.

The reason this premise resonates strongly with a large audience is that many of us have gone through the realization that the beliefs we had acquired early in life turned out to be false. Sometimes the dismantling of such beliefs may be relatively harmless; mostly it is not traumatic to find out that there is really no Santa Claus or that fairies do not exist.

But sometimes the rude awakening can be painful, and it can happen to us as adults. A poignant example was the gradual realization of Western intellectuals from the 1930s onward that Soviet Communism was not the ideal political arrangement that had finally created a just society based on equality. For many of these intellectuals who had been fervent believers in Communism as the advent of freedom and justice, the shock of finding out the truth about the horrors of Stalinism was very difficult to bear. Some writers and intellectuals like Arthur Koestler and George Orwell drew the consequences, and changed their worldview dramatically.[25] Others like Jean-Paul Sartre were completely incapable of renouncing the belief in

Communism as the ideal alternative to capitalism.[26] No evidence about the atrocities of Stalin's regime and the bleakness and terror of life in the Soviet Union in mid-twentieth century could make them give up their ideological convictions.

I believe that currently many neoliberals, who have fervently believed that unregulated markets were the royal road to stable prosperity for all and the guarantors of liberal democracy, are going through a similarly painful process of having to reevaluate the foundations of their worldview. It can certainly not have been easy for Alan Greenspan, who had been chairman of the U.S. Federal Reserve from 1987 to 2006 and described himself as a "lifelong libertarian Republican," to admit recently that his unfettered belief in unregulated markets had been a mistake and had contributed massively to the current economic crisis.[27]

Personally I have gone through two such upheavals: The first occurred in my adolescence, when I gradually realized that the Jewish faith that I had been brought up in did not stand up to the critical scrutiny of rational thought. The gradual process of realizing that my worldview was crumbling was excruciatingly difficult. I will never forget the day, shortly after I turned 18, when I woke up with a crystal clear thought: there is no God.[28]

While this thought was liberating, because it meant that I had finally come to the logical conclusion of a process that had taken a few years, it was also absolutely terrifying. For months I had unbearable anxiety attacks and thought that I was losing my sanity. I now know that what I went through is not unusual: the crumbling of a worldview is exceedingly difficult to bear, even if it leads to a more authentic and truthful way of life in the long run.

In many ways I have gone through a similar process in the last decade. Along with many others, I had been deeply convinced by the philosophic-historical narrative of the European Enlightenment. I had believed that history would inevitably lead to the triumph of liberal democracy, and that rationality would, in the long run, lead humanity to believe that reason rather than faith needed to be the basis for running human affairs.

After the fall of the Berlin Wall and the dismantling of the Soviet Union I believed, along with Francis Fukuyama[29] and many others, that history had basically come to an end, and that it was a matter of time until the world would gradually evolve institutional mechanisms that would guarantee stability and peace for all. And like many others the last decade forced me to go through the painful process of abandoning the optimistic Enlightenment narrative that had become the replacement of the religious beliefs of my childhood. This book is, in many ways, an attempt to salvage the core value of the European Enlightenment from the wreckage of its optimistic philosophy of history.[30]

But is that really a tragedy? There is the erroneous conception that worldviews are something that you acquire early in life and that if you have character, you will stick to them for a lifetime. Changing basic beliefs later in life is often taken to be a sign of weakness, instability, or immaturity. I believe that nothing could be further from the truth. I have deep admiration for people like Koestler and Orwell who were willing to change fundamental tenets of their value system on the basis of empirical evidence.

My personal experience therefore is that escaping the Platonic cave is a process that never ends and that we must always be prepared to rethink and possibly abandon beliefs no matter how cherished they may be. And while this process can, at times, be painful, it is also one of the most sustaining and nourishing activities that humans can engage in—as philosophers from Plato to Michel Foucault have argued for millennia.

Thinking about Basic Questions

There are incisive, moving, and thought-provoking examples of such scrutiny that have been published during the last decade. *The Monk and the Philosopher*, first published in 1997,[31] is a trenchant, searching, and at the same time moving document. Jean-Francois Revel is a French philosopher, an atheist and fervent believer in the ideals of the Enlightenment. A modern day Voltaire, his sharp pen has lashed those who are going astray in ignorance, totalitarian ideologies, or irrational sentiments. He has criticized totalitarian ideologies, the deleterious impact of the mass media, and taken his fellow Frenchmen to task for what he takes to be an irrational anti-Americanism.

His son, Matthieu Ricard, completed a doctorate in molecular biology at the prestigious Louis Pasteur Institute before renouncing his scientific career to devote his life to the study of Buddhism. He became a Buddhist monk, a translator of many classic Buddhist texts as well as writings of the Dalai Lama, whom he often accompanies as his personal interpreter.

The dialogue between father and son, while respectful is sharp. Ricard explains the tenets of Buddhism with rare clarity and describes the reasons that led him to leave behind the Western way of life and to turn to Buddhism. His father is an intent listener and incisive critic. While he wants to understand his son's belief in depth, he does not shy away from pointing out how idealized many Western conceptions of Tibetan Buddhism are, how much belief in magic, and how much downright superstition it contains.

Revel and Ricard are respectful but profoundly critical of each other, and the reader of the book may be in for a powerful personal and intellectual journey. For some, the book may shatter idealizations and pre-conceptions. But few may get away without feeling that while the searching dialogue neither produces a "winner" nor presents easy enlightenment, it leaves the reader enriched because of its depth, precision, and total lack of obscurantism.

Another example is Leon Wieseltier's *Kaddish*.[32] Wieseltier, literary editor at *The New Republic*, had left behind the Jewish faith of his childhood in early adulthood. When his father died in 1996, Wieseltier decided to follow the ritual of mourning as prescribed by Jewish faith despite the distance that he had gained from Judaism. It requires a son whose father has passed away to go three times a day to synagogue and to say the prayer of the bereaved, the Kaddish. Its text is a glorification of God, hailing and establishing his Lordship over the world that he has created. In itself, this is, of course, an emotionally complex experience to praise the God who, in a religious believer's view, rules over the world, and hence over life and death.

Wieseltier turned the year of mourning into a deep and sustained immersion into Jewish tradition, the writings of Jewish scholars and commentators of all ages about mourning, death, and faith. This journey elicits reactions from irritation to rapture and from rage to the yearning for faith in Wieseltier's soul. The book is not the documentation of a process of the return to the faith of his childhood and family. It is an attempt to link to the tradition of his ancestors, to connect to the culture that shaped Wieseltier, but it is not a tearful admission of his sins or a document that seeks resolution. At times, it is even humorous. Wieseltier ends up writing a text that in genre comes close to the Talmudic and interpretive texts of the Jewish tradition; and like these texts, it is a cascade of interpretive lines rather than a striving toward conclusions.

I have witnessed personal processes in which people went through a sustained dialogue with the culture of their upbringing in the last decades, even though they were not turned into literary documents; processes in which individuals chose to delve into the deep waters of *weltanschauung* without wanting either quick fixes or easy solutions. For many the investment in their intellectual development made a great difference. Their lives became more balanced and their self-esteem stabilized when they took up studies in humanistic disciplines like philosophy, the history of science, or the history of religion.

Alas, the examples are fewer than I would like, and certainly outnumbered by the uncountable instances of those who wasted precious time on half baked and hardly understood forms of pop spirituality. Nevertheless the examples of serious immersion are multiplying. I have met clients, friends, and acquaintances who at some point in their lives concluded that their intellectual resources in tackling ultimate existential concerns were insufficient and that they needed to invest more time and energy in thinking about basic issues.

Some of them came to question religious "truths" they had never truly thought through and entered an active dialogue with the philosophy of religion; they began to learn about their religions in depth and reached a more profound understanding of their history and structure. Others became enthralled by the beauties of current cosmological thought or evolutionary biology and began to see that science is not the enemy of the soul, but can help us see the world in richer and more rewarding ways. In all these journeys, a clarification and deepening of worldviews took place. And all those who were willing to embark on such a journey came to feel that they were less prone to crises of meaning than they had been before they had tackled the great existential question in depth.

Reinstating the Value of Intellectual Pursuit

I believe that most members of the global creative class have many resources to tackle these questions. While many of them may be afraid that they will be out of their depths if they want to read up on questions like "where is history headed?" or "is the European Enlightenment basically superior to other cultures?" they are bound to find out that with some effort they have all the intellectual tools required to tackle these issues.

I am saying this on the basis of long experience. For years I have made it a point to give interdisciplinary courses on topics like "evolutionary perspectives on religion," "Is there a war of ideas, and is the West losing it?" "philosophical and psychological perspectives on the Middle Eastern conflict," or "What is nonreligious Jewish identity?" to students who had no particular preparation for such questions.

After providing the students with some background on positions that are held on these issues, I let them plunge into the writings of the leading scholars on these issues. Time and again students of psychology, economics, biology, brain science, or literature who had never taken a class in history, political philosophy, or the history of religion have given first-rate presentations on their readings that generate spirited classroom discussion.

I always leave some room in these classes for students in their thirties, forties, and fifties who have decided to return to university to widen their horizons. The result is invariably positive: while it sometimes takes them a bit longer to regain the habit of reading texts in unfamiliar disciplines, they soon join the class discussion, and many of them make fruitful use of their experience in business, law, medicine, and other professions in their contributions.

I am often moved by the quality of the papers turned in by students who have no formal background in the course's topic. They show the extent to which intellectual investment in sustained reading, inquiry, and discussion can open minds and prepare them for careful and spirited analysis of large-scale questions. Of course such a course will not turn anybody into a specialist on the intricate topic of the evolutionary psychology and anthropology of religion, the philosophy of history, or the Middle Eastern conflict. But such investment certainly provides the tools to make up minds on these intricate issues in ways that go way beyond the knee-jerk reactions of those who are convinced liberals or conservatives, secularists, or religious believers without having invested careful thought in these issues.

Even during the long reign of anti-intellectualism, leading thinkers have generated important thought on the nature of liberal education. One of the best texts known to me on the topic is Martha Nussbaum's *Cultivating Humanity*.[33] Nussbaum is a philosopher and classical scholar of breathtaking breadth and depth of knowledge. Her work on classical Greek philosophy and Greco-Roman stoicism has established her as a leading authority in these fields, and she has also contributed first-rate work on political and legal philosophy.

Cultivating Humanity is an astonishing feat. Nussbaum shows how the Socratic ideal of the examined life and the Stoic idea of world citizenship can be applied to the present. While Nussbaum's academic grounding is in Western culture, she is also a staunch defender of the ideal that to be a fully rounded human being you need knowledge of at least one culture very different from your own.

Nussbaum makes a very strong case for the relevance and applicability of the classical ideal of liberal education—that is, an education that is geared primarily at providing humans with the tools to have truly free, educated, and informed minds. This idea originated in classical Greece, was deeply rooted in ancient Rome, and was revived during the European Renaissance. It received its modern form through Wilhelm von Humboldt, a philosopher and linguist who served as minister of education in Prussia in the early nineteenth century. He formulated the idea of the modern research university, in which those who teach are also researchers, the model along which all major universities today are structured. A staunch defender of liberalism, he believed that the modern university should provide the formation of rounded personalities who could be truly free citizens, besides advancement of knowledge.

While the classical forms of liberal education were geared toward a very small elite of free citizens who had the intellectual and material resources for such an education, Nussbaum shows that it is perfectly applicable to modern democracies. Her writing exemplifies this convincingly. While she draws her ideas from an immense store of knowledge ranging from Greek and Roman philosophy through gender studies to political philosophy, *Cultivating Humanity* is a book that anyone with a good college education can read without any problems. The only effort required is to follow a complex argument that is lucidly presented and enlivened by Nussbaum's extensive experience in researching various such university programs.

The Idea of Liberal Education

Nussbaum's conception touches on one of the most contentious issues of the last decades about the nature of higher education. For many years there has been a heated debate between liberals and conservatives about what universities should teach. Should they help students escape the Platonic cave or should they primarily dismantle the West's claims to superiority and show that the Western canon is nothing but a collection of "dead white males"? Nussbaum skillfully avoids the Scylla of arguing that the Western tradition is superior to all others and the Charybdis of the tyranny of political correctness.

Yet I think that the whole framing of the discussion as a debate between liberals and conservatives has obscured the real issue. Along with distinctly liberal thinkers like Daniel Bell,[34] Alain Finkielkraut,[35] Bernard-Henry Lévy,[36] and Benjamin Barber,[37] I believe there is no intrinsic connection whatsoever between the ideal of escaping the Platonic Cave and political conservatism. I want to make this case by having a closer look at the bête noire (black beast) of many liberals: Leo Strauss (1899–1973). Here is a somewhat caricaturist, but adequate, rendering of the picture you might get from newspapers and magazines about this dangerous man and his influence.

Leo Strauss was a German-Jewish émigré professor of political philosophy at the University of Chicago. He thought that democracy is untenable, and that elites need to fool the masses and run the country and the world according to their superior insight, like the philosopher-king described by Plato. He had many students who founded the neoconservative school of thought. Most of these are Jewish, and during the 1990s created what would become the blueprint of the foreign policy of George W. Bush. Some of them, particularly Paul Wolfowitz, Richard Perle, and Elliot Abrams rose into influential positions in the ranks of the Bush administration. They made Bush mislead the American people about Iraq and follow a policy that suited the interests of Israel rather that of the American people.

This caricature is the background to a recent wave of books that have been written about Leo Strauss in the United States. Most of these books are intended to set the record straight.[38] Strauss is often painted as a cynical Machiavellian who believes in manipulating the masses who cannot be trusted to know the truth, a portrait based primarily on confusion. A number of pundits and advisors linked to the Bush administration indeed had some, mostly rather fleeting association with Strauss. But the policies of George W. Bush have nothing to do with Strauss's thought as Francis Fukuyama has argued forcefully.[39] Strauss never believed in American exceptionalism or in the view that America should unilaterally rule the world. In fact he hardly ever took a stance on current affairs.

Strauss was neither an enemy of liberal democracy nor a believer in manipulating the masses by feeding them lies. But he did see great dangers in the machinations and mechanisms of mass democracy: "We are not permitted to be flatterers of democracy precisely because we are friends and allies of democracy . . . we are not permitted to remain silent on the dangers to which democracy exposes itself as well as human excellence."[40]

So why has this reclusive, bespectacled philosophy professor who mostly wrote rather esoteric books on ancient and medieval philosophy become a symbol for everything that has been wrong in recent American policies? I believe that the deeper, more interesting reason is that Strauss is associated with one of the most popular curses in current political discourse: *elitism*.

The United States, the world's most powerful nation, has been ruled for eight years by a man who made skillful use of attacking elites by presenting himself as an affable man of the people (never mind that George W. Bush comes from a wealthy family and carries degrees from Yale and Harvard), thus defeating Al Gore and John Kerry, whose style seemed elitist and uncommunicative even though their political platform was far more attuned to the needs of all but the richest.

The demonizing of elites and the self-presentation of candidates as populist is a political vice that is as widespread as democracy. Deep and searching thought about the nature of the body politic and the common good has been replaced by strategies and tactics devised by advisors paid to manipulate the electorate's feelings.

Strauss was far removed from politics as it is practiced today, where political advisors make their clients mindlessly repeat the slogans that research has shown to play the electorate's emotions effectively, and coach them in coming across affably on television. Politics as we see it in our daily lives is exactly the danger "to which democracy exposes itself as well as human excellence."

What is Strauss's modicum for the dismal state of mass democracy as we see it on television? "Liberal education is the ladder by which we try to ascend from mass democracy to democracy as originally meant. Liberal education is the necessary attempt to found an aristocracy within democratic mass society. Liberal education reminds those members of a mass democracy who have ears to hear, of human greatness."[41]

In the current era of political correctness a sentence like this can easily evoke fury. The very use of the term "aristocracy" can easily be misunderstood as a call to keep political power in the hands of a few advantaged people who have connections and whose money allows them to pay for higher education.

Again, nothing could be further from the truth: Strauss himself came from a lower-middle-class family. In Berlin he taught at the Freies Jüdisches Lehrhaus, an institution for adult education; until he was appointed professor at the University of Chicago in his late forties, he could hardly make ends meet. Throughout his life, Strauss's enduring love was the study of the great texts of the history of philosophy, and he thought that there was nothing that could ennoble the mind more than this experience.

Strauss writes, "Liberal education, which consists in the constant intercourse with the greatest minds, is a training in the highest form of modesty, not to say of humility . . . It demands from us the boldness implied in the resolve to regard the accepted views as mere opinions, or to regard the average opinions as extreme opinions which are at least as likely to be wrong as the most strange or the least popular opinions. Liberal education is liberation from vulgarity."[42]

Here again Strauss says something that can evoke outcries of rage in our era of political correctness. Who is he to call anyone or anything vulgar? So let's clarify what is at issue. Strauss's best-known student, Allan Bloom, loved watching basketball. One of the great pleasures of watching team sports is that we can give free reign to a tendency deeply engrained in our genetic makeup: to love our kin and hate all others. We enjoy that we do not need to refine our feelings and thoughts, that we can curse our adversaries and be as one-sided as our animal nature pushes us to be.

The same Allan Bloom, who enjoyed cursing the opponents of the Chicago Bulls, joined Strauss's demand that we strive for aristocracy of mind, which is a matter neither of birth nor of connections, in his bestselling *The Closing of the American Mind*. It is something we need to work on every day, a discipline of thought and feeling even though we can allow ourselves the respite of being carried away by the primitive edge of emotions at harmless occasions like watching sports.

This discipline, rather the creation of an oligarchy of power, is what Strauss wants liberal education to achieve. He strives for an aristocracy of mind that provides individuals with the inner strength and stamina not to be carried away by opinions just because they are popular.

Strauss's paradigm for such thinking is, of course, the Platonic rendering of Socrates, who accepted no opinion, however entrenched and popular, at

face value. Socrates, who was poor, spent his life questioning such opinion endlessly, trying to get Athenian citizens to break the spell of popular
mindlessness and to liberate them for clear and unimpeded thought. The
Athenian polis would finally put Socrates to death for this quest, a fate that
shows how much hatred independent thought can generate.

Strauss was painfully aware that in mass democracies, deep and differentiated thought was unlikely to prevail in political processes. Born in Germany in 1899 into a religious Jewish family, he saw with his very eyes how
the Weimar Republic democratically brought the Nazis to power. He had
seen how anti-Semitism poisoned the minds of the German electorate to
the point of electing the author of *Mein Kampf.*

But he never gave up on the hope that immersing ourselves in the greatest philosophical texts might inoculate human minds from the tendency
to be swept away by grandiose and yet false beliefs. "Wisdom cannot be
separated from moderation and hence to understand that wisdom requires
unhesitating loyalty to a decent constitution and even to the cause of con-
stitutionalism. Moderation will protect us against the twin dangers of
visionary expectations of politics and unmanly contempt for politics. Thus
it may again become true that all liberally educated men will be politically
moderate men."[43]

How far is this call toward humility, careful thought, and moderation
separated from the stereotype of the cynical manipulator of the masses! So
why does Strauss's call to "found an aristocracy in mass democracy" sound
so ominous to many?

It is, I believe, a basic hatred of thought; hatred of the idea that to be
wise, our minds need training, and our souls need the strength to contain
conflict and take into account complexity; that all of us at moments do not
live up to the ideal of being truly free minds who think clearly and that our
opinions may be wrong-headed and simplistic.

Liberal education in Strauss's sense tries to act against the rule of our
lower passions. It calls on us to choose our leaders wisely. And wise choices
require overcoming the tendency toward simplistic emotional reaction and
siding with whom we like just because he or she is like us. It is, in other
words, very different from what Bush consistently addressed as "folksy"
and John McCain's gamble of choosing Sarah Palin as his running mate
in the 2008 elections. Strauss calls on a responsibility of thought that goes
against the grain of populist politics as we see it nowadays.

I have many disagreements with Strauss; in particular I believe he
greatly underestimated the importance of empirical science in the formation of critical minds. If he had followed Plato's injunction, he would have
come to the conclusion that without knowledge of the natural sciences,
we are stuck in the cave of illusion. In addition he would have said that to

hone political judgment, we need to be factually informed about the subject matter of politics. For this we must have historical, economical, and sociological knowledge.

More importantly, I believe that Strauss's argument that, since our lives are short, we should focus exclusively on our own, in this case Western, culture, is harmful. Martha Nussbaum's conception of liberal education toward world citizenship requires the study of at least one culture other than our own, and her argument has been powerfully corroborated by other scholars who have investigated the topic.[44]

I do therefore not share his belief that reading classical texts is the only way to engender aristocracy of mind, even if the experience can, indeed, have a lasting impact. Despite my reservations about aspects of his views, Strauss's call to maintain the idea of liberal education and striving toward independence (what he calls aristocracy) of mind to me seems both timely and urgent.

Twenty-five years of teaching at universities have convinced me that aristocracy of mind in Strauss's sense can be achieved by students from all venues and socioeconomic backgrounds. Aristocracy of mind has nothing to do with birth, but it does have a lot to do with the spirit in which students are taught.

In today's discussions about higher education only two questions seem to matter: how many students are accepted and how much they should pay. If academic institutions are seen as nothing but providers of degrees that allow entry to professions, they cannot produce aristocracy of mind, no matter how high the tuition. And academic institutions are under great political and popular pressure to become mass producers of degrees.[45]

The modern university is one of the great creations of humanity. The structure was conceived of in the early nineteenth century in Germany. Its guiding idea is that an education for freedom of mind must do more than impart knowledge, even though knowledge is a sine qua non. Students must experience how knowledge is generated. This was the reason that the modern research university needed to combine research and teaching. Professors are not supposed to be only involved in transmitting knowledge, but they should be actively involved in the search for truth, and students need to participate in this experience.

Karl Jaspers reformulated this ideal movingly in his *The Idea of the University*, which he published in 1946. He had been asked by the Allied Powers to assist in rebuilding the German university system that had been harmed enormously during the Third Reich. Jaspers's emphasis was on the integration of students into the community of those who search for truth. He believed that it was this community and its endless striving for objectivity that should form the character of the students—and as we saw in

Chapter 6, he embodied this ideal of striving for lucidity in both his life and his work.

Jaspers's formulation of the idea of the university seems quaintly out of touch with contemporary reality. Universities, like companies, brands, and indeed individuals, are under relentless pressure to rise in ranking systems and to produce results that make them attractive for donors and businesses that want to cooperate with them.[46] Hence they are supposed to produce knowledge of immediate usefulness and to prepare students for entry into lucrative professions.

Our societies need to stand up to this pressure. We see the price of citizenry unschooled in the basics of sound political thinking daily through the sad spectacle of sound-bite politics on television, which has turned into an entertainment spectacle rather than a deliberation about the public good.[47] The replacement of such deliberation by the arena of television showdowns extracts a terrible price in the form of policies based on fear and hatred rather than on lucid thought.[48] This price tag is rising in a world that needs to deal with the great complexity of clashes between worldviews and between religion and secularism.

8

Religion and Science

Civilized Disdain and Epicurean Laughter

The single problem that has led Homo globalis to shy away from the investigation of its worldviews more than any other is the thorny problem of the tensions between religion, secularism, and science. The rude awakening described in the previous chapter and the realization that religions can lead to a type of intransigence, which only allows for fighting, has led many of us to think that dialogue between religion and science is impossible.

From a global point of view, the great religions are still by far the most important meaning systems. Recent studies converge on the estimate that around 85 percent of the world's population are religious. The largest group, comprising around two billion believers, is Christianity, followed by Islam (approximately 1.5 billion), Hinduism (approximately 900 million), and Buddhism (approximately 375 million). These four religions alone account for more than 70 percent of the world population.[1]

Atheists and agnostics account for about 12 to 15 percent, but this is a problematic estimate because it is difficult to get data about the real situation in China; the actual number may be smaller. Only Europe has a well-documented substantial proportion of agnostics and atheists.[2]

From the point of view of existential psychology, it is not surprising that religion has remained so enormously powerful. Given that defending against death anxiety is, psychologically speaking, the most important function of worldviews, religion has a huge advantage on secular meaning-systems. Most religions, particularly the great monotheistic religions, promise the believer that our individual, physical death is not truly our end: we will survive one way or another. Others like Hinduism and Buddhism have a more complex relation to individual death, for example, through belief in reincarnation. Religions are, in any case, the most effi-cient forms of the denial of death.

Existential psychology provides a strong rationale for the assumption that the European Enlightenment's prediction during the nineteenth cen-tury that the rule of religion would one day be replaced by secular ideolo-gies based on science is unlikely to come true. The human need to deny death is too powerful. And the likelihood that humans will continue to be willing to kill for their beliefs to protect them is high, especially if they are threatened.

This was one of the deepest reasons for the recent retreat into the rela-tivism of political correctness. The ideology of political correctness stated that the only civilized way of coexistence was to respect other peoples' beliefs, just because they are held by someone. The hope behind this ideol-ogy was that if we would just be nice and respectful to each other, we would somehow be able to coexist in the same polity.

This ideology failed because it was a profoundly inauthentic prescrip-tion: it is humanly impossible to genuinely respect beliefs no matter how irrational, immoral, or absurd. The resulting culture was emotionally fro-zen and often did not lead to fruitful discussion between worldviews in general, and between secularism and religion in particular.

This chapter argues for civilized disdain, an alternative to political cor-rectness that is more authentic and more attuned to what we really feel toward worldviews that we do not approve of on moral or intellectual grounds. The difference between civilized disdain and political correctness is that the former allows one to feel disdain for a person's or group's views or beliefs while maintaining respect for the human beings that hold them. In my experience of political argument and effort to create practical com-mon ground with Jewish ultraorthodoxy and adherents of political Islam, civilized disdain has turned out to be surprisingly productive in creating human bonds of lasting value. The mental discipline required for civilized disdain may be crucial for the type of world citizenship that will allow fruitful cooperation across ideological divides.

The Four Apocalyptic Riders: Atheism Strikes Back

Secularists, for a long time, felt that the principle of political correctness required shutting up and at least pretending to respect religious beliefs. Two factors changed this in the last decade: the first was the attack on sci-ence, particularly evolutionary theory, by Christian fundamentalists in the United States. It became clear that an influence of religion on science and on scientific education was a real possibility, particularly through the attempts to introduce intelligent design theory into high school curricula. The second was the jihad declared on the West by radical Islam. This had started much earlier, as the fatwa against Salman Rushdie in 1989 shows, but at the time most of the West had meekly tried to appease radical Islam rather than fighting it. The combination of the attacks on science and modernity by Christian and Islamic fundamentalism[3] has finally brought many Western intellectuals to the point of realizing that the time has come for Western culture and secularism to defend itself.

This has generated a series of books of varying quality that espouse rationalism and science, attacking religion upfront by a quartet, which the anthropologist Scott Atran has humorously called, the "four apocalyptic riders."[4] Sam Harris fired the opening salvo with *The End of Faith*, a courageous, if not always, carefully argued critique of religion and its role in world affairs.[5] Philosopher Daniel Dennett[6] followed suit with *Breaking the Spell*, a forceful critique of religion combined with an explanation of its power based on evolutionary psychology. Dawkins published *The God Delusion* in 2006, a work that has the virtue of great clarity and accessibility. Journalist and writer Christopher Hitchens's *God Is Not Great: How Religion Poisons Everything*[7] added his spirited, if unsystematic, voice to the quartet. These four apocalyptic riders have been joined by French philosopher Michel Onfray with his *The Atheist Manifesto*.[8]

These books vary widely in tone and approach: Harris tries to show how religion is bad and how noxious is its impact on human affairs. His *The End of Faith* is angry and aggressive. Dennett tries to explain the evolutionary foundations of religion and to show in detail why religion does not make humans more moral. Dawkins's book, which reached by far the largest audience, is less disdainful than Dennett's, is more motivated by a deep sense of outrage at the cruelty and injustice of crippling children's minds, and attempts to show that scientific thought is by far the highest achievement of the human species. Hitchens, as is his habit, pulls no punches, takes no prisoners, and pays no dues to political correctness. His book is an unsystematic and verbally brilliant salvo of condemnations of religion that does not follow any logical thread. Onfray's book is more philosophical in nature and primarily makes a sustained argument for a humanism clean of all vestiges of religion.

Richard Dawkins's *The God Delusion*[9] has by far achieved the greatest prominence, mostly because of its author's eminence and well-deserved fame for having reformulated the basic tenets of Darwinian evolutionary biology[10] and making it accessible to the wider educated public. It has sold more than 1.5 million copies to date and been translated into 35 languages. Dawkins had long been a very outspoken critic of creationism, pseudoscience, and attempts by religious groups to disqualify evolution.[11] But in *The*

God Delusion Dawkins goes one step further and mounts a full-fledged attack on religion as such.

The God Delusion is not ecumenist in spirit: Dawkins does not allow for any compromise between religion and science. He is intransigent in that he does not attempt to find bridges between religion and science by trying to interpret religious texts in the spirit of modern morality or drop those parts of the religious canon that are offensive to modern sensibilities (e.g., the Old Testament injunction to kill all the tribes that do not believe in the biblical God) and show that other parts are consistent with currently accepted moral precepts.[12]

He goes all the way by arguing that religion is bad. Period. He expresses outrage at religious education, the irrational fears it implants in the minds of children, deforming them, often for life. Using evolutionary psychology, he argues that religion abuses a trait of the infantile mind that has great evolutionary importance: children's credulity. This credulity is important so children will follow adult precepts that will save their lives (e.g., "*Never* come close to a lion because it will eat you!" or "Never put your fingers into electric sockets because you will be electrocuted!"). But religious education abuses this trait by inculcating fears of eternal damnation, hell, or eternal torture for "sins" like questioning God's existence, questioning the validity of the Bible, or masturbating.

For Dawkins there is absolutely nothing to recommend about religion. It does not make people more moral nor does it create more openness for the suffering of others. Dawkins presents us with a choice: either we take the road of modern science and the Enlightenment or we become mired forever in irrationality, inhumanity, and impediments for free and rational inquiry into the world and the flourishing of human nature.[13]

Ridiculing Religion Is a Self-Defeating Strategy

I have been an admirer of Richard Dawkins's work since I first read *The Selfish Gene*[14] some 25 years ago. His now canonical reformulation of the tenets of Darwinian thought, the enormous lucidity of his thinking, and his ability to present highly complex arguments accessibly are exemplary for the spirit of science and Enlightenment values.

Yet I have been bothered by an inconsistency in his approach, particularly in the years since his *The God Delusion*. In this book he basically tries to demonstrate (a) that arguments for God's existence and the truth of sacred texts of the various monotheistic traditions are invalid, (b) that arguments that religion makes people more moral are fallacious, and

(c) that religious education is largely noxious and mostly prevents human beings who have been subjected to it from becoming truly free thinkers.

I happen to agree with him on all three points, but I wonder what he is trying to achieve. He has recently said that he hopes to convince religious people who haven't given the issue much thought by ridiculing their religious beliefs, which he thinks might be a useful way to win them over the scientific worldview.

Given his deep commitment to science, it somewhat surprises me that in formulating this strategy of ridicule and frontal attack he does not take into account scientific knowledge about the functioning of the human mind. The findings of existential psychology are pertinent to the question of how to deal with the conflict between science and religion. As we have seen when people's belief systems are attacked, the result is inevitably that they dig more deeply into the trenches of their worldview. Even if you agree with Dawkins, Dennett, and Hitchens that liberalism should no longer tolerate attacks while being sensitive toward the feelings of the religiously inclined; no rational person can expect that their polemic will convince the religious to leave their creed, certainly not after the data produced by existential psychology. The statistics about the prevalence of religious belief worldwide and the findings of existential psychology make it very unlikely that religion will disappear from the human landscape. The instinctive terror of death, which we all need to defend against, requires the worldview defense, which we have encountered in this book time and again.

If we look at religions from a Darwinian point of view, they are memes, cultural units that compete for the minds of individuals and groups. Their adaptive advantage is enormous, because most major religions simply deny death of the individual quite literally and promise their believers eternal life of some sort (ranging from survival of the soul to the promise of physical resurrection in a number of religious creeds). Memes, as we saw, spread neither as a function of their intrinsic truth value nor for their contribution to humanity's well-being but as a function of their catchiness and the extent to which they serve psychological needs like consolation.

This is exactly what has happened in the last decades: the more Western secular culture impacted traditional forms of life in all three Abrahamic religions, the more they moved toward fundamentalist versions that vehemently attacked science and Western liberalism as decadent and corrupting. If Dawkins's theory were right, the technological superiority of the scientific worldview should have made them feel ridiculous, and hence they should have given up on their belief systems. But the opposite happened: from Wahabists' insistence on purifying Islam from Western influence to the frontal attack on evolutionary theory by the American religious Right, the fundamentalist backlash has been rather disheartening.

Equally dismaying was the timid way in which secularism, both in Europe and the United States, tried to appease religious attacks ranging from Ruholla Khomeini's fatwa against Salman Rushdie to stopping funding of stem-cell research by the Bush administration. Such appeasement only encouraged further attacks.

Within this context there was great value of the four apocalyptic riders' salvos against religion and the fiery insistence of philosophers like Bernard-Henri Lévi[15] and Alain Finkielkraut[16] that the Western tradition of freedom of thought needs to be defended.

But let us not delude ourselves: the value of these books is to raise the spirits of liberal atheists who had been made to feel that they had no right to fight for their views. These spirited counterattacks certainly succeeded in reestablishing some esprit de corps of those committed to Enlightenment values and the scientific worldview. But the primary effect of such aggressive rhetoric is primarily to rally our side. We should not think that all-out attacks on religion will convert *anybody*. The scientific evidence shows that the opposite is likely to be true. Hence the frontal attack on religion may have the positive effect of lifting the spirits of secularists who have felt on the defensive for years, but it certainly is not a fruitful strategy to solve the world's problems, as they will only reach the converted at best and outrage those criticized at worst.

I am in no way arguing for a return to the timid and politically correct tactic of seemingly paying respect to views that are irrational, morally repugnant, or both. But I believe that it is of crucial importance to get religious communities, particularly in third world countries, to accept scientific precepts on global problems ranging from the population explosion to the epidemic spread of HIV. In so doing we will have to find ways to convince religious leaders to endorse scientifically established methods of dealing with these issues. The strategy of ridiculing religious belief is very unlikely to achieve this and may only increase resistance to science where it is most sorely needed.

Hence, along with anthropologist Scott Atran,[17] I believe that the secular humanists among us will have to ask the question how science and democracy can not only achieve some form of status quo with religion but also find ways of crossing the chasms that have made communication so difficult, particularly in the last decades.

From Political Correctness to Civilized Disdain

But before thinking about the common ground, the emotional truth of the divide must be addressed. I simply do not believe that genuine respect for views that we consider to be irrational, immoral, or plain stupid is a human possibility. I believe that the obsessive attempt to empty discourse of anything that might hurt anybody's feelings is a strategy doomed to failure. Political correctness often hides unacknowledged aggression and disdain that belies its saccharin-flavored tone. Such disdain needs to be acknowledged, expressed, and faced squarely—and yet we must find ways of living together in the same polity with individuals and groups whose views we do *not* respect.

The prerogative religious believers have recently taken to react to any perceived lack of respect for their beliefs with often exorbitant violence has led the four apocalyptic riders to argue that religion "poisons everything." "Why indeed should we atheists have to respect the feelings of people who have absurd beliefs, and why should the world have to suffer because fanatics are willing to kill and die for a few square kilometers in the Old City of Jerusalem?" the argument runs. If you use a sufficiently narrow lens, religion indeed seems to be the one, huge problem of humanity.

In a nutshell my claim is that the new knights of the Enlightenment are both right and wrong. They are right in that the Enlightenment value of universal criticism at its best can be a safeguard against fanaticism; however, they are wrong in thinking that the problem is uniquely with religion because they disregard the whole history of the twentieth century. After all, the worst crimes against humanity were perpetrated in the name of secular ideologies by Adolf Hitler, Joseph Stalin, Pol Pot, and so on. Going back a bit further we may remember that even the values of *liberté, egalité, fraternité* were used to justify systematic terror (the term gained its notoriety from Maximilien Robespierre).

The real problem is not religion but our human nature: we tend to be very attached to the belief systems and worldviews that provide us with meaning, and we are willing to go to great lengths to defend them. This human tendency can become lethal by virtue of a simple fact of logic: the very existence of competing worldviews constitutes a threat for any belief system that claims unique validity.

How do humans deal with this? Mostly by arguing that our own belief system (Islam, Communism, free market fundamentalism, dianetics) is greatly superior to all others. If that doesn't work, we resort to violence. The biblical injunction to kill the Canaanite tribes that did not believe in Israel's deity Yahweh is the archetypal solution: just wipe out anybody who offends my beliefs by not sharing them. But we shouldn't forget that the Jacobins dealt with "counterrevolutionaries" in the same way by making the guillotine (an enlightened, humane way to kill people) work overtime.

My point is that no belief system is immune from the dangers inherent to the human propensity to violent worldview defense, as history from the inquisition to the Gulags sadly shows.

"But that isn't true for Enlightenment values!" is the counterargument of Dawkins, Hitchens, Dennett, and others. I admit that I have a weakness for this position, because I, too, think that the Enlightenment has created an idea of immense importance: no human belief is above criticism, no authority is infallible, and no worldview can claim ultimate validity. Hence unbridled fanaticism is the ultimate human vice responsible for more human-made suffering than any other.

Yet there is a catch: it doesn't take much philosophical sophistication to realize that if this argument applies to all belief systems, it applies to the ideas of the Enlightenment, too. They should not be above criticism either. History shows that Enlightenment values can indeed be perverted into fanatical belief systems. Just think of the "Dr. Strangeloves" of past U.S. administrations who were willing to wipe humanity off the face of the earth in the name of freedom, and the—less dramatic but no less dismaying—tendency of Dick Cheney and Donald Rumsfeld of the Bush administration to trample human rights in the name of democracy.

Are Enlightenment values no better than any others then? I do have a suggestion to the contrary that is borne out by the fact that Enlightenment movements emerged several times in history: in India in the seventh century BCE, Greece in the fifth and fourth centuries BCE, Islam in the ninth century, and then in Europe in the seventeenth century.

The saving grace of all of these Enlightenment movements was to realize that the tribal inheritance that pushes humans to think their belief system is unique is dangerous and irrational. At its best, enlightenment creates the capacity for irony and a sense of humor; it enables us to look at all human forms of life from a vantage point of solidarity: we all need meaning and we all need protection from the unbearable knowledge that we are mortal.

We should be able to marvel at the variety of collectively created fictions invented to provide meaning to human life rather than thundering at those we like least. Of course anti-theists and religious believers will continue to disdain each other's worldviews, which is fine as long as it doesn't turn into a matter of life and death. Civilized and cheerful disdain could provide a model for all ideologies—religious and secular—by replacing bilious self-righteousness with laughter; and it could make us see human history as something more akin to a contest for best collective work of fiction than to a mortal clash of civilizations.

Tolerance and Toleration

Political philosopher Michael Walzer[18] has suggested an important differentiation between tolerance and toleration. Tolerance is full-fledged acceptance of a point of view, group, or ideology. Toleration is the state of affairs in which we say that we are willing to tolerate a point of view, religion, or political attitude even though we condemn it. Toleration demands nothing more from us than to feel that we can live with a certain form of life or worldview in our society, even though we find it primitive, immoral, and reprehensible. For example believing Christians, Jews, or Muslims may decide upon toleration of liberal atheists even though they think that they are depraved, devoid of moral values, and spiritually shallow. In contrast, atheist liberals may decide upon toleration of a group like ultraorthodox Jews or fundamentalist Muslims even though we strongly disapprove of their treatment of women as less than equal.

Let me make this concrete. Israeli documentarian Shosh Shlam has created a haunting documentary on the plight of ultraorthodox Jewish women, on which I advised.[19] These women are raised with the certainty that it is their sacred task to bear as many children as possible, often while at the same time making a living to support these children and their husbands, who are supposed to study the Torah and the Talmud throughout the day without investing a moment in materially supporting their family. While women's role in Jewish ultraorthodox society is idealized, it is clear that this physically, emotionally, and existentially draining mode of life (we are talking about women who often have their fourth child when they are in their early twenties and end up giving birth to up to 12 children) is really subservient and inferior to the husband's role of being a Talmudic scholar in the society that indoctrinates women to accept their plight as the way to serve God's will.[20]

Personally I am outraged by this mode of existence forced on women. Yet I feel that I cannot initiate any political or legal way of preventing it. As opposed to female genital mutilation, it is not forced physically on ultraorthodox Jewish women, but "only" the result of indoctrination. I would greatly prefer to live in a world where women are not subjected to such brainwashing and in which children can grow up with proper parental care (such families rely on older daughters taking care of their younger siblings, because their mothers are not able to directly raise so many children). Nevertheless the principle of toleration leads me to accept this practice as legal, even though I find it appalling.

I know that my way of life, with the intellectual, political, and personal liberties that define it, is disdained by ultraorthodox Jews. They think that I am devoid of real values, that freedom of thought is nothing but the royal road to moral depravity, and that secularism is responsible for the maladies of the world. Conversely, I disdain some aspects of their way of life. I feel that it is immoral to deprive their children of experiencing the impact of the best of science and philosophy. I believe that it is unacceptable that they live along the lines formulated by the Jesuit founder Ignatius of Loyola who said, "Give me a child until age seven, and I'll give you a faithful Christian" even though most of them have never heard of Ignatius of Loyola. I believe that this robs their children of the right to make up their minds and to value ideas, instilling fear instead.

How are we to live with this reality? The idea of a civilization of mutual disdain occurred to me more than a decade ago. For two years I was a constant member of the weekly political talk show on Israel's largest ultra-orthodox radio station. For many of the talk-show guests I was like a visitor from Mars. My hairstyle (i.e., clean shaved skull) is typical for secular liberals in Israel; so is the way I dress. The reason the station wanted me on the small team of constant participants was simple: on the one hand, I represented the political end of the spectrum farthest away from ultraorthodoxy. On the other hand, when things heated up too much, they could count on me to chip in jokes in Yiddish or make some other gesture that helped overcome often bitter animosity; often some guest who hadn't met me before would say something like "but you have a real Jewish soul! It can't be that you don't believe in God."

One night, in the midst of a heated debate, another participant said, "I am confused. You seem to understand us (the ultraorthodox world), but you don't really respect our views." Without much thinking I answered, "Tell me the truth. You have come to the conclusion that I'm actually a human being and maybe a nice guy, but you really feel deep disdain for what I stand for. You think I'm immoral, devoid of spirituality, a sensual materialist, and that the world is worse off because of people like me." He didn't confirm, but he didn't deny, either.

So I continued, "You see, it's the same thing for me. I think you're a great guy, but I feel deep aversion for everything you stand for. Just take the fact that this show will never have a woman, because you believe that women need to be kept out of the public eye. I think the way you raise your children is scandalous, because you prevent them from making up their minds about the most basic issues. You don't let them study science, philosophy, and literature, and you indoctrinate them instead. I also can't understand how a rational human being would actually believe what you do. Instead of faking mutual respect, why don't we settle for civilized disdain?"

This term, born on the spur of a moment, became a constant feature of the program. At crucial junctures it would be conjured by one of the participants. What made the program a hit was that we mostly managed to season the inevitable acrimony with humor and human warmth. The result was interesting: as I have many ultraorthodox relatives, who in turn have a lot of children who get married at a very early age, I quite often end up at weddings in Bnei Brak, one of the strongholds of Israel's ultraorthodoxy. At the time I was a bit apprehensive, wondering if my status as the representative of the "enemy" on the highest-rated talk show would create a problem. I was quite surprised when many of my relatives and acquaintances would tell me "we enjoy the program greatly. Even though you vent your anger toward us without mincing your words, there is always warmth there. We can live with that easily."

The idea of civilized disdain makes dialogue across chasms much deeper than those between atheists and ultraorthodox Jews possible. It allows communication across very deep divides indeed. For a number of years I have been a member of the Permanent Monitoring Panel on Terrorism of the World Federation of Scientists (WFS), a Swiss-based international body of researchers around the world that investigates global emergencies. After 9/11 the WFS decided that terrorism had become such an emergency and set up a permanent monitoring panel on the topic.

One of the members, Khurshid Ahmed, is a Pakistani Senator, a legal scholar, a specialist on Islamic Law, and a professor at the University of Islamabad. He is also one of the founders of Jamaat' Islamyie, one of the most radical Islamic groups in Pakistan, and spent long times in Pakistani prisons for his political activities. Pervez Hoodbhoy, another member, is professor and chairman of the Department of Physics at the same university. He was an outspoken critic of the Musharraf regime both for its undemocratic nature and because of its lenient approach to Islamic fundamentalists, including the Taliban and Jamaat' Islamyie.

In one of the sessions, Ahmed argued that no connection should be made between Islam per se and terrorism. In the corner of my eye I noticed that Hoodbhoy became more and more agitated until he burst out, "How can you say this? Students associated with your party have destroyed the equipment of our musicology department, because musicology is un-Islamic; I have two female students who will be disfigured for the rest of their lives, because your people threw acid in their faces because they came to the university without their faces veiled? How can you say that Islam has no connection to terrorism?"

Khurshid and I have spent many hours together, sometimes arguing hotly debated questions, sometimes exchanging anecdotes, and at times joking (even though it is not easy to make Khurshid smile). I have no illusions about Khurshid's views about my atheist liberalism; he thinks it is shallow, devoid of spiritual depth, sinful, and depraved—even though he may like me as a person.

I deeply respect Khurshid as a human being and admire the unbeliev-able resilience he showed during periods of incarceration and torture, and his incredible intellect. Nevertheless I condemn his worldview without res-ervation. I assume that he has no illusions about my view of his extremist form of Islam and his endorsement of jihad. I think it is a dark, dangerous form of religious fanaticism that has already cost millions of lives, and that could, under certain circumstances, bring our world to the brink of total catastrophe, if Islamic terrorists indeed manage to lay their hands on a nuclear device.

I think that civilized disdain is a much more authentic way of dealing with deep differences than political correctness, with its emotional frozen-ness, which is the result of trying to inculcate feelings nobody genuinely feels, like universal respect for the beliefs and views of all humans. I offer it to my fellow Homo globalis as an alternative in the spirit of Voltaire, the immortal beacon of the European Enlightenment who supposedly told a Catholic cleric "I despise every word you utter—and I will give my last drop of blood for your right to express your views."

By speaking about civilized disdain I am not just arguing for more authenticity or claiming that anti-theists are entitled to their feelings as much as are religious people. The emphasis is no less on "civilized" than it is on "disdain." The history of religious strife and also of conflict between worldviews in general shows that it takes a lot of mental discipline to feel disdain while remaining civilized. The process of civilization, as Norbert Elias[21] has shown, is about the ability to interiorize processes and to keep the public space clean of physical and mental products that this sphere cannot contain without deterioration. To feel anger, hurt, and disdain without violence and to maintain communication with those whose views we do not respect and who do not respect ours are the basis for the type of world citizenship that has become a vital necessity in a globally intercon-nected world.

Judith: In Search of Desire

How real can communication across the divide of secularism and religion be? Is it indeed possible to have ongoing, close working relationships across such a deep divide? I hope that the following story will show how fruitful such dialogue can be.

Judith consulted me because she felt stuck in her professional develop-ment. She had done well for herself in most parameters of life. She was a senior partner in one of the largest international accounting firms.[22] She had gotten married early and raised four children; the youngest was about to finish college. She described her marriage as "fine," her family life as "warm," and her career as "successful." These characterizations seemed warranted by her descriptions. The problem? She found it progressively more difficult to get through her workdays. Nothing in what she did truly interested her—neither her clients nor the management of the firm in which she was actively involved.

At the beginning it was a bit difficult to have a fruitful dialogue. Judith was prim, well dressed (a bit on the conservative side), and her self-presentation focused on the fact that "basically everything is OK," which indeed it was. There were no indications of any acute suffering except for the boredom at work.

So we spoke about work. Judith felt that she had done well. She had been very invested in her children's upbringing and it was therefore quite a feat that she had managed to build a successful career. It was very interesting, though, to hear what she had to say about her choice of profession: "I can't really say that I chose to be an accountant. In a good Jewish family the choices were between law, medicine, and accounting. Medicine was impossible, because you can't raise a family and do an internship, and my hunch was that accounting would be less time-consuming, which turned out to be right."

Judith felt that I was a bit taken aback by the dryness of her description. "I'm sorry to tell you, but I've lived my life in a very practical manner. It will be difficult for you to find any wild fantasies in my psyche. I was raised with the idea that you needed to be able to account for your time, and the way to do so was to show you had been productive." She laughed. "Maybe it isn't so surprising that I became an accountant."

It had been Judith's belief that it was a bad idea to waste time and energies on dreams that could not be fulfilled anyway. She felt that this just complicated life unnecessarily. This did make it rather difficult to connect to any dreams she might have had about another career; she simply didn't have any.

In short, Judith was a classic case of the normotic personality described so well by Joyce McDougall and Christopher Bollas.[23] Her life had been about normality, living up to standards that she fully identified with, and efficiency in combining the demands of family, life, and career. I need to emphasize, though, that Judith by no means came across as inwardly dead or emotionally detached. The opposite was true. Her vitality was often contagious, and she was full of energy. But we still didn't know how to proceed; we were stuck.

The opening came from a most surprising angle. When I came into the consulting room with coffee, Judith was standing in front of my library.

She seemed very intently concentrated but her hands were clasped on her back as if to say, "I mustn't touch this."

"Anything grabbed your attention?" I asked. She said, "Yes; you have this book here *God: A Biography*. What is it about?" I described briefly Jack Miles's brilliant idea of approaching the figure of God in the Old Testament from a purely literary point of view as a character that evolves along the text, and then I asked her, "Why do you think this book in particular caught your eye?"

Judith began to talk about her relationship to religion. She had grown up in an orthodox Jewish family. Religion was not something that you questioned and theological issues were rarely discussed. The emphasis was rather on how Judaism prescribed a way of life. It was clear, though, that the divine origin of the Old Testament was to be accepted, as she said: "The one time my father addressed this issue it was within the context of explaining to me what Reform Judaism was and why he saw it as lethal for Judaism. "If you question that, my beloved daughter, everything falls apart."

Judith felt that she firmly believed in God, and he was basically a benevolent presence in her life. She did feel, though, that the painstaking attention of orthodox Judaism to details of commandments and prohibitions in daily life had been quite a bother for her for at least 15 years. "I can't really believe that God cares how long I wait between eating meat and milk. But that's what the Talmud says."

As long as her children were at home, she had not wanted to rock the boat, though. She had no idea how you could raise children as religious Jews if you started to question things like that. But anyway, even with her children gone, she didn't know how to go about even thinking about these issues.

I asked her whether she had ever read any of the vast literature on interpretations of Judaism. She said, "No; I know only that there are orthodox Jews and then there are all those who mount the slippery slope that is the end of Judaism, and I've never read any of those." I asked her whether she knew that there were orthodox Jewish thinkers who had formulated very interesting philosophies of Judaism like Franz Rosenzweig, Emanuel Levinas, and Yeshayahu Leibovitz. She said she had never taken an interest in this and then, surprisingly, said, "I think I would rather read the Jack Miles book. I think it's better to read *goyyim* (gentiles) than Jews if we're touching such dangerous stuff."

For a number of months our meetings looked a bit more like a private tutorial in the philosophy of religion than therapy. Jack Miles's book had an immediate impact on Judith. As Miles does not confront theological issues, but approaches the Bible from a purely literary point of view, Judith didn't feel that this was "dangerous stuff." She was rather struck by the character of God as it emerges from Miles's interpretation, and by the idea that this character changes through the various books of the Bible. She said, "If you look at it from outside, the God of Genesis and Deuteronomy isn't such a nice character. He really seems too concerned with whether he's accepted as a sole authority and God. Frankly, I don't really experience God that way; my God is rather concerned with whether we're doing well, and whether we need help and solace."

After some sessions in which we discussed her thoughts and feelings about what she was reading, we also discussed the subtext of our encounter. Judith knew from a newspaper interview that I had grown up in an orthodox family and she had noticed right away that I was quite familiar with the terminology of the yeshiva world. She asked me whether I had an agenda talking to her about the historicity of Judaism. "Wouldn't you love to turn me into an apikores as well?"

The term is of Talmudic origin. It serves to denote hedonistic, gluttonous unbelievers, and it is derived from the name of the Greek philosopher Epicurus (341–270 BCE). For orthodox Jews the connotation of apikores is distinctly negative, even though Judith used the term with a warm smile. She did not know it, but at the time I had, for some years, felt a deep affinity to Epicurean philosophy.

I couldn't help laughing. I told her that, at least consciously, I had no such wish. I thought, though, that it was very important that she tell me if she felt that I was pushing her in any particular direction, because I was not transparent to myself and might enact an agenda I was not conscious of.

There was one point on which I did put quite a bit of emphasis. Judith had asked herself about the discrepancies between the way some prohibitions were formulated in the biblical text and the Talmudic interpretation. The classical case was that the Bible prohibits cooking a goat in his mother's milk, whereas Jewish orthodox practice forbids eating any meat and milk in temporal proximity in general. Time and again I asked her what she thought about this. It seemed to me that she simply refused to truly think about the question, and preferred to block it out.

I told her that in this respect I *did* have an agenda. Judith was exceptionally intelligent and it seemed to me that she simply chose not to think at all when the issue of the historicity of Judaism came up.

Judith looked confused for a while and then said, "But once you start saying that Judaism has evolved historically, you don't know where you end!" "Do you actually think so?" I asked. Judith stopped, and a look of surprise filled her eyes. "I . . . I'm not sure. I mean, I've never really thought about it. Thinking about it, that's just what I was told. And anyway, you start with this historicity thing, and then end up an apikores like you."

I answered her, "I think I was not really the believing type to begin with. I had very little of a sense of God's presence. You talk to God on a personal basis, so to speak. What matters to me is that I feel you don't allow yourself to explore thoughts. I'm not invested in the result. My issue is not with what you'll end up believing. It's rather with the fact that you don't feel that your mind belongs to you."

Judith looked at me intently and replied, "Maybe. Don't forget that one of the basic principles of Judaism is first we will do as commanded and only then we'll understand (נעשה ונשמע). We don't trust the human mind; we believe in action and in a way of life."

I nodded. "Judith, I feel you've caught me here. I am aware of this principle and there is no doubt that I am guided by a very different principle. *Sapere aude*, 'dare to know,' as Immanuel Kant said in his famous article 'What is Enlightenment.' It is true that I am quite convinced that human beings cannot develop fully if they don't take responsibility for their minds, and I also believe that taking such responsibility entails not to shy away from knowledge like textual criticism of the Bible and evolutionary theory. It is your choice whether you accept this principle of mine or not."

It was quite clear that Judith indeed needed to make a choice. Freedom of the mind is not a religious principle; it is a principle of various Enlightenment movements from India through Greece to eighteenth-century Europe, and this principle historically and philosophically clashes with the principle of the superiority of faith.

Judith made her choice through her course of action. Not only did she continue to read, but after a while she followed my suggestion and joined study groups of orthodox Jews who were reading texts by Emanuel Levinas, the famed French-Lithuanian philosopher. She convinced her husband to join her, and soon she became quite active in organizing study groups of this sort herself.

After about a year in which she was quite invested in this, something in Judith loosened up, and she entered a process through which it became clear to her what in her work did not interest her. She has since joined a venture capital fund and feels that she has found a new career that satisfies her. Toward the end of our consultations she said, "If you had told me that reading philosophy would become the opening through which I became capable of finding a new career, I would have laughed at you."

Judith was by no means a fanatic or narrow in her emotional life. She was warm, vital, and full of feeling. Nevertheless she had difficulty in knowing her deeper desires, because she had grown up to fear them and to think that listening to desires was likely to rock the boat too much and make life difficult. Entering into a dialogue with the prohibitions against free thought she had internalized in childhood helped Judith to reconnect to her desires.

She did not leave the faith in which she was brought up and has remained an orthodox Jew. Her relation to her faith did change, though. If before the analytic journey she felt that she was not allowed to think freely about the most basic questions of the philosophy of religion, she no longer feels that she needs to protect herself against knowledge that could have any impact on her faith. Not only does she freely read orthodox Jewish philosophers, but she has developed an interest in general philosophy because she came to the conclusion that she could not truly understand twentieth-century Jewish philosophy of religion without this background.

Judith certainly hasn't become an apikores, she still believes that there is a God and that he is in some way connected to the Jewish tradition that she cherishes and feels attached to. But she no longer closes herself off from other ways of thinking, whether secular or religious. In fact she has also developed some interest in the history of religion in general, and she now feels that there are affinities between religious traditions, and she sometimes speaks of the unity of religious experience.

Toward the end of our journey we would often joke about our differences. She would sometimes say, half seriously and half jokingly, that I would forever be limited because of my lack of religious feeling, and I countered by saying that it was such a pity that she would never know full freedom of thought and how wonderful a universe without gods could be.

But there was no enmity in these exchanges. Neither of us felt threatened by the differences between us. I feel that something essential to Judith would have been lost if she had left religion. A certain aspect of Jewish *menshlichkeit* (the Yiddish expression for humaneness with a specifically Jewish tinge) to me seems essential to her in the same way as being Muslim seems to me an essential characteristic of a Pakistani friend of mine.

Epicureanism and Evolutionary Psychology of Religion

Judith was by no means my first client with whom religious issues played a role, and I was keenly aware of the major source of potential conflict in this constellation. One of my most deeply held assumptions about human life is that without freedom of thought humans cannot fully evolve. Our brains have been hardwired to seek knowledge, and if humans are actively prohibited from using knowledge and information (whether by external or internalized) authority, they cannot fully develop.

Judith had called me an apikores at several stages of our encounter. Epicureanism is generally associated with the unbridled search for pleasure.

The term "hedonism" is also understood basically as a gluttonous conception of life. This is often mistakenly associated with Epicurus, whose goal was to liberate humankind from irrational fears, including fear of the gods.

In this he was one of Freud's great predecessors. A substantial part of Freud's work is an attempt to provide an account of the psychological roots of religion. His approach was basically evolutionary even though this is rarely addressed nowadays.[24] It is a generally neglected aspect of Freud's work that he sought to formulate the phylogenetic origins of the superego.[25] His explanation is not relevant nowadays because Freud was Lamarckian, an explanatory frame of reference long since rejected by the scientific community.

Contemporary evolutionary psychology, in many ways, has rehabilitated Freud's evolutionary program on a Darwinist basis. The recent decade has brought some very interesting attempts to formulate the phylogenetic basis of religion.[26] The evolutionary psychology of religion, based on a wealth of anthropological and experimental data, is based on two major findings.[27] One is that we humans are hardwired to overdetect intentional agents. We see a shadow in the woods and tend to overinterpret it as either animal or human. This is often called the "hyperactive agent detector device" or HADD, because it leads to many false positives. The reason the hardwired HADD was advantageous in an evolutionary sense is simple: under jungle conditions, false positives are better than false negatives because they alert us to the possibility of dangerous predators, and a single false negative can be lethal.

The HADD leads to our tendency to overuse intentional explanations for natural events. Thunders are expressions of Zeus's wrath, droughts occur because of Demeter's grief, and the Temple in Jerusalem was burned because God punishes the Jewish people for its sins. In other words, our brain is biologically programmed not for science but for religion.

A second major reason religion is a ubiquitous phenomenon is its singular effectiveness in guaranteeing the cohesion of societies. Most religions require the public display of rituals costly in time and other resources. The performance of these rituals provides a stronger guarantee than anything else that the members of a society will abide by its rules. In addition, most religions assert that the gods know our most intimate thoughts and desires. As opposed to human agents, the gods can know whether we *really* live according to our society's rules or not. Hence belief in gods binds the members of a society together with very strong ties indeed.

The price of religious belief is life in the shadow of the fear of the gods. We must please and appease them to avoid their wrath and incur their favor. And we must, of course, not question either the gods' existence or their influence on nature. We cling to the gods that protect us from death awareness, and enslave us at the same time, because we are forever doomed to fear them.

This is the source of the age-old conflict between religion and science. Science, the open-minded investigation of laws of nature, invariably leads to naturalistic explanations of human events. There were good reasons, therefore, why religions have been hostile to science, because it undermines the cognitive and ethical foundations of religion. This hostility is what led an Athenian court to condemn Socrates to death at the beginning of the fourth century BCE; it made the Catholic Church burn Giordano Bruno at the stake in 1605; led the Jewish community of Amsterdam to excommunicate Baruch de Spinoza in 1656; and it made the Catholic Church put Darwin's *Origin of Species* on the index of forbidden books.

As mentioned earlier, European Enlightenment movements occurred at a variety of places and at different times. These movements celebrated the freedom of thought; some of them valued the virtue of doubt over those of faith, others tried to combine the two.

Epicurus was part of the Greek Enlightenment. He believed that true freedom was not possible as long as humans are afraid of the gods. Only when we understand that the world is ruled by blind natural law can we finally begin to live our lives rationally and be free or experience eudaemonia ("human flourishing," often misleadingly translated as "happiness").

Here we reach the third salient feature of Epicureanism. Lucretius in *De Rerum Natura* argues at length that the fear of death is irrational. In a famed argument that has attracted a lot of attention through the history of philosophy, Lucretius says, "Death is not an event that happens to *me*, because when I am dead, *nothing* can happen to me because I don't exist. Hence the fear of death itself is irrational."

The Epicurean tradition points to a deep logical mistake engrained in human psychology. We tend to try to *imagine what it would be like* to be dead. We do so even if we don't believe in an afterlife. In doing so we imagine being dead and what it would feel like. But this involves a contradiction in terms: when we are dead (assuming that there is no afterlife and this is not the issue) there is no thinking or feeling subject that can feel anything. As a logical consequence, the very attempt to imagine what it is like to be dead misleads and leads us to irrational fears: "it will be lonely in the grave," or "I will be subjected to torments of all sorts."

Lucretius's then moves on the next point: assuming that we are no longer afraid of death itself, because we understand that death is not something that happens to us, we see death as a misfortune because we are saddened by the fact that we will no longer be there. Or as a friend of mine once succinctly put it, "I can't believe the party will go on without me!"

Lucretius argues that none of us is saddened by the fact that there was an infinite time span before we were born in which we didn't exist. Why should it sadden us that there will be an infinite time span after we die in which we will not exist? Why should the infinity of time before we were born be less of a reason to mourn than the infinity of time after we die? Ergo, death cannot be a misfortune.

I don't think that anybody today truly expects the Epicurean arguments to completely abolish the human fear of death. Most of this fear is not rationally based. It is part of our evolutionary heritage that like all animals we are terrorized by anything that threatens our lives. This terror of death is an evolutionary necessity since no animal that doesn't try avoiding death would survive long enough to reproduce.

One of the most important functions of cultural belief systems is to protect us from death awareness. These beliefs make us feel special because we belong to some special group (whites, Christian, Muslim, Jewish, American, etc.) or because we have the "right" beliefs (religious or otherwise). Many of these belief systems contain an outright denial of death (they assert immortality of some sort).

Existential psychology shows that whenever something reminds us of death, our adherence to our cultural belief system will be mobilized to strengthen our defense against death awareness. As a result, we become less tolerant, more judgmental, and less accepting of difference. And finally, the strengthened worldview is protected against further intrusion by self-righteously judging and rejecting members of groups that do not share our worldview. Because one of the intrinsic problems of worldview defense is very simple: the very fact that others do not share our worldview presents a threat to our worldview because it, by its nature, claims exclusive rightness.

Existential psychology shows that the defense against death awareness is the deepest root of fanaticism. By ferociously believing in our cultural belief system, we immunize ourselves against death awareness, making us capable of murder to defend the belief in our specialness or immortality. The most destructive manifestations of fanaticism in recent history (i.e., suicide and terror attacks) are to be explained by the denial of death. Even physical death, to the fanatic, is preferable to accepting our mortality, paradoxical as this may sound.[28]

Epicureanism attempts to help us live with our fear of death. Maybe its ambition to cure us of this terror is too optimistic by assuming that reason is capable of completely overcoming our phylogenetic inheritance. But meditating on death and facing it certainly helps us to become less attached to our parochial beliefs, which may likely make us more humane and thus more human.

It is this feature that attracts me most to Epicureanism. It is, I think, utterly impossible to be Epicurean and to be a fanatic, for the deepest root of fanaticism is the denial of death. On the other hand, Epicureanism makes us do all we can to understand that there is no use in fighting death awareness and that accepting death can bring us more serenity and, paradoxically, joie de vivre.

Epicureanism invites us to celebrate life because it argues that neither the wrath of the gods nor their favor matter once we understand that nothing can protect us from death. Hence no belief system should any longer be a matter of life and death, and it doesn't make any sense to be cruel and intolerant if we understand that no belief can protect us from death awareness. As we will see in the final chapter, this insight is the foundation for the type of worldviews that can tolerate the insight that all human knowledge is tentative—an insight that is crucial to the survival of humanity.

Toward World Citizenship and a Coalition of Open Worldviews

Worldviews that give us meaning need to be more than cognitive maps of the world. They need to generate a sense about why life is worth living, and to do so they must tell us what the ends of life are. Such basic values are what we experience as sacred. Without such an experience of the sacred, no worldview can provide the existential mooring that we humans need. Could there be a sacred principle common to most members of Homo globalis that could help us deepen our experience of meaning?

If indeed such a principle could be formulated, this would accomplish two goals: The first is that as individuals, we would feel that there is a cause over and above the cultures in which we happen to have been reared; we would feel that there is a core to our worldview that indeed takes us out of the Platonic cave of the belief systems into which each of us has been born. The second is that Homo globalis might come to evolve a sense of being part of a global community united by a common sacred purpose. As we will see, our survival as a species may depend on this possibility, which I will call the "coalition of open worldviews."

In a nutshell my hypothesis is that there are two basic types of world-views: the open worldview, which accepts that humans can never have complete and final certainty, and the closed worldview, which claims to have the ultimate truth and the final solution to all human problems. Closed worldviews by their very nature are likely to lead to the catastrophic implications described by existential psychology, whereas open worldviews are, if not immune, less likely to fall into the fanaticism the consequences of which we have witnessed for millennia but never more so than in the bloodiest century of human history.

Homo globalis's awareness of global interconnectedness may also lead us to form a coalition with those who want to transcend the tribal past of humanity by endorsing open worldviews because they enable the type of cooperation that is needed to save our species. Our access to the huge store of human knowledge and the technological means to connect to new, possibly global movements may bring about a victory of reason and humaneness over bigotry, greed, and ignorance. Thus the community of Homo globalis will grow daily because of the spread and ubiquity of communication technology and education.

This coalition may create a world citizenship that goes beyond the glib worldliness often denoted by "cosmopolitanism." The charge against cosmopolitans has often been that they are just out to raid the globe in search of gain and have no commitment to any polity.[1] The world citizenship I am talking about is of a very different sort. It is based on the realization that globalization has led to the point where there is no longer a space on earth that is outside civilization and that political consciousness can no longer be restricted to one country, culture, or religion and thus needs to address the fate of humanity as a whole.[2]

The Common Ground of Homo Globalis

For ethical and political reasons we should probe into the possibility that there could be a coalition of members of Homo globalis that crosses the lines between different religions and between secularism and religion. This would be a coalition united by the insight that at this stage of history all humans are interconnected by a nexus of fate that excludes nobody; it should be united by the ideal of global communication between ethnic, national, and religious groups designed to solve huge problems that all inhabitants of our planet have in common.

This ideal is, of course, not new. In the second half of the twentieth century, a large number of religious leaders understood that interreligious dialogue is a vital necessity. They realized that the tribal origins of religion could no longer determine how religions could function in the present world of global interconnectedness. There had to be a way for religions to communicate between each other and to accommodate each other's claim to truth. Ecumenical conferences abounded and the idea of a plurality of religions began to take root in the minds of adherents of religions such as Christianity, Hinduism, Buddhism, Judaism, Islam, and so on.

In addition, many religious authorities began a serious investigation of how religion could incorporate the findings of modern science. They understood that the fight of the Catholic Church against the Copernican

TOWARD WORLD CITIZENSHIP   173

Revolution had been a big mistake, and a growing number of them realized that repeating the same error vis-à-vis Darwin's theory of biological
evolution would end up looking seemingly misguided in retrospect. Hence
the possibility of a dialogue between religion and secularism seemed to
become a realistic possibility.

There are, of course, vast differences between different conceptions of
the good life, and the differences do not exclusively reside in the chasm
between religion and secularism. Many capitalists ardently believe that
human freedom without the right to amass wealth is a sham. Socialists
believe that only societies that provide a minimum of equality and liberate
all its members from the threat of poverty can foster true human flourishing. Conservatives in Western cultures have argued that a fully human life
can only be based on cultural tradition with deep historical roots. Progres-
sives have countered that human flourishing is only possible if every social
institution, tradition, and belief is subjected to critical inquiry, and that the
liberation of humankind from the shackles of prejudice and irrationality
requires putting no tradition above critical inquiry.

The chasm between different conceptions of the good life deepens
when we consider the difference between religions and secular worldviews.
Almost all religions put the virtue of faith over that of the liberty of mind
and critical inquiry.[3] They claim that social and individual morality not
sanctioned by a supernatural agency are bound to be shallow. They also
claim that those who do not experience religious faith and rapture are
spiritually impaired.

Some of my fellow anti-theists like Richard Dawkins, Daniel Dennett,
and Christopher Hitchens argue that religions cannot be truly tolerant.
Interconfessional dialogue is a sham. Deep down every religion is based on
the idea that it contains the ultimate truth, the final revelation. The very
idea of revelation, they would claim, is that there is an infallible source of
truth and hence toleration of other religions—never mind secularism and
atheism—cannot be completely genuine.

I certainly agree to the extent that there is an inevitable tension between
religion and open-mindedness, the idea of supernatural revelation and
critical thought. But this is where the idea of civilized disdain comes in.
Anti-theists like Dawkins, Dennett, and I will always feel disdain for those
who are in need of revealed truth and religious authority.[4] But then we
shouldn't forget that religious people feel the same disdain for us: they
think we lack spiritual depth, and many of them will always distrust us and
think that we are morally flawed humans beings.

Liberal secularists like Dawkins, Hitchens, and I fume against papal
injunctions against contraceptives, condoms in particular. We think that
it is immoral, absurd, and inhuman to preach against condoms in Africa,

where millions are infected by HIV. We think that Catholicism and Pope Benedict XVI live according to a deeply flawed belief system. But I don't think that any of us would disqualify the current pope as a partner for dialogue. He has in fact shown that despite his theological conservatism he is able to enter dialogue with evolutionary theory. I have no doubt that Pope Benedict XVI has plenty of bad things to say about us liberal secularists. But we can argue with each other. Despite Dawkins and Hitchens's claims to the contrary, and despite my own misgivings about religion, I think that dialogue and even fruitful cooperation across the divide of civilized disdain is possible.

The goal of civilized disdain is not to respect each other's beliefs, although anti-theists may respect religious leaders like John Paul II or the Dalai Lama as human beings and religious believers may respect some anti-theists for their human qualities. It is to find a way to coexist, cooperate, and gain respect for each other as human beings. And we, the new species of Homo globalis, whether religious, agnostic, or anti-theist, knowing that there is no way around coexistence and interdependence, need to form a coalition with those who are willing and able to communicate with each other across divides of beliefs and ideology.[5]

Homo globalis can be found in all colors, shapes, and with the strangest beliefs. We must train ourselves to widen our moral imagination to understand that we can cooperate across worldviews very different from ours, because we have a common cause.[6] We should be able to cheerfully disdain each other's lifestyles, beliefs, and religions and yet try to save the possibility of humanity to continue its history. This final chapter's task is to sketch the nature of this potential global coalition.[7]

Can Homo Globalis Have a Common Sacred Cause?

What could unite those who want to enter this dialogue is a common element of the sacred, one that is perfectly fine with anti-theists—the ideal of human flourishing and the continuation of the human race and civilization. This is less impossible than it sounds. After all, religions, as Emile Durkheim[8] has argued, are cultural systems designed to sanctify the social bonds that make a fully human life possible. This is well in tune with the values of all secularists. No human being can survive alone, and the richer, more complex forms of human existence require rather complex social organization.

In speaking of the sacred, I do not make any religious assumptions in the narrow sense. Durkheim, one of the great early theorists of modern sociology, gave a very interesting definition of the notion of the sacred, which serves our purpose. Durkheim's intuition was generated by his observation of the Dreyfusard movement, which was essentially secular.

In the 1890s and early 1900s France was divided by a trenchant debate about the Dreyfus affair. Captain Alfred Dreyfus was a young, Jewish artillery captain who was accused and convicted of treason for spying for Germany in 1894. In 1896 new evidence came to light that showed that he was not implicated in the spying scandal, and the real culprit, Major Ferdinand Halzy Esterhazy, was found guilty. But the army and the French government tried to avoid dealing with this new evidence and did not revoke Dreyfus's conviction, and instead chose to acquit Esterhazy, making use of fabricated evidence. The ploy was soon uncovered and made public, through, among others, Emile Zola's famous letter to the French prime minister, titled "J'accuse!" (I accuse). It was not until 1906 that Dreyfus was reinstated as a major in the French army, with which he was to fight during World War I, ending his service as a lieutenant colonel.

Durkheim was struck by the enthusiasm and the sense of purpose that penetrated the ranks of the Dreyfusards, the faction that defended Dreyfus. People who only months before had led quiet and relatively purposeless lives were fueled by a deep sense of meaning. Their lives revolved around the Dreyfus affair, the idea of universal rights, and the equality of all citizens without regard for ethnicity or religion.

This experience led Durkheim to his theory of religion, which he expounded most fully in his classic *The Elementary Forms of Religion*.[9] Durkheim's basic argument was that the essence of religion was to differentiate between the extraordinary realm of the sacred and the ordinary realm of the profane. The sacred was an object, a ritual, or an idea that symbolized the social order and its sublime status. Durkheim's argument was that no society could function without such a notion of the sacred and that this was the thread that connected between elementary forms of religious life like totemism (the monotheistic religions of high civilization) and the secular movements like the Dreyfusards, who elevated the idea of equality of values into a sacred principle. They defended the ideas of the French revolution and yet it was clear that the fervor and enthusiasm generated by the Dreyfusard cause had something in common with religion. Those who, like Emile Zola, were willing to take on the French government and the French army in their fight for justice felt that their cause was sacred.

Durkheim thought that the cohesiveness of societies hinged on a common idealized goal that acquires a sacred quality. His models were restricted to society that had some kind of geographical contiguity even though there were already several examples for transnational communities at the beginning of the twentieth century. Like the community of Enlightenment scholars, which came into being in the seventeenth century, some constituted a network of thinkers who created the ideas for representative democracy that were put into action, like the U.S. Constitution. Others, like the Communist movement that consumed Europe, were to lead to much darker results.

In the last two chapters we have primarily dealt with the question of how authentic communication between different worldviews is possible. But could there be a conception of the sacred that could conceivably connect between members of Homo globalis who live in different cultures, languages, ethnicities, and convictions? The very idea seems preposterous. Wouldn't this mean that we need something like a universal religion or at least a universally accepted set of values? But if there were such a thing, we wouldn't have all these differences, conflicts, and clashes that are making life on earth miserable, and so the very idea of such a universal set of values must be a chimera.

Nevertheless there are reasons to believe that humanity could unite around at least one basic principle. Robert Wright in his book *Nonzero*[10] argues that human history, like biological evolution, exhibits directionality toward higher complexity. This course of history is based on the principle that win-win interactions tend to be more fruitful than win-lose or lose-lose situations.

Historically this principle was formulated because evolutionary theory had to account for a fact that seems to contradict basic Darwinian principles. In many species, behavior is perceived as "altruistic" if an individual endangers herself while protecting others. The most basic example is a parent caring for her offspring. Another example is an animal alerting the flock or herd of an approaching predator despite exposing itself to danger in the course of doing so. The question is whether this contradicts the principle of the survival of the fittest. Why should a gene that endangers the individual be successful in evolutionary terms?

In a series of classic papers in the 1960s Robert Trivers and George C. Williams showed through a game of theoretical analysis that altruistic behavior made evolutionary sense.[11] If you looked at the likelihood of a gene's survival chance, it makes sense for a mother to defend her offspring against predators and even for an individual to warn the flock or herd at some expense for personal security. In fact these calculations led to Dawkins's classic reformulation of evolutionary theory in terms of genes rather than individual organisms or groups.

The principle of nonzero is manifested in the fact that over billions of years, biological evolution has resulted in organisms of growing complexity. As Wright shows this does not contradict basic Darwinian principles. It has just turned out that cellular organisms (composed of complex organelles) are superior to subcellular organisms and multicellular organisms, which are basically huge aggregations of interrelated suborganisms, developed properties that go way beyond those of simpler biological creatures. Darwinian logic of the survival of the fittest has turned out to favor organizational principles that are based on cooperation rather than blunt competition.

The advancement of technology furthers the possibilities of win-win interactions (e.g., global commerce). The new global communication system may be about to generate a new form of global awareness. The formation of global communities has become easier than ever. Instant communication between human rights organizations, and between nongovernmental organizations committed to ecological preservation, has made these communities more effective and capable of reacting very quickly to events anywhere on the globe. Because there is no corner on the globe about which we cannot get information, Homo globalis is more likely than any previous generation of history to be able to overcome parochialism, bigotry, and chauvinisms of all sorts and to connect to a universalist conception of humanity, potentially Homo globalis's unifying for a sacred cause.

I will argue that Wright's prediction—that the course of history toward higher complexity and more cooperation will shape the human destiny—hinges on one factor: the spread of open worldviews that reduce the propensity for mutual destruction. This may lead to an ever-growing community of Homo globalis united around the goals of preserving human civilization and the planet that supports it.

The problem is that many worldviews don't see things like that. They assume that the flourishing of one's way of life (e.g., liberal democracy) can only lead to the decline of another (e.g., Communism or Islam). In other words, they assume that human history is ultimately a zero-sum game between competing ideologies that can neither communicate nor find a common denominator. Let us therefore start with the reasons for the scenario of pending apocalypse.

To some extent the results of existential psychology provide more reasons for pessimism than for optimism. Here are some of the questions: Are worldviews, as some proponents of existential psychology claim, inevitably destructive in their implications? Will all of them, of necessity, lead us to intolerance, to the willingness of being cruel, to inflict destruction, suffering, and death in order to defend them? Why then should anybody be optimistic about any positive impact of the global communication system? Why should it possibly enhance the chances of anything as grandiose as a universalist consciousness of the interconnectedness of humanity as a whole and of humanity with nature?

At the end of this journey about regaining our minds and our sense of individuality, one threatening question looms large: could it be too late? Could it be that we are regaining sanity at a point when the human species is already headed toward inevitable self-destruction? Much of the world's current affairs are not governed by nonzero cooperation and not even by civilized disdain but by violent clashes involving totalitarian worldviews.

A Place to Kill For

For quite a few years I have shunned the Old City of Jerusalem, even though it is one of the most beautiful, captivating, and historically complex places on earth; and it is only sixty kilometers from Tel Aviv, where I live. In the early 2000s it was dangerous to go there because the second Intifada (Palestinian uprising) led to many terrorist attacks on visitors. After that I felt reluctant to visit the Old City because in my mind it is inevitably associated with religious fanaticism of all sorts.

Jerusalem's Old City is divided into four quarters: Muslim, Christian, Armenian, and Jewish. The Muslim quarter is the most colorful. Its market, composed of narrow alleys filled with shops, is a tourist attraction and its atmosphere is that of a busy Middle Eastern souk. Vendors of all kinds and youngsters who transport merchandise ranging from pitas to carpets mix with the odors of spices, grilled meat, and sweets. The Christian and Armenian quarters are quieter. The Via Dolorosa winds through these passageways, following the various sites of Christ's suffering according to tradition, and it is an essential item on the trip of every Christian pilgrim. The Jewish quarter has changed greatly since Israel conquered the Old City in the 1967 Six-Day War. It has been modernized, and many yeshivas (schools for Jewish religious studies) were erected by right-wing zealots who took care to place some of these yeshivas in the Muslim quarter to enlarge the Jewish presence in the Old City.

The southeastern corner of the Old City is one of the most contested pieces of land on earth: the Temple Mount (as it is called by Jews) or Haram al-Sharif (as it is called by Muslims). Until 70 CE it was the site of the Jewish temple before it was destroyed by Roman legions. Since the end of the seventh century, it has been one of Islam's holiest sites with two mosques: the Dome of the Rock and the al-Aqsa Mosque. Both traditions believe that this is the site at which Abraham went to sacrifice his son Isaac following God's command only to be stopped by God at the very last minute. It is, of course, important to note that the Muslim tradition states that it was Abraham's firstborn son Ishmael, the ancestor of the Arab people, who was on the verge of being slaughtered. Jewish and Muslim zealots are willing to kill and to die because they believe that the Temple Mount must absolutely be under Jewish or Muslim rule, respectively.

Julia, my wife, and I were in Jerusalem a while ago to celebrate our wedding anniversary, and Julia convinced me to visit the Old City despite my misgivings. Very soon we were taking in its charm and walking through its four quarters until we ended up at a point where you can see the Temple Mount as a whole. It is a splendid sight, dominated by the golden dome on one of its mosques.

We sat down, staring at its beauty, and looked at each other wondering why people need to kill for the sovereignty over this place, why it can't simply be declared as belonging to humanity and have the United Nations be its guardian. This solution has been proposed countless times, and you cannot help wondering what on earth prevents the human species from endorsing this most logical of all solutions. Instead hundreds of millions of Muslims swear solemnly that Islam will one day reconquer its holy sites. Jewish extremist plots have been uncovered to blow up the mosques on the Temple Mount and to liberate it for the third temple that will come down from heaven along with the Messiah.[12] We didn't know whether to be taken by the beauty of the site or the tragic absurdity of what it symbolizes.

The Temple Mount is the epicenter of a murderous fanaticism that is keeping the world on its toes. It is the embodiment of all the deleterious effects of worldview defense against death awareness. It shows the catastrophic impact of the need to cling to a worldview that provides symbolic immortality to its most extreme manifestations: the willingness to kill and, even more paradoxically, to die for it.

Is the effect of worldviews invariably deleterious at best and catastrophic at worst?

The worst crimes against humanity such as religious persecution and genocide (on the basis of spurious claims about racial or cultural superiority) have indeed been perpetrated in the name of ideologies and religions that give meaning to millions of people. The holy inquisition tortured and/or executed hundreds of thousands in the name of Christianity; al Qaeda leaders felt that they were morally and religiously justified to kill thousands of innocent citizens in an act designed to protect the purity of Islam and to punish its enemies. Dr. Baruch Goldstein, an orthodox Jewish settler in the West Bank occupied by Israel believed that he performed a holy duty when he entered the tomb of Abraham and killed 29 Muslims who were praying at this holy place Goldstein thought to be desecrated by their very presence.

Is the problem, then, primarily with religion? This is a tempting line of thought that has been taken by some of the recent critics of religion like Dawkins, Hitchens, Dennett, and Sam Harris. Hitchens in particular is avid in pursuing all forms of religion and lambasting all religious authorities by accusing them of anything from obscurantism to immorality.

Yet this is misleading. Religions are by no means the only worldviews that have led to atrocities. The greatest crimes against humanity in history were perpetrated in the name of secular ideologies that promised to create a paradise on earth. Nazi Germany killed six million Jews in the name of its racial theory of Aryan superiority. The Soviet Communist regime killed more than twenty million Russians during the Stalinist purges; and Pol Pot, the Communist dictator of Cambodia during the 1970s, killed more than three million of his compatriots in an attempt to impose a purified version of Communist ideology on his country.

Hannah Arendt has characterized such worldviews as totalitarian.[13] Because they are supposed to be final and to lead humanity to the end of all suffering, any means to defend them against dissent, criticism, and investigation must be crushed by all means. The belief that there is a protection or a protector who holds all the truths and will provide for us is so dear to those who hold it that it justifies any means to enforce it. The history of totalitarianism in the twentieth century makes clear beyond any doubt that the line between open and closed worldviews does not run along the boundary between religious and secular worldviews.[14] What, then, characterizes the worldviews that are bound to lead to intolerance and bigotry at best, and to slaughter at worst?

Closed Worldviews and Final Solutions

The main characteristic is the belief in what Isaiah Berlin calls "the final solution."[15] It is the belief that humankind can arrive at a truth that will stay there forever; a truth that will finally resolve all our problems. I will call such positions "closed worldviews." They are closed for several reasons: First, they are supposed to be final; thus, they are no longer subjected to criticism, inquiry, and revision. Second, they make recourse to an authority that is beyond criticism. This authority may be a revelation of supposedly divine origin or it may be the set of pronouncements of a führer, comrade, prophet, church, or a political party.

I will never forget the sunny day in which I was lying on the lawn of the campus of the Hebrew University of Jerusalem, reading political philosopher Berlin's article "Two Concepts of Liberty," possibly the most influential piece of writing in political thought of the twentieth century.[16] It was the day when I realized the nature of closed worldviews and the importance and difficulty of living with an open worldview.

I was in my early twenties, a few years after I had left religion behind. Ever since I had sought for an irrefutable foundation of my worldview, which at the time was not quite spelled out but was associated with the tradition of liberal thought. I felt that if it wasn't possible to *prove* the superiority of this worldview, then strife, war, and irrational slaughter would never stop. In other words, I was looking for a transcendental justification of the principles of liberalism.

Berlin was, at the time, seen by many as the greatest living philosopher. I didn't quite understand why. Berlin had not constructed some grand philosophical theory that integrated everything with everything. He had not even written a single systematic treatise outlining his philosophy. So why on earth was he so revered? Why did people speak of him with such admiration and, often quite simply, with love?

I was gradually coming toward the end of "Two Concepts of Liberty" when I read the following passage:

> One belief, more than any other, is responsible for the slaughter of individuals on the altars of the great historical ideals—justice or progress or the happiness of future generations, or the sacred mission or emancipation of a nation or race or class, or even liberty itself, which demands the sacrifice of individuals for the freedom of society. This is the belief that somewhere, in the past or in the future, in divine revelation or in the mind of an individual thinker, in the pronouncements of history or science, or in the simple heart of an uncorrupted good man, there is a final solution. This ancient faith rests on the conviction that all the positive values in which men have believed must, in the end, be compatible, and perhaps even entail one another. "Nature binds truth, happiness, and virtue together as by an indissoluble chain," said one of the best men who ever lived.[17]

I was thunderstruck. Here, in a single paragraph, Isaiah Berlin summarized the essence of all the worldviews responsible for human-made misery. It was the belief that there is, as he says, "a final solution." Berlin did not choose this term lightly or inadvertently. "Two Concepts of Liberty" was his inaugural lecture as the Chichelle Professor of Political Thought at Oxford University, and he delivered it in 1958, just 13 years after the end of World War II, and after the horror of the Nazi's concept of the *final solution*—that is, the extermination of all Jews—had become known to all.

But Berlin included some of my ideals (i.e., justice and liberty) in the list of values that if pushed to the extreme could lead to "the slaughter of individuals on the altars of the great historical ideals." How, then, was it possible to prove, as I wanted to do, beyond any doubt that my current worldview was the only rational possibility? A few pages later I arrived at the final paragraph of Berlin's article:

> It may be that the ideal of freedom to choose ends without claiming eternal validity for them, and the pluralism of values connected with this, is only the late fruit of our declining capitalist civilisation: an ideal which remote ages and primitive societies have not recognised, and one which posterity will regard with curiosity, even sympathy, but little comprehension. This may be so; but no skeptical conclusions seem to me to follow. Principles are not less sacred because their duration cannot be guaranteed. Indeed, the very desire for guarantees that our values are eternal and secure in some objective heaven is perhaps only a craving for the certainties of childhood or the absolute values of our primitive past. "To realise the relative validity of one's convictions," said an admirable writer of our time, "and yet stand for them unflinchingly is what distinguishes a civilised man from a barbarian." To demand more than this is perhaps a deep and incurable metaphysical need; but to allow it to determine one's practice is a symptom of an equally deep, and more dangerous, moral and political immaturity.[18]

I was shaken. Here one of the twentieth century's greatest proponents of liberalism proclaimed my goal of proving the truth of liberalism to be impossible. Not only that, he called on us to accept that the process of formulating a worldview was an open-ended quest, that we could never be sure to have arrived at the final solution, and worse that the very *desire* for the final solution, the final worldview, was the greatest source of suffering inflicted by humans on humans.

While Berlin's insight was not easy for me to stomach, it changed my mind-set forever. I understood that under the guise of openness and tolerance, I had been headed in the wrong direction. I had sought more certainty than we humans are capable of and I would have to live with the endless process of inquiry, the search for answers that, of necessity, had to remain tentative.

Over the years I would also come to understand why Isaiah Berlin was revered and loved by so many. He had, indeed, not produced an integrative system of philosophical thought. But his incredible ability to empathize with a variety of worldviews, his staunch defense of liberalism without turning it into a dogma, the warmth of his voice and the richness of his thought more than made up for that. Berlin was the embodiment of humanism and humaneness by his willingness to look for the human core of every cultural manifestation. Berlin showed the possibility of accepting the historical contingency of one's own position without falling into cynicism. His ability to stick to his beliefs without being dogmatic about them may indeed be one of the marks of the civilized mind and "the ultimate test of character for the individual."

The Psychodynamics of Closed Worldviews

As Berlin says, the lure of closed worldviews is enormous. The desire for ultimate protection is deeply rooted in our psychology. Humans have always hoped that there is some infallible guidance to help them through the maze of life, whether it is a holy text, a seer, the stars, or an all-knowing ancestral voice. We are all too aware of the fragility of life. We know that there are no guarantees for our lives to work out well. We know that making wrong decisions can lead to disastrous consequences and that sometimes even good decisions cannot protect us from calamities like illness, divorce, bankruptcy, difficult relationships with our children, and so forth. This fragility of goodness is difficult to bear and we all want protection from it.

But why should humankind ever have thought that there is such protection? After all, both personal and empirical experience should convince us that there is no such thing. Sigmund Freud's hypothesis about the origins of this idea seems compelling to me to this day.[19] He argued that we have all experienced such protection in our lifetimes. As infants we did not know about the world's vastness or its dangers. We were protected from it by humans whose powers seemed unlimited. Our caretakers provided us with all that we needed and we had no idea about what it took for them to do so. It seemed to depend on nothing but their will on whether we would receive food, shelter, and comfort. Freud's argument was that this experience, while not consciously remembered, leaves an indelible mark on our unconscious and we are left with a lifelong yearning for unbounded protection.

Freud's argument provides one of the powerful reasons why even Homo globalis, despite access to the best extant knowledge, often flocks to obscurantist sources of comfort. After all, lucid knowledge is never completely reassuring. Most scientific knowledge pertaining to our personal life is statistical in nature. If a beloved enters the operating theater, the outcome can never be certain; there are only statistics. If we go to a job interview, nothing guarantees our success. When we love, we can never be certain that our love will be returned forever. No human knowledge will ever arrive at levels of certainty that satisfy our yearning for total protection. The one thing we know for certain is that we will die. And this, as existential psychology shows, is the one certainty that we cannot bear—and the consequences can be truly lethal.

Research about the functioning of terror networks has shown the extent to which they are a function of ideologies, states of mind, resentments, and religious fanaticism that circulate the globe through the Internet.[20] The sexual frustrations and sense of humiliation of a few young men in some

Western cities is what led to the terror cells in London and Madrid and to the formation of the group that would end up shaking the world on September 11, 2001.

Many of us may feel that what is happening in the provinces of Pakistan that border Afghanistan is of little relevance to our daily lives. Nothing could be further from the truth. Anthropologist Scott Atran took considerable risk to interview terrorist leaders there in 2004. One of them explained to Atran that he considered it to be his religious duty to kill four million American women and children with an atomic device because he needed to avenge the killing of four million Muslim women and children by the United States. Given that Pakistan is a nuclear power and that its political system is unstable, the possibility that nuclear material or even a fully functioning nuclear warhead could fall into the hands of Islamic terrorists is unfortunately not a scenario developed by the hyperactive minds of Hollywood screenwriters, but an actual likelihood.

For some it would be comforting to think that such grandiose apocalyptic thinking is only typical of Islam. Unfortunately, nothing could be further from the truth. In the 1990s Israel's secret services uncovered a group of Jewish zealots whose explicit goal was to blow up the mosques on the Haram al-Sharif or the Temple Mount. They believed that the presence of mosques on the location of the Jewish temple was a blasphemy that could not be accepted. They were very well aware that blowing up these mosques would cause an eruption of violence in the Muslim world that could easily lead to a third world war. But they had no problem with this scenario: they believed that this war would be the war of Gog and Magog that was prophesied in the Bible and that its result would be the coming of the Messiah and the establishment of the third temple and the new kingdom of Israel. This faith, with some variations, is shared by substantial fundamentalist groups in the United States who, through a literal interpretation of the book of Revelation, actually believe in an apocalyptic scenario that will be the harbinger of the second coming of Christ.

Of course there is a point at which civilized disdain is likely to become impossible and at which conflict is difficult to avoid. This is the point when human flourishing becomes secondary to a belief in an ideal that is supposed to override it. I can hardly imagine an open-minded dialogue based on competing conceptions of human flourishing with Hitler, Stalin, Pol Pot, Mahmud Ahmadinejad, or Osama bin Laden.

The problem is not that extremists of this sort are devoid of values or immoral. Osama bin Laden, to stick to the most contemporary example, was deeply convinced of his rightness. He was sure beyond any doubt that Western conceptions of liberty were debased and corrupt conceptions of human flourishing, and that Islam needed to be purged of this corrupting influence at any price and by any means.

Bin Laden's worldview is an extreme example of a closed worldview. He saw neither the necessity nor the possibility to enter into dialogue with those whom he considered his total enemies. As Paul Berman has argued forcefully, it is a great mistake to try to reduce a belief system like Bin Laden's to the expression of grievances and injustices. Closed, totalitarian belief systems need to be taken seriously. Well-meaning liberals who believe that any worldview that is too different from theirs is a pathological reaction to Western misdeeds are empirically wrong and ideologically misguided. Reducing such belief systems to psychopathology is a form of naiveté, as it assumes that any worldview that doesn't correspond can be brushed aside as nothing but a reaction to some grievances and fails to realize that the human mind is prone to the seduction of closed worldviews.[21]

While the worldview for Homo globalis I have developed throughout this book tries to stretch dialogue to its limits, it does recognize that these limits exist. Sometimes the moment comes when civilized disdain will have to be replaced by the use of force. I say this even though I am aware that this will turn some of my liberal brethren and sisters against me. And we will continue our disagreement about these questions in trenchant argument and enjoy the civilized disdain we feel toward each other because between open worldviews there is, in principle, never a need to resort to violence, because dialogue remains a possibility.

Ecological Self-Destruction

These are just the scenarios of humankind's self-destruction derived from politics, religion, and extremist ideologies. There are other ways in which we humans may be about to realize the same goal. In the 1960s James Lovelock, an independent researcher, was working for NASA in developing sensitive instruments that would be able to determine the existence and composition of atmospheres on other planets. This research led him to formulate a hypothesis of far-reaching importance. He argued that planet earth was an interlinked system in which biological organisms were part of the generation and maintenance of the atmosphere that in turn sustained the earth's biosphere.[22] Lovelock's hypothesis, if true, had one mind-boggling implication: by disturbing the equilibrium of the biosphere beyond a certain point, humankind would destroy the foundation of earth's biosystem to the point where earth would be able to support little or no life—and certainly not the ever-growing number of humans with their staggering consumption of food and energy.

The hypothesis was formulated in perfectly acceptable scientific terms. It was testable and at least consistent with established background knowledge. Lovelock's choice for the name of the hypothesis was problematic, though, he called it the "Gaia hypothesis," using the name of the Greek goddess of earth. This led the scientific establishment to disregard Lovelock's hypothesis for decades; it was assumed to be another New Age nonsense and not a theory that was well founded and provable.

In the last twenty years, Lovelock's hypothesis has found its way into mainstream research, and there are strong indications that he may be right. Lovelock now believes that the destruction humankind has inflicted on the Earth's biosphere may be beyond repair, and that at the present rate of growth, humankind may be on the way to extinction already during the twenty-first century.[23] In Lovelock's terms, the human species is behaving like a parasite that in the process of taking over its host organism, Earth, and is killing it—taking itself down along the way. I do not have the competence to judge the conflicting opinions about how likely Lovelock's prediction is, but the scientific case for his view is very strong.

All of humankind is therefore interlinked not just through trade, the Internet, the financial markets, and the infotainment network. We are now interlinked in a nexus that is literally a matter of life and death for all of us. Whatever the exact truth about global warming, Lovelock's Gaia hypothesis, and the dwindling of earth's energy resources is, we can no longer live with the illusion that it is enough for us to care about our immediate environment and communities and that the world at large is not our business.

The quality of the air that Australians breathe depends on factors occurring on the other side of the globe. Amazonian rainforests are among the major producers of oxygen and their decimation will have far-reaching implications for all of us. The Bush administration's refusal to ratify the Kyoto agreements in 2002 had another far-reaching implication. Given that the United States is responsible for 25 percent of the world's greenhouse gases, this refusal cast doubt on the ability of humankind to reach an agreed-upon strategy to reduce both the consumption of fossil oils and the pollution of earth's atmosphere. Humankind simply seems incapable of construing global institutions that protect our irreplaceable, basic means of survival.

The Race between Destruction and the Nonzero Principle

All this has led some thinkers to come to profoundly pessimistic conclusions. British political philosopher John Gray has completely abandoned the hope of the European and American Enlightenment that the history of

humankind is predetermined to reach a positive conclusion.[24] The opposite seems to be true. All indicators point to the possibility that humankind
is about to self-destruct in one way or another or, as Gray gloomily says,
that the human species is but a temporary illness that has befallen planet
Earth, and that it will soon be eradicated from its face.

I have become pretty convinced that Lovelock and Gray are right. The
question is what consequences we draw from this. Are we supposed to
withdraw into a disgust of humankind and watch the catastrophe unfold?
Gray has been criticized as being a misanthrope in the style of Arthur Schopenhauer, the great nineteenth-century philosophical pessimist who could
see no alternative to philosophical contemplation of the tragic-comic spectacle that is human history. I think that this criticism is not justified. The
ability of looking the facts in the eye and accepting the truth is one of our
species' saving graces.

Then again, something in me rebels against the idea that the grand story
of the development of humanity will end in an apocalyptic scenario devoid
of meaning. Will humans, in the end, be nothing but a kind of bacterium
that has, by its biological nature, led to nothing but another global calam-
ity? It is difficult to resist the powerful logic of the arguments put forth by
Lovelock and Gray. So what are we supposed to do?

Of course Lovelock and Gray are right when they say that our species
is governed by the Darwinian logic that governs any other species. But no
lesser man than Richard Dawkins, the celebrated and much-hated grand
proponent of Darwinian evolution, has argued that the human species is
special in one respect. We are the one species that has been able to grasp the
iron laws that govern the biological world, and he has called upon all of us
to use this knowledge to change our fate. Dawkins is, for example, a strong
proponent of social democracy rather than of social Darwinism.

It might be argued that this call suffers from an intrinsic contradiction:
if indeed Darwinian logic governs the kingdom of living beings, there is no
reason we should be able to escape it. Gray and Lovelock must be right: we
cannot escape the nexus of natural law that governs the universe.

But biological evolution also has been governed by Robert Wright's
nonzero principle.[25] The nonzero principle is manifested throughout
human history. Its direction is clearly toward ever-growing complexity. To
be more precise, history in the full sense of the word has only arisen in
cultures beyond a certain complexity. Only when humans moved toward
social organization with a high degree of division of labor was it possible
for professions to arise that allowed for the recording of history. Priests,
scribes, and later writers and historians had the leisure to write down history and thus to allow humankind to learn about its own development
only in societies that were complex enough to support such functions.

The most convincing recent example of the nonzero principle is the history of the Internet's emergence, which is recounted in fascinating detail by sociologist Manuel Castells.[26] Without a governing body, and mostly without the motivation of material gain, a large number of individuals and groups that often did not know each other personally cooperated in creating a system, which has immeasurably increased the reach and organizing power of human knowledge. The emergence of the Internet has shown that the principle of cooperative complexity is indeed at work at any moment of evolution.

Yet, as anthropologist Jared Diamond has shown,[27] complex systems do not necessarily attain the intelligence to survive. Diamond has documented in often depressing detail how human societies can evolve to the point where they wipe out the ecosystems on which they depend. Humankind seems to be at a fascinating, exhilarating, and totally frightening crossroads. We are the onlookers to a race between the sheer inertia of humanity's destroying the planet's resources, and the emergence of sufficient collective understanding of the fact that we need to change course to survive. Is the pooling of human intelligence through the Internet— this exponential empowerment of human knowledge going to win the race against inertia—greed and ignorance? Personally I believe that the odds are against us, that authors like Lovelock, Diamond, and Gray are pointing the way for things to come.

The uses of the Internet are a good example. The Internet is a carrier of memes, and as we have seen in Part III, memes, like viruses, have the unfortunate tendency to spread without regard to the well-being of their carriers, who, in this case, happen to be us, the human species. The Internet carries invaluable information and has made research easier and more effective than ever. On the negative side, it also carries pornography and gambling, the two businesses that make the largest amount of money on the Internet. It also carries crackpot theories about anything from numerological indications that the apocalypse is close to downright lethal content, like information distributed by jihadist websites on how to prepare explosives for terror attacks.

Looking at recent history, it is difficult to be optimistic: the number of people who believe in the apocalypse is larger than the number of people who understand the basics of evolutionary theory. The number of people who subscribe to the theory that 9/11 was the result of a conspiracy between the CIA and the Mossad surpasses the number of people who understand the theory of relativity by a factor of thousands. Between the various forms of fundamentalism and those who wish for an apocalypse, those of us who are trying to come up with constructive solutions to global problems, such as deforestation to AIDS, seem to be hopelessly outnumbered. In other words, it looks like we are lost.

The Empowerment of Homo Globalis
and the Possibility of Universalism

This is unfortunately combined with a strong sense that there is nothing we can do to influence the course of history. Those of us that are not part of David Rothkopf's "superclass" that runs the world's affairs—and that's 99.999 percent—often feel that there isn't much use in getting involved in politics. Governments throughout the world are bogged down in their power struggles, institutional inertia, and dynamics typical of all bureaucracies: groupthink and the tendency to think in entrenched terms. The intelligence community by nature thinks in terms of conspiracies and likes to work in secrecy. Governments are generally motivated by short-term political considerations, allegiances, and alliances that need to be maintained and often mindless principles and slogans that drive their activities.

So most ordinary citizens feel that they can vote once every few years, but for the rest, their influence is negligible. If they are not willing to get involved in party politics, they will have no impact on the functioning of parties. And mostly only powerful interest groups with strong financial muscle will truly determine policy through lobbying and prodding.

And yet I think that it's worth picking the fight. After all, it is more interesting, more exhilarating, and more productive to go for one more round of defending what is valuable in our species than just to give into the rather ugly possibility of watching our own demise with the glee of the pessimistic philosopher. Despite the evidence to the contrary, I do not want to give up on Sigmund Freud's saying: "The voice of the intellect is a soft one. But it does not rest until it gets a hearing."[28] There have been some indications lately that the human species has powers of regeneration that are quite amazing. The prime example is the election of a black man for the U.S. presidency. In addition to its being a historical moment per se, the process of Barack Obama's election is unprecedented in its use of the Internet and the empowerment of a large, previously unorganized polity of liberals against the power of special interest groups. Obama's election to the U.S. presidency is but one, very powerful exemplification of the small chance we have to save our species for another round.

Let me make it clear, Obama is just a human being and his election is not a miracle. Without the economic meltdown he would probably not have carried the day. But he also wouldn't have done so, in any case, if it hadn't been for a fascinating and completely new phenomenon: Obama managed to raise funds that dwarfed any previous election. The secret was simple because Obama was the first major politician who truly understood the Internet's power.

Obama got elected because liberals discovered that they could override the power of big finance and special interest—that by pooling their intelligence and their financial assets through the Internet, they could vastly outmaneuver the powers that had governed American politics for decades. Millions of individuals were stronger than the combined assets of the world's largest corporations and they could offset the power of special interest and its impact in traditional Washington. The principle of nonzero outperformed the principle of mimetic infection.

The result was impressive. Many members of Homo globalis, even outside the United States, felt that the principle of nonzero—the universalist belief that humankind needs to rise over its primate and tribal ancestry—had won over tribal divisiveness. At the time of writing, there is a strong sense that Obama is living up to the expectation of embodying the universalist spirit of world citizenship by reaching the hearts and minds even of those who have felt for years that they are hardly connected by the bond of common humanity with the Free World.

The question is, can we do it again? Can we, as members of the new Homo globalis, with our access to the vast array of human knowledge once again pull it off to overcome our animalistic past? Will we able to win the race against ignorance, bigotry, and worldviews governed by the limitations of upbringing, custom, and the narrow-mindedness engendered by lack of education?

There are models for initiatives that may change our rush toward self-destruction. Al Gore has done a tremendous job in putting the fight against global warming into global awareness. Greenpeace has forced even those who didn't want to listen to realize that we are about to destroy the biodiversity of our planet. The Bill and Melinda Gates Foundation is providing models of how the bureaucratic inefficiencies of national governments can be bypassed to create research programs and distribution networks that fight global scourges like AIDS with innovative efficiency. Every day millions contribute to the stock of human knowledge and resourcefulness. Wikipedia, one of the most impressive proofs of the validity of the nonzero principle keeps growing at an incredible pace.

Homo globalis is no longer limited to any particular geographic, ethnic, or political sphere. This new species is spreading in primarily Hindu India, as well as primarily Christian California, and primarily Jewish Israel; and the number of Homo globalis in the primarily Muslim Arab world is rising steadily. Will we be able to counteract the divisive nature that we have inherited from our primate ancestors?

In all likelihood we'll lose the race: the destructiveness of some terrorist fanatics may bring us one step closer to catastrophe by initiating the Armageddon that they are dying to bring about. The sheer inertia of government bureaucracies may prevent the implementation of programs that could cut down the consumption of fossil oils that will kill Earth's atmosphere. And the bigotry of religious leaders may make it impossible to stop the population of third world countries from multiplying to the point where Earth's population can no longer be sustained by her resources.

And yet the temptation to write, "Members of Homo globalis of all nations, unite!" is too great to resist. Maybe the pooled creativity of those who understand that humankind has been united by fate, if not by design and intelligence, will carry the day once more; not by competing with other species and erasing them, but by creating a new form of solidarity of the human species that, by blind chance, has reached both the abysses of genocide and environmental havoc and the heights of individual and collective creation that surpass anything our scarred globe has ever seen.

Notes

The author wishes to thank the editors of *Psychoanalytic Psychology*, *Journal of Humanistic Psychology*, and *American Journal of Psychotherapy* for their permission to use material for Chapters 5, 6, and 8.

Introduction

1. Kant, I. (1783). *Prolegomena to any future metaphysics that will be able to present itself as science*. This introduction and this book as a whole is in many ways an extended meditation on Kant's celebrated essay "What Is Enlightenment?" (1784). the canonical text of eighteenth-century Enlightenment thought. For English translation, see Kant, I. (2001). *The basic writings of Immanuel Kant*. Allen Wood (Ed.). New York, NY: Modern Library. His *Critique of Pure Reason* (1781/1787) set the agenda for subsequent epistemology, philosophy of science, and cognitive psychology.

2. For such a triumphalist view, see Mandelbaum, M. (2002). *The ideas that conquered the world: Peace, democracy, and the free markets in the twenty-first century*. New York, NY: Public Affairs.

3. The idea that capitalism tends to turn the self into a commodity was raised by theorists of the Frankfurt school since the 1930s onward—most famously in Marcuse, H. (1964). *One-dimensional man*. London, UK: Routledge. But it was the global infotainment system that made this commoditization into a lived reality. For the first time, members of Homo globalis could indeed check their "I" commodity value by plugging into the infotainment system and watch its fluctuation daily.

4. The argument of this book, along with many other critiques of neoliberal dogmas like those of Paul Krugman, George Soros, and Nouriel Roubini, is not meant to argue for some form of statism, but to limit capitalism's impact on the way we understand the meaningful life.

5. There have been previous enlightenment movements ranging from India in the seventh century, classical Greece in the fifth and fourth centuries through the Islamic Enlightenment in the ninth century. Since this book focuses on Western culture, I will focus on the European Enlightenment that started in the seventeenth century and, at times, on classical Greece.

6. Mill, J. S. (1974). *On liberty*. G. Himmelfarb (Ed.). Harmondsworth, UK: Penguin. (Original work published 1859). A contemporary examination of Mill's

project can be found in Appiah, K. A. (2005). *The ethics of identity*. Princeton, NJ: Princeton University Press.

7. The goal of this book is restricted to rethinking aspects of individualist liberalism. I do not wish to imply, the way Fukuyama did, that this is the one, final political and ideological arrangement of the world. Nevertheless I think that it is a valuable form of life that needs to recover from its conflation with fundamentalist free market capitalism. For a brilliant critique of this conflation, see Gray, J. (1998). *False dawn: The delusion of global capitalism*. London, UK: Granta. I differ from Gray in that I think that the core value of *Selbstdenken* (Gotthold Ephraim Lessing's term for independent thinking much beloved to Hannah Arendt). is an aspect of Enlightenment thought that is not necessarily linked to the triumphalist idea of the West's superiority.

8. In the last decade any reference to Plato and the allegory of the cave evokes the suspicion of cultural and political conservatism, mostly associated with Leo Strauss, popularized through Allan Bloom's 1987 work, which is then seamlessly connected to the neoliberal ideology of Wolfowitz, Perle, and other founders of neoconservatism; see Bloom, A. (1987). *The closing of the American mind*. New York, NY: Simon & Schuster. Francis Fukuyama, John Gray, and most exhaustively, Steven Smith have shown beyond any doubt that this associative chain has no historical foundation. Cf. Smith, S. (2006). *Reading Leo Strauss: Politics, philosophy, Judaism*. Chicago, IL: University of Chicago Press. Strauss quite explicitly spoke against grandiose political schemes like Neo-Conservatism—more about this at the end of Chapter 7. While the cultural agenda of this book may be interpreted as conservative, its political message is certainly not. My own political views are social democratic and primarily shaped by classical European Liberalism.

9. The contemporary relevance of the stoic notion of world-citizenship was formulated by Martha Nussbaum. See Nussbaum, M. (1995). *Cultivating humanity*. Cambridge, MA: Harvard University Press, which will be discussed in Chapter 8.

10. The term is not always used pejoratively but is often taken to denote what I mean by "world-citizenship." Cf. Appiah, K. A. (2006). *Cosmopolitanism: Ethics in a world of strangers*. New York, NY: Norton.

11. Pierre Hadot must be credited with the idea that classical Greek philosophy needs to be understood as a set of spiritual exercises designed to liberate the mind rather than a set of theoretical propositions. See Hadot, P. (1995). *Philosophy as a way of life*. Oxford, UK: Blackwell. Michel Foucault showed that this notion can be fruitfully applied to the present by developing his notion of disciplines of the self. Cf Foucault, M. (1984). *The care of the self*. New York, NY: Random House. Foucault's notion of disciplines of the self has been given an interesting reformulation by Peter Sloterdijk. See Sloterdijk, P. (2009). *Du mußt dein Leben ändern!* Frankfurt am Main, Germany: Suhrkamp.

Chapter 1

1. See Fukuyama, F. (1992). *The end of history and the last man*. New York, NY: Free Press. Of course Fukuyama himself never understood his thesis this way.

He was trying to revive Hegel's idea that there was an end-state in which political structure reaches a balance in which all tensions are balanced out (*aufgehoben*, to use Hegel's term). In addition Fukuyama was not too happy with the outcome of this historical process, which he, with Nietzsche, also saw as a takeover of bourgeois values that were not particularly inspiring ("The last man"). Nevertheless John Gray has made a strong argument that even though this was not Fukuyama's intention, his argument ends up being a form of Western triumphalism. Cf. Gray, J. (2007). *Black mass: Apocalyptic religion and the death of utopia*. New York, NY: Farrar, Strauss & Giroux.

2. Atran, S. (2003). The genesis of suicide terrorism. *Science, 299,* 234–239.

3. See Becker, E. (1973). *The denial of death.* New York, NY: Free Press. This is the classic book that is in many ways the foundation of contemporary experimental existential psychology (EEP).

4. See Heidegger, M. (1927). *Sein und zeit.* Tübingen, Germany: Niemeyer. English translation, Heidigger, M. (2008). *Being and time.* J. Macquarrie and E. Robinson (Trans.). San Francisco, CA: Harper Perennial; Sartre, J-P. (1992). *Being and nothingness.* H. E. Barnes (Trans.). New York, NY: Gramercy (Originally published in French as *L'Être et le Néant* in 1943); Becker, E. (1973). *The denial of death.* New York, NY: Free Press.

5. This theme has been investigated phenomenologically by Robert Stolorow. See Stolorow, R. (2007). *Trauma and human existence: Autobiographical, clinical, and philosophical reflections.* Hillsdale, NJ: Analytic Press.

6. For his most sustained presentation of the application of existentialism, see Yalom, I. (1980). *Existential psychotherapy.* New York, NY: Basic Books.

7. See Greenberg, J., Koole, S. L., & Pyszczynski, T. (Eds.). (2004). *Handbook of experimental existential psychology.* New York, NY: Guilford Press. This is the most extensive collection of essays summarizing the results and ideas of EEP to date.

8. See Becker, E. (1971). *The birth and death of meaning.* New York, NY: Free Press; Becker, E. (1973). *The denial of death.* New York, NY: Free Press.

9. See Pyszczynski, T. A., Solomon, S., & Greenberg, J. (2003). *In the wake of 9/11: The psychology of terror.* Washington, DC: American Psychological Association.

10. See Solomon, S., Greenberg, J., Schimel, J., Arndt J., & Pyszczynski T. (2003). Human awareness of death and the evolution of culture. In M. Schaller & C. Crandal (Eds.). *The psychological foundations of culture* (pp. 15–40). Mahwah, NJ: Erlbaum.

11. This book will not deal with this factor, even though it is of great importance. See Florian, V., & Mikulincer, M. (2004). A multifaceted perspective on the existential meanings, manifestations, and consequences of the fear of personal death. In J. Greenberg, S. L. Koole, & T. Pyszczynski (Eds.), *Handbook of experimental existential psychology* (pp. 54–70). New York, NY: Guilford Press. Insightful analyses of the changes in intimate relations can be found in the work of Anthony Giddens: see Giddens, A. (1992). *The transformation of intimacy.* London, UK: Polity; and in Bauman, Z. (2003). *Liquid love: On the frailty of human bonds.* London, UK: Polity.

12. See Solomon, S., Greenberg, J., Schimel, J., Arndt, J., & Pyszczynski, T. (2003). Human awareness of death and the evolution of culture. In M. Schaller & C. Crandal (Eds.). *The psychological foundations of culture* (pp. 15–40). Mahwah, NJ: Erlbaum.

13. The relational embeddedness of the self has been the central theme of relational psychoanalyis in the last decades. Its conceptual foundation is presented in Aron, L. (1996). *A meeting of minds: Mutuality in psychoanalysis.* Hillsdale, NJ: Analytic Press.

14. For a comprehensive picture of the topic, see Buss, D. (2004). *Evolutionary psychology* (2nd ed.). New York, NY: Pearson. For a highly readable introduction to the basic ideas of evolutionary psychology, see Wright, R. (1994). *The moral animal.* New York, NY: Pantheon.

15. See Buss, D. (2004). *Evolutionary psychology* (2nd ed.). New York, NY: Pearson; Wright, R. (1994). *The moral animal.* New York, NY: Pantheon.

16. See Castells, M. (2001). *The Internet galaxy: Reflections on the Internet, business, and society.* Oxford, UK: Oxford University Press.

17. See Fukuyama, F. (1992). *The end of history and the last man.* New York, NY: Free Press.

18. See Friedman, T. (1999). *The Lexus and the olive tree.* New York, NY: Farrar, Strauss & Giroux.

19. See Barber, B. (2003). *Jihad vs. McWorld* (augmented ed.). New York, NY: Random House.

20. See Armstrong, K. (2000). *The battle for God.* New York, NY: Knopf.

21. See Gray, J. (2003). *Al Qaeda and what it means to be modern.* New York, NY: Norton.

22. There are already a number of analyses of cultural, historical, and economic factors that led to the meltdown of 2007 and 2008. See some prime examples in Taleb, N. N. (2007). *Black swan: The impact of the highly improbable.* New York, NY: Random House. The book provides an insider's view of the falsity of the assumptions of the manageability of all types of financial risks. See George Soros, who had been warning about the inevitability of this meltdown for more than a decade; he restates his points in his recent book: Soros, G., *The new paradigm for financial markets: The 2008 credit crisis and what it means.* New York, NY: Public Affairs. For a collage of perspectives on the current crisis and those that preceded it, see Lewis, M. (2008). *Panic: The story of modern financial insanity.* New York, NY: Norton. An analysis that takes into account a much wider historical perspective is given in Ferguson, N. (2008). *The ascent of money: A financial history of the world.* New York, NY: Penguin.

23. See Mandelbaum, M. (2002). *The ideas that conquered the world: Peace, democracy, and the free markets in the twenty-first century.* New York, NY: Public Affairs.

24. See Florida, R. (2002). *The rise of the creative class.* New York, NY: Basic Books.

25. For a riveting account of how the system refused to listen, see Lewis, M. (2008, December 8). The end of Wall Street. *Portfolio.*

26. The evidence for Iraq's weapon of mass destruction was fabricated in a concerted effort by the Bush administration and has been made convincingly by

Suskind, R. (2008). *The way of the world: A story of hope in an age of extremism.* New York, NY: Harper.

27. Olofson, M., & Marcus, S. C. (2009). National patterns in antidepressant medication treatment. *Archives of General Psychiatry, 66*(8), 848–856; Compton, W. M., Conway, K. P., Stinson, F. S., & Grant, B. F. (2006, December). Changes in the prevalence of major depression and comorbid substance use disorders in the United States between 1991–1992 and 2001–2002. *American Journal of Psychiatry, 163*(12), 2141–2147.

Chapter 2

1. See Brooks, D. (2000). *Bobos in paradise.* New York, NY: Simon & Schuster.
2. These commercials can be accessed either through YouTube or Google Video.
3. See Fukuyama, F. (1992). *The end of history and the last man.* New York, NY: Free Press.
4. Sir Anthony Giddens was instrumental in formulating the tenets of the "Third Way." See Giddens, A. (1993). *Beyond left and right: The future of radical politics.* New York, NY: Polity.
5. History of the personal computer. Wikipedia. Retrieved from http://en.wikipedia.org/wiki/History_of_the_personal_computer; History of the Internet. Wikipedia. Retrieved from http://en.wikipedia.org/wiki/History_of_the_Internet. For a systematic account, see Castells, M. (2001). *The Internet galaxy: Reflections on the Internet, business, and society.* Oxford, UK: Oxford University Press.
6. Microsoft. Wikipedia. Retrieved from http://en.wikipedia.org/wiki/Microsoft.
7. Google. Wikipedia. Retrieved from http://en.wikipedia.org/wiki/Google.
8. A comprehensive overview is given by Aron, R. (1967). *Main currents in sociological thought.* Harmondworth, UK: Penguin.
9. See Reich, R. (2005, December). The new rich-rich gap. *American Prospect.*
10. See Conley, D. (2009). *Elsewhere, U.S.A.: How we got from the company man, family dinners, and the affluent society to the home office, BlackBerry moms, and economic anxiety.* New York, NY: Pantheon.
11. See Rothkopf, D. (2008). *Superclass.* New York, NY: Farrar, Strauss & Giroux.
12. See Barber, B. (2003). *Jihad vs. McWorld* (augmented ed.). New York, NY: Random House. Barber provides a detailed and insightful account of the centralization of the infotainment system and its interdependence.
13. See Seabrook, J. (2000). *Nobrow: The culture of marketing and the marketing of culture.* New York, NY: Knopf.
14. This and the following commercials are all accessible through YouTube.
15. Csikszentmihalyi, M. (1990). *Flow: The psychology of optimal experience.* New York, NY: HarperPerennial.
16. Couldry, N. (2002). Playing for celebrity. Big brother as ritual event. *Television New Media, 3,* 283.
17. See Miller, M. (Ed.). (2008, June). The celebrity 100. *Forbes.*

18. See Benjamin, W. (1969). The work of art in the age of mechanical reproduction. In W. Benjamin, *Illumination* (pp. 217–252). H. Arendt (Ed.) & H. Zohn (Trans.). New York, NY: Schocken. (Originally published 1935).
19. I have analyzed this fantasy of limitlessness and its impact on identity formation in Strenger, C. (2004). *The designed self*. Hillsdale, NJ: Analytic Press.
20. Correspondents of *The New York Times*. (2005). *Class matters*. New York, NY: Times Books.

Chapter 3

1. Atran, S. (2002). *In gods we trust: The evolutionary landscape of religion*. Oxford, UK: Oxford University Press.
2. See Bauman, Z. (2007). *Liquid times: Living in an age of uncertainty*. London, UK: Polity. Bauman has written a series of books building on his characterization of late capitalist society as liquid. His basic thesis is that those I call Homo globalis are characterized by a high degree of detachment from communities, and that they no longer trust any of the existing institutions and hence move from place to place, attachment to attachment in an attempt to maximize their chances.
3. See Sassen, S. (2000). *The global city: New York, London, Tokyo*. Princeton, NJ: Princeton University Press. The book provides an in-depth analysis of the economic structure of modern economies.
4. See Conley, D. (2009). *Elsewhere, U.S.A.: How we got from the company man, family dinners, and the affluent society to the home office, BlackBerry moms, and economic anxiety*. New York, NY: Pantheon.
5. Olofson, M., & Marcus, S. C. (2009). National patterns in antidepressant medication treatment. *Archives of General Psychiatry, 66*(8): 848–856; Compton, W. M., Conway, K. P., Stinson, F. S., & Grant, B. F. (2006, December). Changes in the prevalence of major depression and comorbid substance use disorders in the United States between 1991–1992 and 2001–2002. *American Journal of Psychiatry, 163*(12), 2141–2147.
6. There are several very good presentations and analyses of the pop spirituality market. A good academic study is Illouz, E. (2008). *Saving the modern soul: Therapy, emotions, and the culture of self help*. Berkeley, CA: University of California Press. A funny, yet trenchant indictment of this culture is Tiede, T. (2001). *Self-help nation: The long overdue, entirely justified, delightfully hostile guide to the snake-oil peddlers who are sapping our nation's soul*. New York, NY: Atlantic Monthly Press.
7. World Values Survey. Retrieved from http://www.worldvaluessurvey.org/ contains a wealth of data on this and the following.
8. See Florida, R. (2007, April). Creativity and religion. Retrieved from Creative Class website: http://www.creativeclass.com/creative_class/2007/04/17/creativity-and-religion. See Richard Florida's blog entry. In general Creative Class is a good source for the type of discourse Florida has created.
9. See Tolle, E. (2004). *The power of now: A guide to spiritual enlightenment*. Novato, CA: New World Library.

10. For this and the following, see Laitman, M. (2006). *Kabbalah science and the meaning of life: Because your life has meaning* (p. 11). Toronto, Canada: Laitman Kabbalah Publishers.

11. See Laitman, M. (2006). *Kabbalah science and the meaning of life: Because your life has meaning* (p. 12). Toronto, Canada: Laitman Kabbalah Publishers.

12. See Scholem, G. (1941). *Major trends in Jewish mysticism.* Jerusalem, Israel: Schocken.

13. This development has been analyzed in depth in Foucault, M. (1966). *The order of things.* New York, NY: Vintage.

14. My examples are taken from Jewish contexts, but the analogous cases can be found in all major religions, and even more in the endless variety of sects that are mushrooming throughout the world.

15. See The Kabbalah Centre. What is kabbalah? Retrieved January 5, 2009 from http://www.kabbalah.com/01.php.

16. The locus classicus for a basic history of Kabbalistic thought to this day is Sholem, G. (1941). *Major trends in Jewish mysticism.* Jerusalem, Israel: Schocken. For a more contemporary account, see Idel, M. (1989). *Kabbalah: New perspectives.* New Haven, CT: Yale University Press.

17. The classic study is Eliade, M. (2004). *Shamanism: Archaic techniques of ecstasy.* Princeton, NJ: Bollingen Series. An invaluable source is Scholem, G. (1964). *Von der mystischen gestalt der gottheit.* Frankfurt am Main, Germany: Suhrkamp.

18. For an incisive discussion of the value of mystical experience, see the dialogue between a Western philosopher and his son who turned from a career in biology to being a Buddhist monk: Revel, J-F., & Ricard, M. (1997). *The monk and the philosopher.* New York, NY: Schocken.

19. See Dawkins, R. (2006). *The God delusion.* New York, NY: Houghton Mifflin.

20. See Sharma, R. (1999). *The monk who sold his Ferrari.* San Francisco, CA: Harper.

21. See Pulsifer, C. (n.d.). A motivational, inspirational book review: Greatness guide. [Review of the book *The greatness guide*, by R. Sharma]. Retrieved from http://www.wow4u.com/the-greatness-guide/index.html.

22. See Byrne, R. (2006). *The secret.* New York, NY: Simon & Schuster; Hicks, E., & Hicks, J. (2008). *The astonishing power of emotions: Let your feelings be your guide by Abraham.* Carlsbad, CA: Hay House.

23. See Adler, J. (2007, April 25). Decoding the secret. *Newsweek.* Retrieved from http://www.newsweek.com/id/36603

24. See Salkin, A. (2007, April 12). Shaking riches out of the cosmos. *The New York Times.* Retrieved from http://www.nytimes.com/2007/02/25/fashion/25attraction.html?_r=1&pagewanted=all.

25. Strenger, C., & Ruttenberg, A. (2008, February 1). The existential necessity of midlife change. *Harvard Business Review,* 82–90.

26. Susan Jacoby makes a strong case for this argument in Jacoby, S. (2008). *The age of American unreason.* New York, NY: Pantheon.

27. For the following, consult primarily Finkielkraut, A. (1995). *The defeat of mind.* New York, NY: Columbia University Press. A more recent trenchant critique of the Left's anti-Westernism and its consequences is to be found in Levy,

B-H. (2008). *Left in dark times: A stand against the new barbarism.* New York, NY: Random House.

28. For a powerful and lucid critique of this tendency, see Eagleton, T. (1996). *The illusions of postmodernism.* New York, NY: Wiley.

29. A good exemplification of this trend is Masson, J. (1993). *Against therapy.* San Francisco, CA: Common Courage Press.

Chapter 4

1. Some of these conditions are outlined in Gellner, E. (1994). *Conditions of liberty: Civil society and its rivals.* London, UK: Hamish Hamilton.

2. See Sen, A. (2006). *Identity and violence: The illusion of destiny.* New York, NY: Norton.

3. See Weber, M. (1905). *The protestant ethics and the spirit of capitalism.* P. Baehr (Trans.) and G. C. Wells (Ed.). Harmondsworth, UK: Penguin.

4. Jaspers, K. (1953). *Way to wisdom: An introduction to philosophy* (2nd ed.). R. Mannheim (Trans.). New Haven, CT: Yale University Press.

5. Chapter 5 presents Jaspers's ideas in more detail.

6. The argument follows Berlin, I. (1999). *The roots of romanticism.* London, UK: Chatto & Windus.

7. See Rousseau, J-J. (1955). *Confessions.* J. M. Cohen (Trans.). Harmondsworth, UK: Penguin. (Original work published 1781).

8. The expressive view of human life is well analyzed by Taylor, C. (1989). *Sources of the self.* Cambridge, MA: Harvard University Press. I am indebted to Taylor's sweeping and yet careful analysis in many ways.

9. See Nietzsche, F. (1985). *The gay science.* In A. Nehamas (Ed.), *Nietzsche: Life as literature* (chap. 4, para. 290). Cambridge, MA: Harvard University Press. (Original work published in 1881).

10. I have developed this theme in depth in Strenger, C. (1998/2000). *Individuality, the impossible project.* Madison, CT: International Universities Press; New York, NY: Other Press.

11. The classical analysis of the metaphysics of identity is Kripke, S. (1980). *Naming and necessity.* Cambridge, MA: Harvard University Press.

12. For the following consult Heidegger, M. (1927). *Sein und zeit.* Tübingen, Germany: Niemeyer. English translation, Heidigger, M. (2008). *Being and time.* J. Macquarrie and E. Robinson (Trans.). San Francisco, CA: Harper Perennial; Sartre, J-P. (1992). *Being and nothingness.* H. E. Barnes (Trans.). New York, NY: Gramercy (Originally published in French as *L'Être et le Néant* in 1943).

13. See Kundera, M. (1986). *The unbearable lightness of being.* London, UK: Faber.

14. See Kundera, M. (1988). *The art of the novel.* New York, NY: Grove Press.

15. See Obama, B. (2004). *Dreams from my father.* New York, NY: Three Rivers Press.

16. I have developed the basic ideas of this chapter in detail in Strenger, C. (1998/2002). *Individuality, the impossible project.* Madison, CT: International Universities Press; New York, NY: Other Press.

17. See Ali Hirsi, A. (2007). *Infidel.* New York, NY: Free Press.
18. Ástor Piazzolla. Wikipedia. Retrieved from http://en.wikipedia.org/wiki/Ástor_Piazzolla.

Chapter 5

1. Jacques, E. (1965). Death and the midlife crisis. *International Journal of Psychoanalysis, 46,* 502–514.
2. Jaspers, K. (1932). *Philosophy* (Vol. 2, Pt. 3). E. B. Ashton (Trans.). Chicago, IL: University of Chicago Press; and Jaspers, K. (1953). *Way to wisdom: An introduction to philosophy* (2nd ed., chap. 2). R. Mannheim (Trans.). New Haven, CT: Yale University Press.
3. See Jaspers, K. (1997). *General psychopathology.* (p. 801). J. Hoenig and M. Hamilton, Trans. Baltimore, MD: Johns Hopkins University Press. (Original work published 1913).
4. See Becker, E. (1974). *The denial of death.* New York, NY: Free Press.
5. See Bion, W. (1962). *Attention and interpretation.* London, UK: Tavistock.
6. Bellow, S. (1994). *It all adds up* (p. 90). London, UK: Penguin.
7. See Bellow, S. (1964). *Herzog.* New York, NY: Viking.
8. See Rembrandt van Rijn. (2007). *Rembrandt's self portraits.* Retrieved from http://www.rembrandtpainting.net/rembrandt_self_portraits.htm.
9. See Schwartz, G. (1985). *Rembrandt: His life, his paintings.* New York, NY: Viking.
10. See Pinker, S. (1997). *How the mind works.* New York, NY: Norton; Rorty, R. (1979). *Philosophy and the mirror of nature.* Princeton, NJ: Princeton University Press.
11. See Nietzsche, F. (1985). *The gay science.* In Nehamas, A. *Nietzsche: Life as literature* (chap. 4, para. 290). Cambridge, MA: Harvard University Press. (Original work published in 1881)
12. The following is based on Saner, H. (2005). *Karl Jaspers.* Hamburg, Germany: Rowohlt.
13. In order to provide a concrete feel for the client's personality, I try to give vivid descriptions. It is important to note that I change every identifying detail, while trying to preserve the client's *Sosein* as much as I can.
14. This type of call to the patient for existential responsibility has been investigated in depth particularly in part 2 in Yalom, I. (1980). *Existential psychotherapy.* New York, NY: Basic Books.
15. See Bion, W. (1961). *Learning from experience.* London, UK: Tavistock; Bion, W. (1961). *Attention and interpretation.* London, UK: Tavistock; see also Eigen, M. (1992). *The electrified tightrope.* New York, NY: Jason Aronson.
16. See Saner, H. (2005). *Karl Jaspers* (pt. 3). Hamburg, Germany: Rowohlt.
17. I have described such examples in Strenger, C. (1998). *Individuality, the impossible project* (chaps. 5 and 6). Madison, CT: International Universities Press.

Chapter 6

1. Jacques, E. (1965). Death and the midlife crisis. *International Journal of Psychoanalysis, 46*, 502–514.
2. The theme of death acceptance as an essential aspect of psychological maturation has recently been elucidated in Yalom, I. (2008). *Staring into the sun: Overcoming the terror of death*. San Francisco, CA: Jossey-Bass. He has investigated the psychodynamics of death denial and death acceptance earlier in Yalom, I. (1980). *Existential psychotherapy* (Pt. 1). New York, NY: Basic Books.
3. See Jacques, E. (2003). *The life and behavior of living organisms: A general theory*. London, UK: Greenwood.
4. See Jacques, E. (1997). *Requisite organization: Total system for effective managerial organization and managerial leadership for the 21st century*. London, UK: Gower; Jacques, E. (2002). *Social power and the CEO: Leadership and trust in a sustainable free enterprise system*. London, UK: Greenwood.
5. See Strenger, C. (1998). *Individuality, the impossible project* (p. 6). Madison, CT: International Universities Press.
6. See Winnicott, D. (1965). *Maturational processes and the facilitating environment*. London, UK: Hogarth.
7. Becker, E. (1973). *The denial of death* (chap. 1). New York, NY: Free Press.
8. See Ellenberger, H. (1970). *The discovery of the unconscious*. New York, NY: Basic Books.
9. Becker, E. (1973). *The denial of death* (chap. 4). New York, NY: Free Press.
10. Foucault, M. (1984). The ethics of the concern of the self as a practice of freedom. In P. Rabinov (Ed.), *The essential Foucault, Vol 1: Ethics* (pp. 281–301). New York, NY: Pantheon.
11. See Miller, J. (1993). *The passion of Michel Foucault*. New York, NY: Simon & Schuster.
12. I have developed this in more detail in Strenger, C. (1998). *Individuality, the impossible project*. Madison, CT: International Universities Press.
13. See Gaskin, J. (1995). *The epicurean philosophers*. New York, NY: Everyman Library; see also Strenger, C. (2003). Mysticism and epicureanism in psychoanalysis: Michael Eigen and Adam Phillips. *Israel Psychoanalytic Journal, 1*(3), 435–461. Modern epicurean perspectives on death are to be found in Phillips, A. (1999). *Darwin's worms: On life stories and death stories*. London, UK: Faber; and in Yalom, I. (1980). *Existential psychotherapy*. New York, NY: Basic Books.
14. For the following, see Handy, C. (1976). *Understanding organizations*. New York, NY: Oxford University Press; Handy, C. (1989). *The age of unreason*. London, UK: Arrows Books; Handy, C. (1996). *Beyond certainty*. London, UK: Arrows Books; Handy, C. (1998). *The hungry spirit: Beyond capitalism: A quest for purpose in the modern world*. New York, NY: Broadway Books; and Handy, C. (2001). *The elephant and the flea*. Cambridge, MA: Harvard Business Publications.

15. Handy, C. (2001), *The elephant and the flea* (p. 29). Cambridge, MA: Harvard Business Publications.
16. Handy, C. (2001), *The elephant and the flea* (p. 31). Cambridge, MA: Harvard Business Publications.
17. Handy, C. (2001). *The elephant and the flea* (p. 29). Cambridge, MA: Harvard Business Publications.
18. Handy, C. (2001). *The elephant and the flea* (pp. 157–160). Cambridge, MA: Harvard Business Publications.
19. See Handy, C., & Handy, E. (2001). *Reinvented lives: Women at sixty, a celebration*. London, UK: Hutchinson; Handy, C., & Handy, E. (2006). *The new philanthropists*. London, UK: Heinemann.
20. See Malakh-Pines, A., & Aronson, E. (1988). *Career burnout: Causes and cures*. New York, NY: Free Press.
21. Freud, S. (1917). Mourning and melancholia. In *The standard edition of the complete psychological works of Sigmund Freud*. Vol. 14: A history of the psychoanalytic movement, papers on metapsychology and other works (1914–1916) (pp. 237–257). London, UK: Hogarth.
22. Strenger, C. (1998). *Individuality, the impossible project* (chap. 5). Madison, CT: International Universities Press.
23. Strenger, C., & Ruttenberg, A. (2008, February 1). The existential necessity of midlife change. *Harvard Business Review*, 82–90.
24. See Handy, C. (1989). *The age of unreason*. London, UK: Arrows Books; Handy, C. (1996). *Beyond certainty*. London, UK: Arrows Books.
25. Handy, C. (2001). *The elephant and the flea* (chap. 2). Cambridge, MA: Harvard Business Publications.
26. See Ellenberger, H. (1970). *The discovery of the unconscious*. New York, NY: Basic Books.
27. See Erikson, E. H. (1963). *Childhood and society* (2nd ed.). New York, NY: Norton; Erikson, E. H. (1964). *Insight and responsibility*. New York, NY: Norton.
28. Handy, C. (2001). *The elephant and the flea* (chap. 1). Cambridge, MA: Harvard Business Publications.
29. Specific strategies for dealing with death anxiety involving both the use of philosophical ideas and personal connection of significance are examined in Yalom, I. (2008). *Staring into the sun: Overcoming the terror of death*. San Francisco, CA: Jossey-Bass.
30. See Csikszentmihalyi, M. (1990). *Flow: The psychology of optimal experience*. New York, NY: HarperPerennial.

Chapter 7

1. This point has been made strongly by the founder of existential psychiatry, the Swiss psychiatrist Ludwig Binswanger. He argued that *Dasein* is never in isolation and that relatedness (or *Mitsein*) is more basic to the structure of human existence than Heidegger, and even more Sartre imply. He developed this perspective most systematically in his magnum opus, Binswanger,

L. (1951). *Ausgewählte Werke.* Vol. 2: *Grundformen und erkenntnis menschlichen daseins.* Bern, Switzerland: Asanger (1993). From a developmental point of view Binswanger's point is strongly corroborated by the findings of contemporary attachment theory; see Fonagy, P., Gerget, G., Jurist, E., & Target, M. (2005). *Affect regulation, mentalization, and the self.* New York, NY: Other Press. "Intersubjective embeddedness" has been elucidated in Stolorow, R., Attwood, G., & Orange, D. (2002). *Worlds of experience: Interweaving philosophical and clinical experience in psychoanalysis.* New York, NY: Basic Books.

2. See Solomon, S., Greenberg, J., & Pyszczynski, T. (2004). The cultural animal— twenty years of terror management theory and research. In J. Greenberg, S. L. Koole, & T. Pyszczynski (Eds.), *Handbook of experimental existential psychology* (pp. 13–34). New York, NY: Guilford Press.

3. See Pyszczynski, T. A., Solomon, S., & Greenberg, J. (2003). *In the wake of 9/11: The psychology of terror.* Washington, DC: American Psychological Association.

4. The relativism of contemporary cultures has been described and analyzed from a variety of points of view. For a culturally conservative critique, see Bloom, A. (1987). *The closing of the American mind.* New York, NY: Simon & Schuster. A European Perspective is given by Finkielkraut, A. (1995). *The defeat of mind.* New York, NY: Columbia University Press. A somewhat different angle is taken by Jacoby, S. (2008). *The age of American unreason.* New York, NY: Pantheon.

5. See Dawkins, R. (1976). *The selfish gene.* Oxford, UK: Oxford University Press.

6. See Riesman, D. (1950). *The lonely crowd: A study of the changing American character.* New Haven, CT: Yale University Press.

7. See Fromm, E. (1942). *Escape from freedom.* New York, NY: Holt.

8. Jacoby, S. (2008). *The age of American unreason.* New York, NY: Pantheon.

9. This has been shown in detail in McEvilley, T. (2001). *The shape of ancient thought: Comparative studies in Greek and Indian philosophies.* New York, NY: Allworth Press.

10. This was one of the most important arguments in Allan Bloom's bestselling *The closing of the American mind.* It has been discussed in depth in Taylor, C. (2005). *A secular age.* Cambridge, MA: Belknap.

11. Rushdie, S. (1989). *The satanic verses.* New York, NY: Penguin.

12. Christopher Hitchens recounts the story lashing out against those who became fainthearted in the face of threat: Hitchens, C. (2001). *Unacknowledged legislation* (pp. 125–135). London, UK: Verso.

13. See Berman, P. (2003). *Terror and liberalism.* New York, NY: Norton.

14. For what follows, see Jacoby, S. (2008). *The age of American unreason.* New York, NY: Pantheon.

15. See Jacoby, S. (2008). *The age of American unreason.* New York, NY: Pantheon.

16. See Woodward, B. (2007). *State of denial: Bush at war part III.* New York, NY: Simon & Schuster; Suskind, R. (2008). *The way of the world: A story of hope in an age of extremism.* New York, NY: Harper.

17. The question was picked up much earlier in a discussion generated by Charles Taylor's thoughtful examination of the multiculturalist ideal. See Taylor, C. (1994). *Multiculturalism*. Princeton, NJ: Princeton University Press.

18. The following is primarily based on the classic work by Putnam, H. (1982). *Reason truth and history*. Cambridge, UK: Cambridge University Press.

19. I have developed the point in more depth in Strenger, C. (1991). *Between hermeneutics and science: An essay on the epistemology of psychoanalysis (psychological issues)*. Madison, CT: International Universities Press; see especially chapter 5.

20. See Goodman, N. (1978). *Ways of worldmaking*. New York, NY: Hackett.

21. John Gray has aptly called Berlin's position "agonistic pluralism." Gray, J. (1995). *Isaiah Berlin*. Princeton, NJ: Princeton University Press.

22. A proviso is needed for the following reflections: I feel competent to discuss only the West, as it is the only culture in which I have a sound grounding. While I expect that the majority of the readers of this book have grown up in Western culture, I hope that those of different backgrounds will be able to translate the thoughts that follow into their own context.

23. For a magisterial comparative picture, see Collins, R. (1998). *The sociology of philosophies: A global theory of intellectual change*. Cambridge, MA: Belknap.

24. Plato. (1968). *The republic* (Book VII, 514a–515b). A. D. Bloom (Trans.). New York, NY: Basic Books.

25. One of the most gripping examples is Arthur Koestler's classic novel in Koestler, A. (1941). *Darkness at noon*. New York, NY: Macmillan.

26. For a trenchant critique of the dogmatic left, see Merleau-Ponty, M. (1957). *Les aventures de la dialectique*. Paris, France: Gallimard.

27. For the background story, see Lewis, M. (2008, December 8). The end of Wall Street. *Portfolio.*

28. I have told the story more fully in Strenger, C. (2003). From Yeshiva to critical pluralism. *Psychoanalytic Inquiry, 22*, 534–558.

29. See Fukuyama, F. (1992). *The end of history and the last man*. New York, NY: Free Press.

30. For a brief and powerful statement of the demise of the "End of History" narrative, and the return of old-fashioned power-politics, see Kagan, R. (2008). *The return of history and the end of dreams*. New York, NY: Knopf.

31. See Revel, J-F., & Ricard, M. (1997). *The monk and the philosopher*. New York, NY: Schocken.

32. See Wieseltier, L. (1997). *Kaddish*. New York, NY: Vintage.

33. See Nussbaum, M. (1995). *Cultivating humanity*. Cambridge, MA: Harvard University Press.

34. See Bell, D. (1996). *The cultural contradictions of capitalism: Twentieth anniversary edition*. New York, NY: Basic Books.

35. See Finkielkraut, A. (1995). *The defeat of mind*. New York, NY: Columbia University Press.

36. See Lévy, B-H. (2008). *Left in dark times: A stand against the new barbarism*. New York, NY: Random House.

37. See Barber, B. (1995). *Jihad vs. McWorld* (augmented ed.). New York, NY: Random House.

38. For a good presentation of Strauss's intricate and complex views on political philosophy, I particularly recommend Smith, S. (2006). *Reading Leo Strauss: Politics, philosophy, Judaism*. Chicago, IL: University of Chicago Press.

39. See Fukuyama, F. (2006) *America at a crossroads*. New Haven, CT: Yale University Press.

40. All quotations from Leo Strauss refer to two of his most famous papers: "What is Liberal Education?" and "Liberal Education and Responsibility." They are quoted as reprinted in Strauss, L. (1989). *Introduction to political philosophy* (p. 344). Detroit, MI: Wayne State University Press.

41. Strauss, L. (1989). *Introduction to political philosophy* (pp. 314–315). Detroit, MI: Wayne State University Press.

42. Strauss, L. (1989). *Introduction to political philosophy* (p. 319). Detroit, MI: Wayne State University Press.

43. Strauss, L. (1989). *Introduction to political philosophy* (p. 345). Detroit, MI: Wayne State University Press.

44. See Nussbaum, M. (1995). *Cultivating humanity*. Cambridge, MA: Harvard University Press; Appiah, K. A. (2006). *Cosmopolitanism: Ethics in a world of strangers*. New York, NY: Norton; Sen, A. (2006). *Identity and violence: The illusion of destiny*. New York, NY: Norton.

45. Spirited defenses of liberal education have been mounted by Kronman, A. (2008). *Education's end: Why our colleges and universities have given up on the meaning of life*. New Haven, CT: Yale University Press; Lewis, H. (2007). *Excellence without a soul: Does liberal education have a future?* New York, NY: Public Affairs.

46. For ways to develop partnership with business without giving up the soul of academia, see Kirp, D. (2004). *Shakespeare, Einstein, and the bottom line: The marketing of higher education*. Cambridge, MA: Harvard University Press.

47. See Sloterdijk, P. (2006). *Zorn und zeit*. Frankfurt am Main, Germany: Suhrkamp. He has made a strong case that the media have turned politics into the heir of the Roman arena.

48. See Sloterdijk, P. (2009). *Du mußt dein Leben ändern!* Frankfurt am Main, Germany: Suhrkamp. This book makes a strong case for the necessity of training the self for civilization, if a globalized world is to survive.

Chapter 8

1. U.S. Religious Landscape Survey (2008). Pew Forum of Religion and Public Life.

2. The World Values Survey contains a wealth of data on this and the following. See World Values Survey. Retrieved from http://www.worldvaluessurvey.org.

3. Jewish fundamentalism was more focused with arguing for the eternal right of Jews to live in the greater Israel or the necessity to implement halakhic restrictions on daily life in Israel. Hence it was less concerned with science and

rationality in these years. For the rise of Jewish Messianic fundamentalism, see Ravitzky, A. (1997). *Messianism, Zionism, and Jewish religious radicalism*. Tel Aviv, Israel: Am Oved.

4. The moniker is attributed to Scott Atran in the Internet. He remembers using it at a much publicized conference *Beyond Belief*, in which Harris and Dawkins participated, but told me that the term didn't originate with him. I will use it without attribution and invite the original author to claim her or his copyright.

5. See also Harris, S. (2004). *The end of faith: Religion, terror, and the future of reason*. New York, NY: Norton.

6. See also Dennett, D. C. (2005). *Breaking the spell: Religion as a natural phenomenon*. New York, NY: Viking.

7. See also Hitchens, C. (2007). *God is not great: How religion poisons absolutely everything*. New York, NY: Twelve Books.

8. See also Onfray, M. (2007). *Atheist manifesto*. New York, NY: Arcade.

9. See also Dawkins, R. (2006). *The God delusion*. New York, NY: Houghton Mifflin.

10. See also Dawkins, R. (1976). *The selfish gene*. Oxford, UK: Oxford University Press. This book achieved a rare feat in intellectual history. Dawkins wrote it in his thirties to present the basic tenets of evolutionary biology in accessible terms. His logical reconstruction of this theory as centered on the gene as the unit of evolutionary selection became the center of what is often called neo-Darwinism and has become a canonical text in the history of science. For a celebration and assessment of Dawkins's contribution thirty years later, see the essays in Grafen, A., & Ridley, M. (2006). *Richard Dawkins: How a scientist changed the way we think*. Oxford, UK: Oxford University Press.

11. See, for example, Dawkins, R. (1998). *Unweaving the rainbow: Science, delusion, and the appetite for wonder*. New York, NY: Houghton Mifflin.

12. There are some points where I believe Dawkins's position needs further refinement. His juxtaposition between science and religion has its problems, because they are not seen by all as actually competing with each other. For a thoughtful, if at times overly polemical, critique, see Eagleton, T. (2009). *Reason, faith, and revolution: Reflections on the God debate*. New Haven, CT: Yale University Press. It should be added that Dawkins at times simplifies the epistemological complexity of science. For a classical statement of this complexity, see Rorty, R. (1980). *Philosophy and the mirror of nature*. Princeton, NJ: Princeton University Press; see especially part 2.

13. For fair disclosure I want to put on record that I very much agree with Dennett, Dawkins, and Onfray on many counts and rather enjoyed Hitchens, who is less bound by academic etiquette and vents his anger and disdain at religion in the contrarian spirit that characterizes all his writings. Having been subjected to religious education, I basically agree with the point of view that religions are bound to often play a destructive role on the world stage in an interconnected world that needs to cooperate across beliefs and customs. I can neither see anything good in the pope's present and previous emphasis

on the sinfulness of contraception when he speaks to his flock in AIDS-ridden Africa or overpopulated South America nor have I seen a great deal of positive impact of Muslim or Jewish clerics on human affairs lately. The fact that the United States is by far the most religious Western democracy has not prevented it from evolving the cruelest form of capitalism in the West, leading to great suffering of most of its poorer citizens, incarceration of almost 2 percent of its male population, and now to a meltdown that is threatening the structure of the world economy.

14. Dawkins, R. (1976). *The selfish gene.* Oxford, UK: Oxford University Press.
15. See Lévy, B-H. (2008). *Left in dark times: A stand against the new barbarism.* New York, NY: Random House.
16. See Finkielkraut, A. (1995). *The defeat of mind.* New York, NY: Columbia University Press.
17. See Atran, S. (2002). *In gods we trust: The evolutionary landscape of religion.* Oxford, UK: Oxford University Press.
18. See Walzer, M. (1997). *On toleration.* New Haven, CT: Yale University Press.
19. Shlam, S. (2005). *Be fruitful and multiply* [Documentary]. Israel: New Israel Foundation for Cinema and Television.
20. This does not prevent me from seeing the beauty and inner coherence of Chassidic Judaism excellently described by Chaim Potok's novels, even though he chose to leave this form of life for more liberal versions of Judaism. It is possible to disagree and even feel disdain while appreciating a form of life on a human and aesthetic level.
21. See Elias, N. (1976). *The civilizing process: Sociogenetic and psychogenetic investigations.* Oxford, UK: Blackwell.
22. A brief remark is in order on how I write case histories: Every identifying detail has been changed, but I try to preserve my patient's basic personality and to get it across to the reader.
23. See McDougall, J. (1989). *Plea for a measure of abnormality.* New York, NY: International Universities Press; Bollas, C. (1989). *Forces of destiny.* London, UK: Free Association.
24. I have analyzed this in depth in Strenger, C. (2006, May). Freud's forgotten evolutionary project. *Psychoanalytic Psychology, 23*(2), 420–429.
25. See Sulloway, F. (1979). *Freud, biologist of the mind.* New York, NY: Vintage.
26. See Atran, S. (2002). *In gods we trust: The evolutionary landscape of religion.* Oxford, UK: Oxford University Press; and Dennett, D. C. (2005). *Breaking the spell: Religion as a natural phenomenon.* New York, NY: Viking.
27. This and the following are based on what I consider the most comprehensive account of the evolutionary basis of religion: Atran, S. (2002). *In gods we trust: The evolutionary landscape of religion.* Oxford, UK: Oxford University Press.
28. Atran, S. (2003). The genesis of suicide terrorism. *Science, 299,* 234–239.

Chapter 9

1. This charge has been formulated within the American context in Lasch, C. (1995). *The revolt of the elites and the betrayal of democracy.* New York, NY:

Norton. It is at the foundation of Naomi Klein's scathing indictment of the tactics of multinational corporations and neoliberal economic policies. Klein, N. (2000). *No logo.* London, UK: Picador; see also Klein, N. (2008). *The shock doctrine: The rise of disaster capitalism.* London, UK: Picador.

2. The point that globalization has led to the point where there is no longer an outsider has been argued in detail by Sloterdijk, P. (2005). *Im weltinnenraum des kapitals.* Frankfurt am Main, Germany: Suhrkamp.

3. Dennett and Dawkins bring home this case tirelessly in Dennett, D. C. (2005). *Breaking the spell: Religion as a natural phenomenon.* New York, NY: Viking; Dawkins, R. (2006). *The God delusion.* New York, NY: Houghton Mifflin.

4. Since my point here is the inevitability of disdain and the necessity to manage it within civilized bounds, I will not go into the deeper intricacies of the philosophy of religion. See Eagleton, T. (2009). *Reason, faith, and revolution: Reflections on the God debate.* New Haven, CT: Yale University Press. In particular I believe that civilized disdain does not preclude an appreciation of the coherence and, in many cases, the beauty of forms of religious life. Paul Berman, while seeing Islamic fundamentalism as one of the great dangers of our times, succeeds admirably well in showing the beauty of the position and even the seductiveness of Sayyid al-Qutb, the great theorist of Sunni political Islam. See Berman, P. (2003). *Terror and liberalism.* New York, NY: Norton.

5. Amartya Sen has brought home this point persuasively with reference to the complex cultural divides in India: Sen, A. (2005). *The argumentative Indian: Writings on Indian history, culture, and identity.* London, UK: Picador.

6. This is the core argument of Robert Wright in Wright, R. (2009). *The evolution of God.* New York, NY: Little Brown. Wright's earlier ideas will play an important role in this chapter.

7. An interesting attempt to formulate some of the bridges for communication has been presented in Appiah, K. A. (2006). *Cosmopolitanism: Ethics in a world of strangers.* New York, NY: Norton. While his prescription of widening the moral imagination is certainly valid, I feel that his tireless insistence on respecting worldviews other than ours at times borders on the political correctness that I criticized in chapter 8.

8. See Durkheim, E. (1915). *The elementary forms of religious life.* Oxford, UK: Oxford University Press.

9. Durkheim, E. (1915). *The elementary forms of religious life.* Oxford, UK: Oxford University Press.

10. See Wright, R. (2000). *Nonzero: The logic of human destiny.* New York, NY: Pantheon.

11. These developments are fully explained in Wright, R. (1994). *The moral animal.* New York, NY: Pantheon.

12. I have investigated this dynamic in more depth in Strenger, C. (2009). The psychodynamics of self-righteousness and its impact in the Middle East. *International Journal of Applied Psychoanalytic Studies, 6,* 178–196.

13. See Arendt, H. (1951). *The origins of totalitarianism.* New York, NY: Schocken.

14. For an encompassing interpretation of the wars of the twentieth century from a different vantage point, see Ferguson, N. (2006). *The war of the world*. New York, NY: Penguin.
15. Berlin, I. (1958). Two concepts of liberty. In *Four essays on liberty* (p. 167). Oxford, UK: Oxford University Press.
16. Berlin, I. (1958). Two concepts of liberty. In *Four essays on liberty* (pp. 118–172). Oxford, UK: Oxford University Press.
17. Berlin, I. (1958). Two concepts of liberty. In *Four essays on liberty* (p. 167). Oxford, UK: Oxford University Press.
18. Berlin, I. (1958). Two concepts of liberty. In *Four essays on liberty* (p. 172). Oxford, UK: Oxford University Press.
19. Freud, S. (1927–1931). *The future of an illusion*. In J. Stratchey (Ed.), *The standard edition of the complete psychological works of Sigmund Freud. Vol. 21 (1927–1931): The future of an illusion, civilization and its discontents, and other works*. London, UK: The Hogarth Press and the Institute of Psycho-analysis.
20. Atran, S. (2010). *Talking to the enemy: Violent extremism, sacred values and what it means to be human*. New York, NY: Ecco.
21. This case has been powerfully stated by Paul Berman: Berman, P. (2003). *Terror and liberalism*. New York, NY: Norton. Berman's incisive analysis of the ideology of political Islam leads to the conclusion that the power of destructive ideologies must never be explained away as nothing but the expression of social grievances. Berman's argument is particularly poignant because he is a card-carrying liberal.
22. See Lovelock, J. (2005). *Gaia: And the theory of the living planet*. New York, NY: Gaia Publications.
23. See Lovelock, J. (2007). *The revenge of Gaia: Earth's climate crisis & the fate of humanity*. New York, NY: Basic Books.
24. See Gray, J. (2007). *Black mass: Apocalyptic religion and the death of utopia*. New York, NY: Farrar, Strauss & Giroux.
25. See Wright, R. (2000). *Nonzero: The logic of human destiny*. New York, NY: Pantheon; see also TEDtalksDirector. (2008, April 15). *Robert Wright: How cooperation (eventually) trumps conflict*. YouTube. Retrieved from http://www.youtube.com/watch?v=wcZFIy2mfyE&feature=related for a lively and often humorous exposition by Wright of the nonzero principle. Nobel Prize laureate Ilya Prigogine, from a different vantage point, has put forth a similar argument; see Prigogine, I., & Stengers, I. (1984). *Order out of chaos: Man's new dialogue with nature*. New York, NY: Bantam.
26. See Castells, M. (2000). *The Internet galaxy: Reflections on the Internet, business, and society*. Oxford, UK: Oxford University Press.
27. See Diamond, J. (2005). *Collapse: How human societies choose to fail or survive*. New York, NY: Viking.
28. Freud, S. (1927–1931). *The future of an illusion*. In J. Stratchey (Ed.), *The standard edition of the complete psychological works of Sigmund Freud. Vol. 21 (1927–1931): The future of an illusion, civilization and its discontents, and other works*. London, UK: The Hogarth Press and the Institute of Psycho-analysis.

Index

Abrams, Elliot, 143
active self- acceptance. *See*
    self-acceptance
Adam and Eve, 86
Adidas
    "Impossible is Nothing," 5, 25
aging, 59, 84, 94–95, 104, 106, 113. *See
    also* death anxiety
agnostics, 149, 174
Ahmed, Khurshid, 159
Alderdice, Lord John, 85–86
Allen, Paul, 26
al Qaeda, 9, 15, 19, 179
analysts, symbolic, 29–32
antidepressants. *See* SSRIs
anti-intellectualism, 4–5, 55–58, 63–
    66, 132, 142
anti-theism and anti-theists, 156, 160,
    173–74
anxiety, 10–11, 22, 49–50, 74, 76, 124,
    138
    death, 35, 122, 149, 203n29
    depression and, 112–13
Appiah, Kwame Anthony, 193n6,
    209n7
Arendt, Hannah, 180, 194n7
aristocracy of mind, 144–47
Armstrong, Karen, 15
"Arnold" (patient), 124–27
art and artists
    active self-acceptance and, 91
    analogy with living a life, 75–76,
        78, 108
    analytic thought and, 58
    bricoleurs, 2
    as craftsmen, 75

defense against mortality and, 12
    obsession for original, 41
    political correctness and, 65–66
    romantic conception of, 41, 74–77,
        123
    religion and, 123, 129–30
    tragic sense of life and, 86–87
art history, 58, 91, 95–99, 134
atheism, 64, 66–67, 82, 124–25, 127,
    132, 139, 149–59, 173
athletes
    celebrity of, 24–25, 35, 38–39
    income of, 44–45
Atran, Scott, 47, 151, 154, 184, 207n4
Atta, Mohammed, 9

Bach, Johann Sebastian, 58, 75, 87, 126
Barber, Benjamin, 15, 143, 197n12
Bauman, Zygmunt, 198n2
Becker, Ernest, 11–12, 37, 105–9, 115–
    17, 195n3
Bell, Daniel, 143
Bellow, Saul
    Herzog, 90–91
Benedict XVI (Pope), 58, 174
Benjamin, Walter, 41
Berg, Rabbi Philip, 55, 57
    Kabbalah, 55–58
Berlin, Isaiah, 135
    "Two Concepts of Liberty," 180–83
Berman, Paul, 185, 209n4, 210n21
bin Laden, Osama, 9, 82, 184–85
Bion, Wilfred, 101
Black Monday, 13–14
Blair, Tony, 25

Bloom, Allan, 145, 194n8, 204n4, 204n10
Bloom, Harold, 84
Bollas, Christopher, 161
Borg, Bjorn, 38–39
Boulanger, Nadia, 87–88
boundary situations, 74, 89–90, 93–94, 102. *See also* Jaspers, Karl
Brooks, David, 23
Brown, Dan
    Da Vinci Code, The, 60
Brown, Norman, 65
Bruno, Giordano, 167
Buddha, 52, 136
Buddhism, 56, 64, 123, 127, 139, 149, 172, 199n18
Buffett, Warren, 104
Bush, George W., 19, 65, 122, 131–32, 143–44, 146, 154, 156, 186, 196n26
Byrne, Rhonda, 60–62
    Secret, The, 19, 47, 60–62

capitalism
    global (free market), 15, 20, 114, 198n2
    neoliberal, 2, 138, 193nn3–4
    social morality and, 9, 18, 25, 65, 73, 112, 114–16, 125, 173, 182, 194n7, 207n13
Castells, Manuel, 188
celebrity and celebrities, 2, 35, 37–40
    culture, 23–45
    economic significance of, 33, 37
    infotainment networks and, 37–43
    listing and ranking of, 1, 4, 39
    reality television and, 41–42
cities, global, 28–31, 49
civilized disdain, 149–70, 178, 184–85
    political correctness vs., 6, 150, 154–56, 160
    religion and, 151, 156–59, 173–74, 207n13, 208n20, 209n4
Clancy, Tom, 40
Clinton, Bill, 25
Communism, 65, 79, 123, 137–38, 176, 180

fall of, 1, 25, 177
computer
    impact on experience, 20, 33, 62, 104
    personal, 26
Conley, Dalton
    economic red-shift effect, 31, 49
conservatives and conservatism
    culture and, 131, 173, 194n8, 204n4
    liberalism vs., 62–67, 123, 143
    relativism and, 63, 67
    theological, 174
correctness, political. *See* political correctness
cosmopolitanism. *See* world citizenship
creationism, 125, 135, 151
creative class, 18, 49, 198n8
    global, 24, 63, 103, 105, 125, 127, 131, 141
    See also Florida, Richard
creativity, 75–77, 83–84, 102, 191
    focus and, 114–17
    at midlife, 104–9, 112
    sculpted, 105–9, 114
Csikszentmihalyi, Mihaly
    Flow, 36, 116
culture heroes, 35–39

Dalai Lama, 58, 139, 174
"Daniel" (patient), active self-acceptance and, 95–102
Darwin, Charles, 124, 151–53, 166–67, 173, 176–77, 187, 207n10. *See also* evolution, theory of
Dasein (existential philosophy), 10, 203n1
Davos men, 32
Dawkins, Richard, 125–26, 156, 173–74, 176, 179, 187, 207n4, 207nn12–13, 209n3
    God Delusion, The, 57, 151–52
    Selfish Gene, The, 152–53, 207n10
death and mortality
    acceptance of, 105–12, 114, 116, 169, 201n2

denial of, 11–12, 106–12, 114–16, 150, 168–69, 201n2
    Epicurean view of, 109, 167–69
    search for meaning and, 11–12, 15–16, 36, 110
death anxiety, 35, 122, 149, 153, 167–68, 203n29
death awareness (mortality salience), 10–12, 35, 42, 74, 92–95, 112–13, 122–23, 166–69, 179
de Beauvoir, Simone, 86
democracy, 9, 17, 25, 138, 154, 156, 176–77, 187
    Fukuyama on, 15
    mass, 143–46
    social, 135, 187, 194n8
    of taste, 33, 125
Dennett, Daniel, 151, 153, 156, 173, 179, 207n13, 209n3
depression, 13, 20, 22, 50, 52, 100, 113
destruction, ecological, 6, 185–86
Diamond, Jared, 126, 188
discipline, mental, 3, 88, 102, 108, 145, 150, 160
disdain, civilized. See civilized disdain
dogmatic slumber, 1
Domingo, Placido, 18
Dreyfus, Alfred, 175
Dreyfusard (movement), 175
Durkheim, Emile, 174–75

economic red-shift effect, 31, 49
economy, 1–2, 11, 15–18, 25–32, 40, 71, 83, 112, 114, 133–35, 198n3, 207n13
    economic crisis of 2008, 65, 138, 189, 196n22
education, 48, 136–37, 172, 190
    higher, 28, 44, 51, 63, 131–33, 143–48
    liberal, 6, 125, 142–47, 206n45
    religious, 150–53, 207n13
EEP. See experimental existential psychology (EEP)
Ellenberger, Henri, 115
elitism, 29, 44, 61, 142–44. See also Davos men

Enlightenment, 82
    European, 2–3, 138–41, 150, 160, 164, 167, 175, 193n5
    vision of, 25, 41, 52, 136, 139–40, 150, 152, 154–56, 167, 186, 194n7
Epicurus, Epicureans, and Epicurean philosophy, 163, 165–66
    death and, 109, 167–69
    fanaticism and, 168–69
    laughter and, 156–65
    paring down life to the essentials and, 108–17, 165–66
Erikson, Erik H., 115
evolution, biological and cultural, 10–11, 40, 47, 71–72, 104, 126, 207n10
    nonzero principle, 6, 176–78, 187–88, 190, 210n25
evolution, theory of
    game theory and, 176–77
    nonzero principle and, 176–78
    psychology and, 124–25, 142, 151–52, 165–69
    religion and, 57, 124, 131–33, 135, 141, 150–53, 164–69, 173–74
existential equation, 78–84, 88
existentialism, 2–3, 11, 73–74, 77–78, 84, 195n6
existential philosophy, 4, 10–11, 77–80, 89
existential psychology, 4, 6, 31, 39
    meaning and, 105–17, 121–22, 168
    self-esteem and, 35–36, 140
    symbolic immortality and, 12, 15–16, 35, 37, 179
    thrownness and, 77–78, 89, 93
    tragic view of life and, 11–12, 74, 78, 86–88
    See also experimental existential psychology (EEP)
experimental existential psychology (EEP), 4, 11–12, 22, 35, 42, 122–23, 195n3, 195n7

facticity, 78, 84–86. See also existential equation, thrownness faith, 37, 41, 51, 54, 63–67, 123, 127, 138–40, 151, 158, 164–67, 173, 184

fame, 4, 39, 42, 83, 91, 109, 117, 129, 151
immortality and, 37–38, 43
symbolic immortality and, 35–37
See also celebrity and celebrities

fatedness (existentialism), 108

fear
of death, 11–12, 35, 109, 167–68, 195n11
of gods, 166–67
of insignificance, 4, 35, 135
of loss of meaning, 4, 35
of loss of self-esteem, 36, 40, 122–26
See also death anxiety

final solution, 180–82

Finkielkraut, Alain, 143, 154, 199n27, 204n4

Florida, Richard
Rise of the Creative Class, The, 18, 51, 198n8

flow (psychology), 36, 116–17. *See also* Csikszentmihalyi, Mihaly

Forbes magazine, 31
list of celebrities, 29, 39

Foucault, Michel, 108, 139, 194n11, 199n13

Freud, Sigmund, 107, 113, 115, 166, 183, 189

Friedman, Thomas, 15

Fromm, Erich, 126

Fukuyama, Francis, 144, 194nn7–8
End of History and the Last Man, The, 9, 14–15, 25, 138, 194–95n1

fundamentalism
Christian, 64, 150–51, 153
as defense against globalization, 15, 63, 153
Enlightenment and, 82
free market, 155
Jewish, 153, 206n3
Muslim, 151, 153, 159–60, 209n4
science and, 150–51

Gaia hypothesis, 185–86. *See also* Lovelock, James

Gates, Bill, 17, 26, 44, 190

Gates, Melinda, 26, 190

genius, 41, 75

Gladwell, Malcolm, 44

global I-Commodity Market. *See* "I" commodity

global infotainment system. *See* infotainment system, global

globalis, Homo. *See* Homo globalis

globalization, 3, 13, 27, 172
global cities, 28–31, 49
global creative class, 24, 63, 103, 105, 125, 127, 131, 141
impact on culture, 14–15, 32
impact on identity and meaning, 206n48, 209n2
moving of jobs, 14
multinational companies, 28–30, 208–9n1
religious fundamentalism and, 15, 63, 153

Gnosticism, 55–56

God, 41, 56–57, 67, 73, 75, 138, 140, 151–52, 157–58, 162–66, 178

Goethe, Johann Wolfgang von, 60, 72

Goldman Sachs, 29

Goldstein, Baruch, 179

Goodman, Nelson, 134

Gore, Al, 144, 190

Gray, John N., 15, 186–88, 194nn7–8, 194–95n1, 205n21

Greenpeace, 190

Greenspan, Alan, 17, 138

Guattari, Felix, 65

Handy, Charles, 109–17

Handy, Elizabeth, 112

Harris, Sam, 151, 179, 207n4

Hegel, Georg Wilhelm Friedrich, 194–95n1

Heidegger, Martin, 10, 73, 77–78, 203n1

heroic attitude, 94, 105–7, 116

Hicks, Esther, 60–61
Hicks, Jerry, 60–61
Hilton, Paris, 37
Hinduism, 64, 127, 149, 172, 190
history, end of, 17, 25, 194–95n1. *See also* Fukuyama, Francis
Hitchens, Christopher, 151, 153, 156, 173–74, 179, 204n12, 207n13
Hofstadter, Richard, 64
Homo globalis
  careers, 48–50
  common cause of, 172–78
  detachment and, 198n2
  emergence of, 1–2, 13–15
  empowerment of, 189–91
  fears of, 22
  global infotainment system and, 1–4, 20–22, 27, 45, 193n3
  identity and, 80–81
  politicization of, 15, 63, 123, 130, 172, 189–90
  pop spirituality and, 4, 51–52, 67
  self-esteem of, 20–22
  spectacular life and, 71, 125
  worldviews and, 5–6, 117, 123–24, 185
Hubbard, L. Ron, 67
Humbold, Wilhelm von, 142
Hussein, Saddam, 19

"I" commodity, 193n3
  drama of individuality and, 76–78, 84
  global I-Commodity Market, 20–22, 23–24, 45, 49, 73, 126
  impact on meaning, 73–74
  individuality and, 23–24, 72, 127
  self-esteem and, 20–22, 43, 45, 49, 71, 125–26
identity
  conflicting aspects of, 15, 80–82
  hyphenated, 80, 130
  impact of infotainment network on, 27–33

  individuality and, 52, 71–72, 77–78, 121
  politics of, 4, 49, 66, 71
  See also individual and individuality
identity politics. *See* politics of identity
Ignatius of Loyola, 158
illusion, 3, 72, 108, 117, 186
  awakening from, 72, 90–91, 117, 146
  of end of history, 17, 71
IMF. *See* International Monetary Fund (IMF)
immortality, symbolic, 12, 15–19, 34–35, 37–38, 179
individual and individuality
  active self-acceptance and, 5, 88–90
  altruism and, 176
  Berlin on, 181–82
  development of, 2, 88–90, 108, 115, 108, 115, 140
  drama of, 2, 71–88
  existentialism and, 4, 79–80, 84, 86, 108, 121, 177–78
  liberalism and, 71–72, 135, 194n7
  memes and, 125–27, 153
  Obama and, 80–81, 84–86
  ranking of, 1, 23, 148
  Romanticism and, 74–77
  sacred principles and, 171
individualism, reflective, 4, 71–72
infotainment system, global
  Homo globalis and, 1–4, 20–22, 27, 31, 45, 193n3
  impact on culture, 4, 15, 23, 27
  impact on personal identity, 27–33, 43, 74, 126
  impact on publishing, 47–48
  impact on self-esteem, 21–22, 40, 126
  need for celebrities, 37–43
insignificance, fear of, 4, 12, 35, 135
intellectual investment, 136, 142
intellectuals, 65, 137, 151. *See also* anti-intellectualism

International Monetary Fund (IMF),
  17
Internet, 14, 20, 25–27, 32–33, 62–63,
  126, 183, 186–89, 207n4
  Facebook, 1, 21, 33
  Google, 1, 14, 20–21, 26, 33
  search engines, 1, 14, 20–21, 26–27,
    33
  Wikipedia, 60, 62, 190
iPhone, 26, 49
Iraq, 132
  invasion of, 14, 144
  WMD, 19, 144, 196n26
irrationality, 5–6, 17, 128, 139, 173,
  181
  ecology and, 185–86
  fear of death and, 109, 167
  psychology and, 85
  religion and, 152–56, 166
Islam and Muslims, 19, 41, 81–82,
  149–50, 156, 178–79, 193n5,
  210n21
  cleansing from Western influence,
    153, 184
  fundamentalism, 151, 159–60, 209n4
  humiliation, sense of, 9
  terrorism and, 82, 130, 159–60, 184
  Western culture and, 129, 151
Israel, 95
  Middle Eastern conflict and, 131,
    178–79
  politics and, 143–44
  religion and, 157–59, 184, 190,
    206–7n3

Jackson, Michael, 17
Jacoby, Susan, 65, 126, 132, 199n26,
  204n4
Jacques, Elliot, 104–9, 114–17
James, William, 62
Jaspers, Karl, 73
  and active self-acceptance, 88–93
  biography, 92–95
  and boundary situations, 74, 89–90,
    93–94, 102

illness of, 94–95, 102
  and universities, 147–48
Jerusalem
  Old City of, 155, 178–80
  Temple Mount (Haram al Sharif),
    166, 178–79, 184
Jews. *See* Judaism and Jews
Jobs, Steven, 20, 33
John Paul II (Pope), 58, 174
Jolie, Angelina, 37, 42
Jordan, Michael, 17, 24, 33–34, 38
Judaism and Jews, 131, 181, 206–7n3
  atheism and, 157, 208n20
  fundamentalist, 153, 206–7n3
  modern orthodox, 57, 162–65, 179
  ultraorthodox, 150, 157–59
"Judith" (patient), 160–65
Jung, Carl Gustav, 62, 107, 115
"Just Do It!"
  campaign, 24–25
  culture of, 4–5, 48, 84, 98
  danger of, 33–34, 38–45, 74, 78, 84,
    103
  fantasy and, 17, 78, 89, 104
  impact of, 26–33
  See also Nike

Kabbalah, 19, 199n16
  anti-intellectualism and, 55–58
  history of, 53–55
  pop spirituality and, 53, 58–62, 127
  popularity of, 53
  science and, 53–55
Kahaneman, Daniel, 16
Kant, Immanuel, 13, 164, 193n1
Kerry, John, 144
Khomeini, Ruholla, 82, 129, 154
Kierkegaard, Søren, 27–23
Klein, Naomi, 208n1
Koestler, Arthur, 137, 139, 205n25
Krugman, Paul, 16, 193n4
Kundera, Milan
  Unbearable Lightness of Being, The,
    78–80

Laitman, Rabbi Michael, 53–55, 60
laughter, Epicurean, 156–65
Lehman Brothers (bank), 2, 29
Lévi, Bernard-Henri, 154
Levinas, Emanuel, 162, 164
liberalism and liberals, 25
    Berlin on, 181–82
    classical European, 135, 194n8
    core values of, 71–72
    democracy, 14–15, 25, 123, 138, 144, 177
    education, 6, 123, 125, 142
    individual and, 71–72, 135, 194n7
    threats on, 153, 159
liberty, 9, 71, 135, 173, 181, 184
limitations
    active self-acceptance and, 5, 89–91
    attitudes toward, 25, 43–44, 50, 89, 117, 137, 190
    confrontation with, 5, 74–78, 93–94, 102
Lovelock, James
    Gaia hypothesis, 185–88
Lucretius, 167–68

Madonna (singer), 125
McCann Erickson (advertising company), 32
McLuhan, Marshall, 39
meaning
    active self-acceptance and, 89–90, 94, 102
    capitalism and, 2, 9, 193n4
    flow and, 116–17
    generation of new, 104, 108
    in global era, 15
    as human need, 9–10, 67, 156
    human relations and, 121
    inner truth and, 75
    "Just Do It" attitude and, 43
    modernity and crisis of, 72–75, 141
    Protestant ethics and, 73
    as reaction to human tragedy, 9
    search for, 53, 56, 58, 128
    systems, 117, 121, 149

worldviews and, 3–4, 11–12, 16, 40, 67, 85, 122, 126, 135, 155, 171, 179
memes, impact of, 125–28, 153, 188
Michelangelo, 114
microcosm and macrocosm, 47, 72–73
Microsoft, 26
Middle Eastern conflict, 131, 141–42, 178–79
Miles, Jack
    God: A Biography, 162–63
Mill, John Stuart, liberal values and, 2, 71–72
mind, aristocracy of, 145–47
mobility, social, 28, 44
Moshe de Leon
    Zohar, 45
MTV, 14
multiculturalism, 63, 130–31, 204n17
multinational companies, power of, 28–30, 208n1
mysticism, 47, 52, 56–57, 62
myth
    of true self, 50–51, 71, 88, 99, 117
    wunderkind, 103
mythology, Greek, 35–37, 186

Nazism, 93–94, 146, 180–81
neoliberalism, 2, 138, 193n4, 208–9n1
Nietzsche, Friedrich, 15, 75–76, 92–93, 102, 194–95n1
Nike, 4, 24–28, 33–35, 98, 125. *See also* "Just Do It!"
Nobrow Culture (Seabrook), 33
nonzero principle, 6, 176–78, 186–88, 190, 210n25. *See also* Wright, Robert
Nussbaum, Martha, 142–43, 147, 194n9

Obama, Barack, 5, 80–81, 84–86, 104
    and Internet, 189–90
Onfray, Michel, 151, 207n13
optimism, 11, 61, 74, 105, 138–39, 168, 177, 188

Orwell, George, 137, 139

paring down life to essentials, 108–17, 165–66. *See also* Epicurus, Epicureans, and Epicurean philosophy
philosophy
  existentialist, 4, 10–11, 77, 89
  Greek, 15, 142–43, 163, 194n11
  See also Epicurus, Epicureans, and Epicurean philosophy
phones, cellular, 26
physics
  modern, 54–55, 57, 73
  quantum physics and Heisenberg's Indeterminacy Principle, 53–55, 60, 126, 135
  success of, 133–35
Piazzolla, Astor, 87–88
Pitt, Brad, 37, 39, 42
Plato, 6, 60, 65
  allegory of the cave, 3, 135–39, 143, 146–47, 171, 194n8
pluralism, 182, 205n21
  relativism vs., 133–35
political correctness, 5, 121, 123, 143, 145, 209n7
  civilized disdain and, 6, 154–56, 160
  inauthenticity of, 130–31, 150
  incoherence of, 6
  liberalism and, 62–67
  religion and, 129, 151
politics of identity, 4, 66, 71
pop spirituality, 4–5, 50–62, 198n6
psychology
  cognitive, 45, 193n1
  evolutionary, 124, 142, 151–52
  existential, 4, 6, 11–12, 31, 35–36, 39, 105, 122, 128, 149–50, 153, 168, 171, 177, 183
  of religion, 165–69
psychotherapy, 49, 66, 110
publishing houses, 32, 47–48, 92

quantification. *See* rankings and ranking scales
Qutb, Sayyid al-, Islamic fundamentalism and, 209n4

rankings and ranking scales
  of companies, 16
  of cultures and worldviews, 16
  of human beings, 1, 4, 20–21, 39, 125–26
  I-Commodity Market and, 21, 23, 45, 73, 126
  of ideas, 18
  self-esteem and, 21–22, 36
  of universities, 148
ratings and rating scales. *See* rankings and ranking scales
rationality
  philosophy and, 127
  relativism and, 128
  religion and, 67, 138, 152–53, 206–7n3
  science and, 123
  See also reason
Reagan, Ronald, 1, 17–18, 64–65
reality TV, 61
  celebrity and, 42–43
  impact of, 41–43, 61
reason
  attack on, 63, 128
  Enlightenment and, 2–3, 25, 139–41, 156, 164
  Epicureanism and, 168
  paring down to essentials and, 113
  retreat from, 124–27
  return of, 172
  worldviews and, 6
  See also rationality
Reich, Robert, 29–31, 44
relativism, 4–5, 63, 67, 128, 132–35, 150, 204n4
religion
  critique of, 150–52
  education, religious, 150–53, 207n13

dialogue with secularism / science, 148–51, 154, 160, 172–74
psychological origins of, 57, 183
in United States, 51, 64, 131, 150, 154, 184
See also atheism; *individual religions*
Rembrandt Harmenszoon van Rijn
active self-acceptance and, 91
self-portraits of, 91
Revel, Jean-Francois
Monk and the Philosopher, The, 139–40
Ricard, Matthieu
Monk and the Philosopher, The, 139
Romanticism, 41, 72, 74–77, 86, 90
Roth, Philip, 5, 20, 82–86
Rothkopf, David
Superclass, 32, 44, 189
Roubini, Nouriel, 193n4
Rousseau, Jean-Jacques, 72, 75
Rubinstein Arthur, 87
Rushdie, Salman, 151, 154
Satanic Verses, The, 82, 129–30

sacred
Durkheim on, 174–75
global conception of, 171, 174–78, 181–82
pop spirituality and, 58–62
religion and, 57, 152–53
Sartre, Jean-Paul, 10, 65, 73–74, 77–78, 86, 96–100, 138, 203n1
Sassen, Saskia, 28–29, 198n3
Scholem, Gershom, 199n17
Schopenhauer, Arthur, 187
science, religion and, 149–69
Scientology, 67, 123, 126
Seabrook, John
Nobrow, 33
secularism, 131, 142, 148–60, 165, 172–75, 180. *See also* atheism; anti-theism
self-acceptance, active, 5, 88
"Daniel" (patient) and, 95–101
Karl Jaspers and, 89–93

at midlife, 104–16
Rembrandt and, 91
self-consciousness, 42, 77–80, 121
death and, 86–87, 116
self-esteem
globalization and, 16
comparative nature of, 12–13, 35–36
components of, 12–13, 124
existentialism and, 35–36, 140
fear of insignificance and, 35–36, 40
humanistic disciplines and, 140
infotainment network and, 21–22, 40, 126
rankings and ranking scales and, 21–22
serotonin and, 13, 35
threats on, 122
worldviews and, 11–13, 40
self-help
literature, 47, 59–60
pop spirituality, 4
shallowness of, 2, 4, 67
Sen, Amartya, 71–72, 209n5
September 11 (terror attack), 9, 12, 14, 82, 122, 130–32, 159, 184, 188
serotonin, 13, 35. See also SSRIs
Sex and the City, 23–24
Sharapova, Maria, 24, 34, 38, 43
Sharma, Robin, 61–62
Monk Who Sold His Ferrari, The, 58–59
Shlam, Shosh, 157
Sinatra, Frank, 90
Sloterdijk, Peter, 194n11, 206nn47–48, 209n2
social democracy, 135, 187, 194n8
Soros, George, 16, 104, 193n4, 196n22
Spinoza, Benedictus de, 167
sport. *See* athletes
SSRIs (antidepressants), 22, 50
Stalin, Joseph, 65, 137–38, 155, 180, 184
status, social, 31, 20–21, 24, 28–31, 38–42, 83

Strauss, Leo, 88, 143–47, 194n8, 206n38, 206n40
suicide terrorism. *See* terror and terrorism
superclass, global, 32, 189. *See also* Rothkopf, David

Taylor, Charles, 200n8, 205n17
terror and terrorism
  impact of, 190–91
  Islamic, 159–60, 184, 188
  Jerusalem, 178
  justification of, 155
  London, 130–31, 183
  Madrid, 130–31, 183
  meaning and, 116–17, 122
  9/11, 9, 12, 14, 82, 122, 130–32, 159, 184, 188
  nuclear, 6
  reaction to, 11–12, 39–40, 153, 168
  religion and, 39
  Stalin and, 138
  suicide, 9
  totalitarianism and, 123, 139, 178, 185
terror management theory (TMT), 11–12, 203n2. *See also* existential psychology; experimental existential psychology (EEP)
Thatcher, Margaret, 1, 17
thrownness (existentialism), 77–78, 89, 93
tolerance, 5, 16, 51, 129–30
  relativism and, 63, 132
  toleration and, 157–60
  worldviews and, 122–23, 177, 180
Tolle, Eckhart
  Power of Now, 52
totalitarianism, 123, 139, 178, 180, 185
Trivers, Robert, 176
Tversky, Amos, 16

ultraorthodox (Jewish), 57, 150, 157–59
  women, 157–59

universities and higher education, 28, 44, 48, 131–32, 143
  Karl Jaspers on, 147–48
  liberal education and, 143–47
  pressure of ranking scales and, 148

values
  comparative, 175–76
  conflict of, 135, 181–82
  Enlightenment, 152–56
  liberal, 71–72
  ranking scales and, 1, 4, 16, 18–22
  religious, 83, 157–58
  Western, 9
  See also Berlin, Isaiah
Van Gogh, Theo, 82, 130
Voltaire, Francois, 139, 160

Wachowski brothers
  Matrix, 17, 137
Walzer, Michael, 157
Weber, Max, 72–73
West, Western values, Western culture, 2, 21, 64, 73, 75, 126–27, 137, 139–43, 173
  attacks on, 9, 15, 65–67, 122, 129–33, 147, 151, 153, 183–84
Wieseltier, Leon
  Kaddish, 140
Williams, George, 176
Winnicott, Donald. W., 99, 106–7, 116
Wolfowitz, Paul, 143, 194n8
World Bank, 17
world citizenship, 190, 194nn9–10
  difficulty of, 142, 147, 150
  importance of, 3, 160, 172
  psychology of, 5
worldview and worldviews
  closed, 171, 180–85
  critical examination of, 4–6, 117–18
  as defense against mortality, 11–12, 40
  defense of, 35
  intellectual foundations of, 67
  need for, 3, 11

open, 171–72, 177, 180, 185
religious, 40, 63, 180
secular, 173, 180
symbolic immortality and, 12
Wright, Robert
Evolution of God, The, 209n6

Nonzero, 176–77
nonzero principle, 176–78, 187–90,
    210n25

Zola, Emile, 175
Zuckerberg, Mark, 33, 44

455
427
1652